▮ SCHOLASTIC

BOok of

ListS

James Buckley, Jr. and Robert Stremme

Scholastic 🔆 Reference

an imprint of

▮ SCHOLASTIC

Produced by Shoreline Publishing Group LLC
Santa Barbara, California
www.shorelinepublishing.com
Editorial Director: James Buckley, Jr.
Designed by Tom Carling, carlingdesign.com
Illustrations by Harry Campbell
Additional editorial help provided by
Beth Adelman, Nanette Cardon (Index),
Jim Gigliotti, David Fischer, and John Walters.

Thanks to Ken Wright and Paula Manzanero at Scholastic for patiently shepherding this book
to completion and enthusiastically supporting it along the way.

Library of Congress Cataloging-in-Publication Data
Stremme, Robert.
Scholastic book of lists / Robert Stremme, James Buckley, Jr.
p. cm.
Includes index.
Summary: A reference book containing lists of information about world history, United States history, social
studies, geography, climate, math, science, language arts, popular culture, animals, and the arts.
1. Handbooks, vade-mecums, etc.— Juvenile literature. [1. Handbooks, manuals, etc.] I. Title: Book of lists.
II. Buckley, James, 1963– III. Title.
AG106.S77 2003
031.02—dc21   2002075818

0-439-83757-X

10 9 8 7 6 5 4 3 2 1   06 07 08 09 10

Printed in the U.S.A.
First printing, September 2006

Table of Contents

Introduction

Peple make them to chart the bestselling books and the top 25 college football teams. Your family makes them to bring home the bacon (and the bread and the milk and all the other groceries). You make them to keep track of your favorite songs or movies. What is everybody making? Lists.

Lists are nothing new. As soon as people started using words, they were using lists to keep track of all sorts of information. Lists keep things in order — they combine a whole pile of information into a handy-dandy format.

Lists are the cereal boxes of information; that is, they're the perfect-size package to contain all sorts of great stuff. You can make lists of things in your pocket, books on your shelves, people in your family, or words that start with *Q*. The alphabet is nothing more than a list of letters. A dictionary is a list of words. A phone book is a list of, well, phone numbers. Even the table of contents to this book is a list, a list of the chapters and pages inside. Whether you know it or not, your name is on dozens of lists, from your classroom atten-dance list to your doctor's patient list. This *Scholastic Book of Lists* is nothing but page after page of lists. You'll find lists in here for just about every subject you might study in school, and some that you might

(i) before (e) except after (c)

Uno Dos Tres

blew/blue

天

JOURNAL MY

not touch with a ten-foot pole (c'mon, opera's not that bad!).

In this book, you'll find lists of everything from Super Bowl winners (page 282) to super bowl–fillers (giant food, that is, on page 262) . . . from muscles for frowns (page 146) to oddly named towns (page 102) . . . from history's best (page 60) to animals that rest (page 238).

Some of these lists won't change a bit from the time we typed them until your grandkids read your tattered copy of this book. The names of the original 13 American colonies (page 24) are always going to be the same. Some of the lists, however, might change as time goes on. Faster roller coasters (page 229) might be built. New movies will leap into the Top 10 (page 217). And, of course, lots of sports records might be set as well as new champions crowned.

So, remember to use this book as a starting point, a way to get a leg up on finding information that you need. We couldn't put everything that you might need for your life at home or school in here. There's a different word for a book like that: an encyclopedia!

At the bottom of most of the lists are little fact boxes like this one. Here we'll add a historical fact, a key word or definition, interesting numbers, gross trivia, an insider's secret, or even spring a pop quiz on you!

You're not just a reader of this book, either — you're a list-maker. At the end of each chapter is a blank list for you to fill in names, dates, or other information about some part of your world or yourself. Get started by filling in number 5 on this first list. Have fun!

Five Ways I Can Use This Book

1. Learn the capital of every country in case I ever get on *Jeopardy!*

2. Use it as a pillow.

3. Find out why I should avoid hippos.

4. Discover where juju, zouk, samba, and kodo come from.

5. _____ .

Abbreviations Used in This Book

Most of the abbreviations used are for measurements. We're using both the "regular" American system and the metric system (read more about them on page 108). Sometimes we also abbreviate the names of states; for a translation of those, see page 97.

ft.	foot	m	meter	yd.	yard
g	gram	ml	milliliter	tsp.	teaspoon
kg	kilogram	sq. km	square kilometer	tbs.	tablespoon
km	kilometer			oz.	ounce
l	liter	sq. mi.	square mile	C	Celsius
lb.	pound			F	Fahrenheit

CHAPTER ONE

History

Just because stuff happened before you were born doesn't mean it isn't important! So, our present to you is a trip to the past.

Ancient
Civilizations

The Fertile Crescent was made up of the land around the Tigris and Euphrates rivers, in what is now known as the Middle East. This area is generally considered to be the birthplace of ancient civilizations. However, people on other continents were establishing cultures that would become civilizations, too. Here are some of the world's oldest civilizations.

CIVILIZATION	AREA	DATES*
Sumerian	Fertile Crescent	3500–2000 B.C.
Indus Valley	India	3000–1500 B.C.
Minoan	Crete	3000–1100 B.C.
Egyptian	Egypt	2850–715 B.C.
Hsia	China	2200–1760 B.C.
Babylonian (old)	Mesopotamia	1800–1686 B.C.
Assyrian	Fertile Crescent	1800–899 B.C.
Hittite	Turkey	1640–1200 B.C.
Shang	China	1500–1122 B.C.
Zhou	China	1123–256 B.C.

The Minoan culture flourished on the island of Crete more than 3,000 years ago. Where is Crete located?

Crete is a Greek island in the Mediterranean Sea.

CIVILIZATION	AREA	DATES*
Phoenician	Fertile Crescent	1100–332 B.C.
Greek	Europe	900–200 B.C.
Celts	Europe	800–500 B.C.
Etruscan	Europe	800–300 B.C.
Babylonian (new)	Mesopotamia	625–539 B.C.
Persian	Iran	559–330 B.C.
Roman	Europe	500 B.C.–A.D. 300
Mauryan	India	185–321
Ch'in	China	206–221
Maya	Yucatán	200–850
Gupta	India	320–500
Ghana	West Africa	700–1200
Chimu	North America	800–1465
Kanem Bornu	West Africa	800–1800
Toltec	Central America	900–1100

*All dates up to Roman are B.C., which stands for "Before Christ." From Roman onward, the dates are A.D., or "Anno Domini," which means "year of the Lord" in Latin. The Western calendar uses the birth of Jesus Christ as the turning point in "counting" years.

In North America, there is evidence of three ancient civilizations: the Hohokam, the Mogollon, and the Anasazi. These cultures lived between A.D. **200** and **1600** in what is now New Mexico, Arizona, Utah, and Colorado.

Hail Caesar!

The Roman Empire lasted for more than 500 years and was the largest empire the world had ever seen. It stretched from Great Britain in the north to parts of Africa in the south and pretty much everywhere else in between. Heading up this empire was a succession of emperors. When they ruled, they were among the most powerful leaders in history.

Augustus (Octavianus)	27 B.C.–A.D. 14	Gordianus	238–244
Tiberius Caesar	14–37	Philippus Arabicus	244–249
Gaius (Caligula)	37–41	Decius	249–251
Claudius Caesar	41–54	Gallus	251–253
Nero	54–68	Aemilianus	253–253
Galba	68–69	Valerianus	253–260
Otho	69–69	Gallienus	260–268
Vitellius	69–69	Claudius Gothicus	268–270
Vespasianus	69–79	Quintillus	270–270
Titus	79–81	Aurelianus	270–275
Domitianus	81–96	Tacitus	275–276
Nerva	96–98	Florianus	276–276
Trajanus	98–117	Probus	276–282
Hadrianus	117–138	Carus	282–283
Antoninus Pius	138–161	Carinus	283–285
Marcus Aurelius	161–180	Diocletianus	285–305
Commodus	180–192	Galerius	305–311
Pertinax	193	Maximinus Daia	311–313
Julianius I	193	Licinius	313–324
Severus	193–211	Constantinus I	324–337
Caracalla	211–217	Constantinus II	337–361
Macrinus	217–218	Julianus II	361–363
Elagabalus	218–222	Jovianus	363–364
Severus Alexander	222–235	Valens	364–378
Maximinus Thrax	235–238	Theodosius I	378–395

The life of the Roman emperor could be very dangerous. Julianius I was murdered, Claudius Caesar was poisoned, and Nero committed suicide.

Extinct Countries

How can you lose a country? Check your parents' or grandparents' atlases and you will find the names of countries that you don't recognize. These are countries that once existed, but today have been swallowed up by other countries, or split up into smaller countries, or given new names. Here are some places you can't get a ticket to anymore.

EXTINCT COUNTRY (NEW NAME, IF ANY)

Abu Dhabi
Austro-Hungarian Empire
Basutoland (Lesotho)
Bechuanaland (Botswana)
Biafra
British Honduras (Belize)
Burma (Myanmar)
Ceylon (Sri Lanka)
Czechoslovakia
    (Czech Republic & Slovakia)
Formosa (Taiwan)
Germany, Democratic
    Republic of (Germany)
Germany, Federal Republic
    of (Germany)
Gold Coast (Ghana)
Kampuchea (Cambodia)

EXTINCT COUNTRY (NEW NAME, IF ANY)

Malagasy Republic
    (Madagascar)
Manchuria
Ottoman Empire
East Pakistan (Bangladesh)
West Pakistan (Pakistan)
Persia (Iran)
Prussia
Rhodesia (Zimbabwe)
Siam (Thailand)
Sumatra (Indonesia)
Union of Soviet Socialist
    Republics
Upper Volta (Burkina Faso)
Yugoslavia (Serbia
    and Montenegro)
Zanzibar

When Germany was divided into two nations (East and West Germany), the city of Berlin was divided into East and West Berlin by the 27-mile (45-km) "Berlin Wall." To escape East Berlin, people dug tunnels under the wall, scaled the wall, and even floated in balloons over it. The wall came down in 1989.

Famous Leaders

Throughout time, there have been many people who have ruled countries or empires. Some passed into history with barely a whisper; others dominated their age. Rulers such as these have been among the most important and influential people of all time. Here's a list of some of the most well known, the dates their reigns began, and where they ruled.

TITLE	BEGAN	AREA RULED OR TITLE
Alexander the Great	332 B.C.	Asia Minor and Egypt
Cleopatra	51 B.C.	Queen of Egypt
Charlemagne	800	Holy Roman Empire
William the Conqueror	1066	Conqueror and King of England
Genghis Khan	1200	Mongolian Empire, much of Asia
Ivan the Great	1462	Russian prince
Henry VIII	1509	King of England
Montezuma II	1519	Aztec ruler in Central America
Elizabeth I	1558	Queen of England
Tokugawa Ieyasu	1603	Shogun of Japan
King Louis XIV, the Sun King	1643	King of France
Peter the Great	1682	Tsar of Russia
Catherine the Great	1762	Empress of Russia
George Washington	1789	First U.S. president
Napoléon Bonaparte	1799	Emperor of France
Simón Bolívar	1810	South American leader
Victoria	1837	Queen of England
Benito Juárez	1858	President of Mexico
Abraham Lincoln	1861	16th U.S. president

TITLE	BEGAN	AREA RULED OR TITLE
Giuseppe Garibaldi	1861	Unified Italy into one country
Otto von Bismarck	1871	Prime minister who unified Germany
Vladimir Lenin	1917	Revolutionary leader of the U.S.S.R.
Mohandas Gandhi	1920	Leader of peaceful revolt in India
Joseph Stalin	1922	Leader of the Soviet Union
Franklin Delano Roosevelt	1933	32nd U.S. president
Adolf Hitler	1933	German dictator; head of Nazis
Mao Tse-tung	1935	Communist leader of China
Winston Churchill	1940	Prime minister of Great Britain
Nikita Khrushchev	1953	Soviet leader
General Charles de Gaulle	1959	President of France
Fidel Castro	1959	Communist leader of Cuba
John F. Kennedy	1961	43rd U.S. president
Golda Meir	1969	Israeli prime minister
Margaret Thatcher	1979	Prime minister of Great Britain
Indira Gandhi	1980	Prime minister of India
Corazon Aquino	1986	President of the Philippines
Lech Walesa	1990	Polish president
Boris Yeltsin	1991	Russian president
Nelson Mandela	1994	South African president

Which of these words or phrases has NOT been used in a country somewhere to describe its leader: Shah, Kaiser, Emperor, Chief, Big Fella, Sultan, Emir, Grand Mufti?

Answer: Unless you count basketball teams as countries, no nation calls its leader "Big Fella." The others are all real, however.

Native Americans

Native Americans are members of individual tribes, and the tribes join together into nations. This list gives the names of the Native American tribes in different geographical regions of the United States before the 1700s. Many of these names will be very familiar, since some are now used for states, geographical features, and even cars. Unfortunately, many of these tribes are no longer around; others now have just a few members.

NORTH/NORTHEAST

Abenaki	Kickapoo	Ottawa
Algonquin	Menominee	Pawtuxet
Conestoga	Miami	Pennacook
Delaware	Mohawk	Pequot
Erie	Mohican	Potawatomi
Fox	Montauk	Sauk
Huron	Narragansett	Seneca
Illinois	Ojibwa	Susquehanna
Iroquois	Oneida	Wampanoag

SOUTHEAST

Apalachee	Chickasaw	Quapaw
Attacapa	Choctaw	Saponi
Biloxi	Creek	Shawnee
Calusa	Croatan	Timucua
Catawba	Natchez	Tuscarora
Cherokee	Powhatan	Tutelo

PLAINS

Arapaho	Cree	Osage
Arikara	Crow	Oto
Blackfoot	Iowa	Pawnee
Brea	Mandan	Shoshone
Caddo	Missouri	Sioux
Cheyenne	Nez Percé	Ute
Comanche	Omaha	Wichita

NORTHWEST

Bannock	Makah	Tillamook
Chinook	Nisqually	Tlingit
Duwamish	Nootka	Tsimshian
Flathead	Paloos	Yakima
Haida	Tenino	Yuki

SOUTHWEST

Apache	Navaho	Serrano
Cochimi	Paiute	Taos
Hopi	Papago	Walapai
Lagunero	Pomo	Yuma
Mohave	Pueblo	Zuni

The 2000 U.S. Census reported 2,475,956 Native Americans living in the United States.

Important Wars

Sad to say, this list could have been much longer. War has been a part of civilization since its earliest days. Wars are key turning points in the course of history. The conflicts listed here had the most long-lasting impact.

WAR	DATES
Peloponnesian War (Greece)	431–404 B.C.
Punic Wars (Greece)	264–146 B.C.
Norman Invasion of England	1066
Hundred Years' War (France vs. England)	1337–1453
War of the Roses (France vs. England)	1455–1485
Thirty Years' War (France vs. England)	1618–1648
English Civil War	1642–1651
American Revolution	1775–1783
Wars of the French Revolution	1789–1799
Napoleonic Wars (France vs. Europe)	1803–1815
War of 1812 (United States vs. England)	1812–1814
Mexican-American War	1846–1848
Italian War of Independence	1848–1849
American Civil War	1861–1865
Chinese-Japanese War	1894–1895

WAR	DATES
Spanish-American War	1898
Boer War (England vs. South Africa)	1899–1902
World War I	1914–1918
Spanish Civil War	1936–1939
Chinese-Japanese War	1937–1945
World War II	1939–1945
Israeli War of Independence	1948–1949
Korean War	1950–1953
Cuban Revolution	1952–1959
Vietnam War	1954–1975
Suez War (Israel vs. Egypt)	1956
Six-Day War (Israel vs. Egypt)	1967
Cambodian Civil War	1970–1975
October War (Israel vs. Egypt)	1973
Iran-Iraq War	1980–1988
Persian Gulf War	1990–1991
War Against Terrorism	2001–

What war involving the United States resulted in the most casualties?

The Civil War, in which more than 600,000 Americans died. Soldiers on both sides of the conflict—Union and Confederate—were citizens of the United States.

Famous Explorers

Explorers take on the challenge of discovering new and unknown areas of our universe. Sometimes it is difficult to determine who was first, but these men faced many hardships and trials in order to reach their goals. What's left to explore? The land under the oceans and the vast area of outer space remain mostly unexplored. Where do you want to explore?

EXPLORER, COUNTRY	DATES	AREA EXPLORED
Chang Ch'ien, China	138–109 B.C.	Silk Road trade route through Asia
Hsuan-tsang, China	629–645	India
Erik the Red, Norway	c. 900	Greenland
Leif Eriksson, Norway	c. 1000	Newfoundland
Marco Polo, Italy	1271–1295	Mongolian Empire
Ibn Battuta, Morocco	1325–1354	Africa
Cheng Ho, China	1405–1433	Pacific Islands
Bartolomeu Dias, Portugal	1487–1488	Cape of Good Hope, Africa
Christopher Columbus, Spain	1492–1502	San Salvador, West Indies
John Cabot, England	1497–1498	Greenland, Newfoundland
Vasco da Gama, Portugal	1497–1498	India, reached by sea
Amerigo Vespucci, Spain	1497–1502	South America, West Indies
Pedro Cabral, Portugal	1500–1501	Sailed from Africa to India and Brazil
Vasco de Balboa, Spain	1513	Pacific Ocean
Juan Ponce de León, Spain	1513, 1521	Florida
Hernando Cortés, Spain	1519–1521	Mexico
Ferdinand Magellan, Spain	1519–1521	First to sail around the world
Giovanni da Verrazzano, Italy	1524, 1528	North American eastern coast

EXPLORER, COUNTRY	DATES	AREA EXPLORED
Pánfilo de Narváez, Spain	1528–1536	Florida, Mexico
Francisco Pizarro, Spain	1531–1533	Peru
Jacques Cartier, France	1535–1541	St. Lawrence River, Canada
Hernando de Soto, Spain	1539–1542	Mississippi River, Southwest America
Francisco de Coronado, Spain	1540–1542	American Southwest
Juan Rodraguez Cabrillo, Spain	1542–1543	California
Sir Francis Drake, England	1577–1580	Sailed around the world
Samuel de Champlain, France	1603–1609	Great Lakes, Quebec
Henry Hudson, England	1607–1611	Hudson River, Hudson Bay
Abel Tasman, Netherlands	1642, 1644	Sailed around Australia
James Cook, England	1772–1779	Tonga, Easter Island, Hawaii
Lewis & Clark, U.S.	1804–1806	Western United States
Charles Darwin, England	1831–1836	Galápagos Islands, Ecuador
David Livingstone, Scotland	1851, 1855	Victoria Falls, Africa
Matthew Henson, U.S.	1909	Co-discovered North Pole
Robert Peary, U.S.	1909	Co-discovered North Pole
Roald Amundsen, Norway	1911	First person to reach South Pole
Bertram Thomas, England	1930	Crossed Rub al-Khali Desert
Jacques Cousteau, France	1943–1997	Undersea world
Neil Armstrong, U.S.	1969	First person to walk on the moon

David Livingstone discovered Victoria Falls in Africa, but then disappeared. American explorer H. M. Stanley finally located Dr. Livingstone, who had been recovering from an illness with the help of a native tribe. Stanley greeted the "missing" man with the famous phrase, "Dr. Livingstone, I presume."

The 13
Original Colonies

Citizens of Great Britain hopped into often-leaky boats and came to America to start colonies. They ended up with 13 before America got around to a revolution. Religion played a very important role in the creation of many of those 13 original colonies. Some settlers created specific areas for their own religious groups, and often other religions were not welcome.

COLONY	FOUNDED	RELIGION	FOUNDER(S)
Virginia	1607	Anglican	John Smith
Massachusetts	1620	Puritan	Pilgrims
New Hampshire	1623	Protestant	Colonists from Mass.
New York	1626	Dutch Reformed	Dutch, then English
Maryland	1634	Catholic, Protestant	Lord Baltimore
Connecticut	1636	Protestant	Thomas Hooker
Rhode Island	1636	All religions	Roger Williams
North Carolina	1654	Protestant	Settlers from Virginia
South Carolina	1663	Protestant	English
New Jersey	1664	Quaker, Reformed	Dutch, Swedish
Pennsylvania	1681	Quaker	William Penn
Delaware	1682	Quaker	William Penn
Georgia	1732	Protestant	James Oglethorpe

Many people list Vermont as one of the 13 original colonies, but Vermont, as it is today, did not exist as a separate area in colonial times. It was claimed as part of the New Hampshire and New York colonies. Also, Maine was then part of the Massachusetts colony.

American Patriotic Sayings

The things people say sometimes become more famous than the people themselves. Throughout American history, some of those "sayings" have become very well known. Here are some of the familiar patriotic sayings that you might run across in your travels through history.

Where liberty dwells, there is my country.
— BENJAMIN FRANKLIN

One man with courage is a majority. — THOMAS JEFFERSON

I regret that I have but one life to give for my country. — NATHAN HALE

I know not what course others may take, but as for me, give me liberty or give me death!
— PATRICK HENRY

We have too many high-sounding words, and too few actions that correspond to them.
— ABIGAIL ADAMS

No man is good enough to govern another man without that other's consent. — ABRAHAM LINCOLN

We have nothing to fear but fear itself.
— FRANKLIN D. ROOSEVELT

Freedom is never given; it is won. — A. PHILIP RANDOLPH

The meaning of America is the possibilities of the common man. — W.E.B. DU BOIS

Ask not what your country can do for you, but what you can do for your country.
— JOHN F. KENNEDY

Democracy is not a fragile flower but it still needs cultivating.
— RONALD REAGAN

There is nothing wrong with America that cannot be cured with what is right in America.
— WILLIAM J. CLINTON

Do you know in what famous situation Nathan Hale (above) made his brave statement? Why was it the last thing he said?

During the American Revolution, Hale was a spy for the Americans. Captured by the British, he made his statement just before they executed him.

Founding Fathers

America was founded on the ideals of liberty, freedom, and democracy. But it was up to citizens to put those ideals into action, first by separating from Great Britain and then by forming a new nation. Here are some of the most prominent of the people known as the "Founding Fathers" of our nation.

John Adams (1735–1826)
Helped write the Declaration of Independence; second president

Benjamin Franklin (1706–1790)
One of the leaders of the Revolution; helped create the Constitution

Alexander Hamilton (1755–1804)
Led effort for the Constitution; first secretary of the Treasury

Patrick Henry (1736–1799)
Virginia leader who spoke eloquently in favor of freedom

Thomas Jefferson (1743–1826)
Wrote the Declaration of Indepedence; third president

James Madison (1751–1836)
Called "Father of the Constitution"; fourth president

Gouverneur Morris (1752–1816)
Helped draft the Constitution; minister to France and England

Thomas Paine (1737–1804)
Author whose writing inspired the Founding Fathers

Edmund Randolph (1753–1813)
Early U.S. attorney general and secretary of state

George Washington (1732–1799)
Commander of Continental army; first president

Everyone knows that George Washington was the first president. But which man from this list was the first vice president?

John Adams.

Founding Mothers

Those Founding Fathers on the opposite page get all the press! Women played a big part in the creation of our country, too. However, since they could not vote at the time, their influence was more behind the scenes. Also, we know about some of these women today because of the fame of their husbands. Hundreds more women helped the Revolution anonymously. Read this list of women who were vital to the cause of liberty, and try to find out more about them at your library. Ye go, thou girls!

Abigail Adams (1744–1818)
Wife of John Adams; wrote about life in the colonies

Penelope Barker (1728–1796)
North Carolinian who led a boycott of British goods

Margaret Corbin (1751–c.1800)
Wounded when taking the place of her soldier husband at cannon

Lydia Darragh (1729–1789)
Housewife-turned-spy; discovered and revealed British plans

Sybil Ludington (1761–1839)
16-year-old who rode to warn Patriots of a coming British attack

Eliza Pinckney (1722–1793)
Englishwoman-turned-influential South Carolina plantation owner

Esther DeBerdt Reed (1746–1780)
Philadelphia woman who helped raise money to support troops

Mercy Otis Warren (1728–1814)
Boston writer who supported and wrote about freedom

Martha Washington (1731–1802)
Wife of George Washington; her visits to troops were inspirational

After being forced to let British soldiers stay at her Pennsylvania home, Lydia Darragh listened through a keyhole as British generals plotted a sneak attack. Darragh carried this news through enemy lines to warn General Washington, and the attack was defeated.

The Confederacy

The Civil War divided our country, as 11 states seceded to form the Confederacy. Here is how the country split up during the war.

THE CONFEDERATE STATES

STATE	DATE SECEDED	DATE READMITTED
South Carolina	December 20, 1860	June 25, 1868
Mississippi	January 9, 1861	February 23, 1870
Florida	January 10, 1861	June 25, 1868
Alabama	January 11, 1861	June 25, 1868
Georgia	January 19, 1861	July 15, 1870
Louisiana	January 26, 1861	June 25, 1868
Texas	February 1, 1861	March 30, 1870
Virginia	April 17, 1861	January 26, 1870
Arkansas	May 6, 1861	June 22, 1868
North Carolina	May 20, 1861	June 25, 1868
Tennessee	June 8, 1861	July 24, 1866

A CONFEDERATE TERRITORY

New Mexico

Although Delaware, Kentucky, Maryland, Missouri, and West Virginia were considered slave states, they remained part of the Union during the Civil War.

and the Union

THE UNION

California	Minnesota
Connecticut	Missouri
Delaware	New Hampshire
Illinois	New Jersey
Indiana	New York
Iowa	Ohio
Kansas	Oregon
Kentucky	Pennsylvania
Maine	Rhode Island
Maryland	Vermont
Massachusetts	West Virginia
Michigan	Wisconsin

THE UNION TERRITORIES

Colorado	Nebraska	Utah
Dakota	Nevada	Washington

U.S. Presidents and Vice Presidents

Hail to the Chiefs

He (and it's always been a he . . . so far!) is the commander in chief, the head of the executive branch, and holds the most powerful office in the world. The rules: You have to be at least 35 years old and born in the United States. Hang on for a few more years and this could be you!

PRESIDENT	VICE PRESIDENT	POLITICAL PARTY	YEARS
1. George Washington	John Adams	Federalist	1789–1797
2. John Adams	Thomas Jefferson	Federalist	1797–1801
3. Thomas Jefferson	Aaron Burr	Dem.-Rep.*	1801–1805
	George Clinton	Dem.-Rep.*	1805–1809
4. James Madison	George Clinton	Dem.-Rep.*	1809–1817
5. James Monroe	Daniel D. Tompkins	Dem.-Rep.*	1817–1825
6. John Quincy Adams	John C. Calhoun	Dem.-Rep.*	1825–1829
7. Andrew Jackson	John C. Calhoun	Democrat	1829–1833
	Martin Van Buren	Democrat	1833–1837
8. Martin Van Buren	Richard M. Johnson	Democrat	1837–1841
9. William H. Harrison	John Tyler	Whig	1841
10. John Tyler		Whig	1841–1845
11. James K. Polk	George M. Dallas	Democrat	1845–1849
12. Zachary Taylor	Millard Fillmore	Whig	1849–1850
13. Millard Fillmore		Whig	1850–1853
14. Franklin Pierce	William R. King	Democrat	1853–1857
15. James Buchanan	John C. Breckenridge	Democrat	1857–1861
16. Abraham Lincoln	Hannibal Hamlin	Republican	1861–1865
	Andrew Johnson	Republican	1865
17. Andrew Johnson		Union	1865–1869
18. Ulysses S. Grant	Schuyler Colfax	Republican	1869–1873
	Henry Wilson	Republican	1873–1877
19. Rutherford B. Hayes	William A. Wheeler	Republican	1877–1881
20. James Garfield	Chester A. Arthur	Republican	1881
21. Chester A. Arthur		Republican	1881–1885

PRESIDENT	VICE PRESIDENT	POLITICAL PARTY	YEARS
22. Grover Cleveland	Thomas A. Hendricks	Democrat	1885–1889
23. Benjamin Harrison	Levi P. Morton	Republican	1889–1893
24. Grover Cleveland	Adlai E. Stevenson	Democrat	1893–1897
25. William McKinley	Garret A. Hobart	Republican	1897–1901
	Theodore Roosevelt	Republican	1901
26. Theodore Roosevelt		Republican	1901–1905
	Charles W. Fairbanks	Republican	1905–1909
27. William H. Taft	James S. Sherman	Republican	1909–1913
28. Woodrow Wilson	Thomas R. Marshall	Democrat	1913–1921
29. Warren G. Harding	Calvin Coolidge	Republican	1921–1923
30. Calvin Coolidge		Republican	1923–1925
	Charles G. Dawes	Republican	1925–1929
31. Herbert C. Hoover	Charles Curtis	Republican	1929–1933
32. Franklin D. Roosevelt	John N. Garner	Democrat	1933–1941
	Henry A. Wallace	Democrat	1941–1945
	Harry S. Truman	Democrat	1945
33. Harry S. Truman		Democrat	1945–1949
	Albert W. Barkley	Democrat	1949–1953
34. Dwight D. Eisenhower	Richard M. Nixon	Republican	1953–1961
35. John F. Kennedy	Lyndon B. Johnson	Democrat	1961–1963
36. Lyndon B. Johnson		Democrat	1963–1965
	Hubert H. Humphrey	Democrat	1965–1969
37. Richard M. Nixon	Spiro T. Agnew	Republican	1969–1973
	Gerald R. Ford	Republican	1973–1974
38. Gerald R. Ford	Nelson A. Rockefeller	Republican	1974–1977
39. James E. Carter, Jr.	Walter F. Mondale	Democrat	1977–1981
40. Ronald Reagan	George Bush	Republican	1981–1989
41. George Bush	J. Danforth Quayle	Republican	1989–1993
42. William J. Clinton	Albert Gore	Democrat	1993–2001
43. George W. Bush	Richard Cheney	Republican	2001–

* Oddly, an early political party was called "Democratic-Republican." Those names were later used for separate parties.

George Washington, the first president, chose what we call the chief executive. Not Your Honor or Your Majesty — just "Mr. President."

Civil Rights Leaders

One of the most important issues facing America during the past two centuries has been the role and rights of minorities. Many brave people have stepped forward to see that freedom was guaranteed for all Americans. Here are some of the leaders of movements that helped work toward equality for all, regardless of race.

NAME	LIFE SPAN
Ralph D. Abernathy	1926–1990
Marion Anderson	1902–1993
James Baldwin	1924–1987
Benjamin Banneker	1731–1806
Mary McLeod Bethune	1875–1955
Ruby Bridges	1954–
Stokely Carmichael	1942–
César Chávez	1927–1993
William (W.E.B.) Du Bois	1868–1963
Medgar Evers	1925–1963
James Farmer	1920–
José Garvey	1944–
Marcus Garvey	1887–1940
Dolores Huerta	1930–
Jesse L. Jackson	1941–
Mahalia Jackson	1911–1972
James Weldon Johnson	1871–1938
Barbara Jordan	1936–1995
Coretta Scott King	1927–2006
Martin Luther King, Jr.	1929–1968
Abraham Lincoln	1809–1865
Malcolm X (Malcolm Little)	1925–1965
Rosa Lee Parks	1913–2005
Adam Clayton Powell	1908–1972
Asa Philip Randolph	1889–1979
Paul Robeson	1898–1976
Harriet Beecher Stowe	1811–1896
Reies Lopez Tijerina	1926–
Sojourner Truth	1797–1883
Roy Wilkins	1901–1981
Hosea Williams	1926–2000
Andrew Young	1932–

PSST Dolores Huerta and César Chávez founded the United Farm Workers of America. Together they fought for the rights of migrant workers. They called the public's attention to the people who helped pick the fruits and vegetables on America's farms. March 31 is César Chávez Day in California.

Civil Rights Speeches

People began making speeches in support of civil rights for African-Americans and other groups long before the 1960s. Some advocated a peaceful path to civil rights, while others demanded action by any means. Here are a few of the most noteworthy such speeches.

DATE	SPEECH	SPEAKER
December 22, 1886	The New South	Henry Grady
July 16, 1901	The Evolution of Negro Leadership	W.E.B. Du Bois
February 13, 1905	Lincoln and the Race Problem	Theodore Roosevelt
August 16, 1906	Men of Niagara	W.E.B. Du Bois
October 10, 1906	Being Colored in the Nation's Capital	Mary Church Terrell
August 1, 1924	Call for a Return to Africa	Marcus Garvey
May 14, 1940	Defense of Civil Liberties	Eleanor Roosevelt
July 14, 1948	Speech in support of Democratic party's civil rights platform	Hubert Humphrey
April 10, 1957	A Realistic Look at the Question of Progress in the Area of Race Relations	Martin Luther King, Jr.
April 16, 1963	Letter from Birmingham Jail	Martin Luther King, Jr.
June 11, 1963	A Moral Issue	John F. Kennedy
August 28, 1963	I Have a Dream	Martin Luther King, Jr.
March 29, 1964	The Ballot or the Bullet	Malcolm X
July 4, 1964	The Civil Rights Movement: Fraud, Sham, and Hoax	George C. Wallace
December 10, 1964	Nobel Peace Prize acceptance speech	Martin Luther King, Jr.
March 8, 1965	Speech on Courage	Martin Luther King, Jr.
April 3, 1968	I've Been to the Mountaintop	Martin Luther King, Jr.
May 21, 1969	Speech urging passage of Equal Rights Amendment	Shirley Chisholm
July 29, 1998	I Am a Man, a Black Man, an American	Clarence Thomas

Martin Luther King, Jr. delivered his famous "I Have a Dream" speech in front of the Lincoln Memorial in Washington, D.C. A crowd of more than 250,000 people heard him speak.

Famous Women in History

She's in Charge

Many important women in world history are remembered for political work. Other women on this list are remembered for being pioneers in a certain area, opening the way for many more women to follow.

NAME, TITLE	LIFE SPAN
Nefertiti, Queen of Egypt	14th century B.C.
Cleopatra, Queen of Egypt	69–30 B.C.
Eleanor of Aquitaine, Queen of England and France	1122–1202
Joan of Arc, Leader of French army	1412–1431
Isabella I, Queen of Spain	1451–1504
Catherine de Medici, Queen of France	1519–1589
Elizabeth I, Queen of England	1533–1603
Mbande Nzinga, Queen of Ndongo and Matamba*	1582–1663
Catherine the Great, Empress of Russia	1729–1796
Marie Antoinette, Queen of France	1755–1793
Elizabeth Cady Stanton, Founder, Woman Suffrage Assoc.#	1815–1902
Victoria, Queen of England	1819–1901
Susan B. Anthony, Founder, Woman Suffrage Assoc.	1820–1906
Clara Barton, Founder, American Red Cross	1821–1912
Mother Jones, Famous labor leader	1830–1930

NAME, TITLE	LIFE SPAN
Tz'u-hsi, Empress of China	1835–1908
Liliuokalani, Queen of Hawaii	1838–1917
Nancy Astor, First woman in British Parliament	1879–1964
Jeannette Rankin, First woman elected to Congress	1880–1973
Francis Perkins, First woman Cabinet member	1882–1965
Amelia Earhart, First female pilot to cross Atlantic	1898–1937
Golda Meir, Prime Minister of Israel	1898–1978
Margaret Mead, Anthropologist	1901–1978
Rachel Carson, Environmental scientist and activist	1907–1964
Mother Teresa, Founder, Missionaries of Charity	1910–1997
Indira Gandhi, Prime Minister of India	1917–1984
Margaret Thatcher, Prime Minister of England	1925–
Elizabeth II, Queen of Great Britain	1926–
Sandra Day O'Connor, First woman on Supreme Court	1930–
Madeleine Albright, First woman Secretary of State	1937–

* Former kingdom in Africa; # This group fought for women's right to vote.

Who's missing from this list? Although the United States has not had a woman president, our first ladies (wives of the presidents) can be listed among the famous leaders. This would include influential first ladies such as Abigail Adams, Edith Wilson, Eleanor Roosevelt, and Jacqueline Kennedy.

More Than Just Words

Today, we get our big news from TV, the radio, or the Internet. Throughout history, however, the biggest news has been made by important books or documents. Here is a list of some influential documents or books in history.

The Republic (360 B.C.)

Greek philosopher Plato's thoughts on government and more.

Magna Carta (1215)

Signed by England's King John and British noblemen, it helped pave the way for democracy many years later.

Principia Mathematica (1687)

Sir Isaac Newton laid out some of the basics of mathematics, gravity, and physics.

Declaration of Independence (1776)

The United States declared itself free from British rule, and inspired many other countries to similar actions.

U.S. Constitution (1789)

Along with the ten-amendment Bill of Rights, this set up the basics of American government.

Communist Manifesto (1848)

Written by Karl Marx and Friedrich Engels, it spelled out a social philosophy later used to help form the Soviet Union.

Origin of Species (1859)

Scientist Charles Darwin described the theory of evolution for the first time.

Quotations from Chairman Mao (1967)

Called "The Little Red Book," it gathered the sayings and thoughts of Chinese Communist leader Mao Tse-tung.

Long Walk to Freedom (1994)

The autobiography of South African leader Nelson Mandela.

The Bible and the Koran (also spelled Qur'an) have also played vital roles in shaping history. The Bible's Old Testament contains the holy book of Judaism, while the entire Bible is scripture for Christianity. The Koran is the holy book of Islam.

Internet Time Line

The Internet dates back to the 1960s, when ARPA (the U.S. Defense Department's Advanced Research Projects Agency) linked university computers together. This "network" let computers in many different places talk to one another. Of course, today, the Internet is about people connecting, not just computers. Here is a time line showing the development of the Internet and the programs and machines that help it work.

1946 ENIAC — first electronic computer created

1951 Ferranti Mark I — first commercially produced computer

1969 ARPANET created; grows to 15 sites in two years

1972 E-mail created by engineer Ray Tomlinson in Connecticut

1973 Transmission Control Protocol/Internet Protocol (TCP/IP) designed; lets computers communicate over the Internet

1981 IBM PC introduced

1984 Macintosh introduced

1989 Silicon memory chips introduced

1990 World Wide Web invented

1993 Mosaic, first graphic Web browser, released

1994 Netscape Navigator browser released

1996 45,000,000+ people using the Internet worldwide

1999 150,000,000+ people using the Internet worldwide

1999 "Melissa" virus infects computers via e-mail, followed by the "Love Bug" virus in 2000

1999 Invention of first tool for creating Web logs, or "blogs"

2001 36,000,000+ Internet domain names registered

2001 Napster ordered to stop distributing copyrighted music

2004 iTunes Music Store opens to sell digital music

Save time on the Web with these easy shortcuts: PLS (please); **LOL** (laugh out loud); **ROTFL** (rolling on the floor laughing); **IMO** (in my opinion); **BTW** (by the way); **HHOK** (ha, ha, only kidding); **TYVM** (thank you very much).

Visit Sites of the
American Revolution

Visiting one of the American Revolution sites gives you a firsthand feel for the difficulties of being a soldier from 1775 to 1781. At most sites, guides will explain the importance of the area and tell you about the people who fought our first battle for freedom.

SITE/NOTES	STATE
Bunker Hill National Historic Site Battle, 1775	Massachusetts
Colonial National Battlefield—Yorktown Site of war's final battle, 1781	Virginia
Cowpens National Battlefield Battle, 1781	South Carolina
Guilford Courthouse National Military Park Battle, 1781	North Carolina
Independence National Historic Park Site of Liberty Bell and Independence Hall	Pennsylvania
Minute Man National Historic Park Site of battles early in war, 1775	Massachusetts
Monmouth Battlefield Battle, 1778	New Jersey
Saratoga National Historic Park Battle, 1777	New York
Valley Forge National Historic Park Site of Continental Army winter camp, 1777–1778	Pennsylvania
Washington's Crossing Site of famous military strike by George Washington	Pennsylvania

PsSST You can watch history come alive each year at Washington's Crossing on Christmas Day. An actor playing George Washington leads a boat of men across the Delaware River to surprise Hessian soldiers encamped in Trenton, New Jersey. They don't use real bullets, of course.

Visit Sites of the
Civil War

From 1861 to 1865, the Civil War was fought between Union states in the northern part of the United States and Confederate states in the South. There are many places you can visit where Americans fought Americans for the only time in our history. Here are a few of the more famous sites.

SITE/NOTES	STATE
Andersonville National Historic Site Largest Confederate military prison	Georgia
Antietam National Battlefield Battle, 1862	Maryland
Appomattox Court House National Historical Park Confederate surrender, April 9, 1865	Virginia
Ford's Theatre National Historic Site Assassination site of President Lincoln	Washington, D.C.
Fort Sumter National Monument Battle, 1861	South Carolina
Gettysburg National Military Park Battle, 1863	Pennsylvania
Harpers Ferry National Historical Park Site of attack by abolitionist John Brown	West Virginia
Manassas National Battlefield (Bull Run) Battles, 1861 and 1862	Virginia
Shiloh National Military Park Battle, 1862	Tennessee
Vicksburg National Military Park Siege, 1863	Mississippi

Andersonville Confederate Military Prison in Georgia was one of the worst prisons ever built in America. More than one-quarter of the Union prisoners held there in 1864–1865 died due to the terrible and crowded conditions.

Kids in U.S. History

You probably won't know these kids. Their names do not appear in many history books, but they are remembered because they played important roles in our history. Listed with their names are their ages and the years during which they first accomplished what made them memorable.

Diego Bermudez, 12   **1492**
Sailed with Columbus on the *Santa María*

Pocahontas, 12   **1607**
Powhatan girl who may have saved
Captain John Smith's life

Tom Savage, 13   **1608**
Spied against Native Americans

Mary Chilton, 15   **1620**
Possibly first female to land at Plymouth

Sybil Ludington, 16   **1777**
Did a "Paul Revere" in Connecticut

Anyokah, 10   **1821**
Helped develop writing system for the
Cherokee language

Allen Jay, 13   **1844**
Quaker who helped slaves escape

William Cody, 14   **1860**
Pony Express rider, later "Buffalo Bill"

Johnny Clem, 9   **1861**
Civil War drummer boy

Vinnie Ream, 17   **1864**
Sculptor who created bust of Lincoln

Rose Cohen, 12   **1892**
Labor union leader

Joseph Miliauskas, 10   **1900**
Famous young coal miner

John Thayer, 17   **1912**
Survived the sinking of the *Titanic*

Jackie Cooper, 8   **1930s**
Child movie star

Calvin Graham, 12   **1942**
Snuck into the Navy; received medals
for bravery

Anna Meyer, 15   **1944**
Played in women's pro baseball league

Elizabeth Eckford, 15   **1957**
One of the Little Rock Nine, civil rights
pioneer

John Tinker, 15   **1965**
Vietnam War protestor

Ryan White, 13   **1984**
AIDS victim who spread information and
understanding about the disease

For more on these kids and many others in history, check out *We Were There, Too*, a book by Phillip Hoose published in 2001. The author tracked down hundreds of children who made an impact on history. Maybe you can be in his next edition . . . get busy!

Obscure Famous People

Over the years, some people who were at one time world famous have faded from view. Although they were once well-known celebrities around the world, the men and women on this list are often forgotten today.

PERSON, LIFE SPAN/ACHIEVEMENT

Nellie Bly, 1865–1922
In 1890, this pioneering journalist traveled around the world in 72 days.

William Jennings Bryan, 1860–1925
One of America's most famous politicians at the turn of the century, he ran for president four times.

Howard Carter, 1874–1939
In 1922, Carter uncovered the tomb of the ancient Egyptian King Tut.

Douglas "Wrong Way" Corrigan, 1907–1995
In 1938, Corrigan made headlines when he filed a flight plan to fly from Brooklyn to California — but ended up in Ireland!

Marcus Garvey, 1887–1940
A native of Jamaica, Garvey led a movement in the 1920s and 1930s that led many African Americans to move back to Africa.

Audie Murphy, 1925–1971
Murphy won more military medals and decorations than any other solider in World War II and later became a popular movie star.

Carry Nation, 1846–1911
Nation led a national campaign against the use of alcohol.

Dan Rice, 1823–1901
During the Civil War era, Rice was America's most famous entertainer. He was supposedly the model for the Uncle Sam character.

Major Taylor, 1878–1932
In the late 1890s, this bicycle racer was the most famous athlete in the world. He was also the first African-American pro athlete.

PsSST

Nellie Bly was one of the first women to become famous as a writer and reporter. Her stories from places around the world, published in newspapers in New York and elsewhere, thrilled millions of Americans in the late 1800s.

My Time Machine

Now that you've read all about the people and places from U.S. and world history, it's time to put on your thinking cap — or should we say your bike helmet? We've created the *Book of Lists* Time Machine. Strap yourself in, sharpen your pencil, and have fun filling out your Time Machine itinerary (that means a list of places you go on a trip).

Year in the past I'd most like to visit _____

What I would do first when I got there

_____

_____

Questions I'd ask the people I met back then

_____

_____

_____

Person from the past (any year) that I'd most like to meet and why

_____

_____

_____

Back to the future: Here's what I think my time machine will find when we go to the year 2106

_____

_____

_____

One thing I'd take on my time machine that I couldn't live without, no matter what year it is

_____

CHAPTER TWO

Social Studies

There's something for everyone in social studies. Whether you need to find the capital of Mongolia, the definition of plutocracy, the inventor of chocolate chips (thanks to whoever that is!), or why the Colossus was so "wonder"-ful, you'll find it in this chapter.

Countries

The number of countries in the world is always changing, as some larger countries break up into smaller ones, or former colonies become independent states. The two newest members of this list of countries are East Timor (2002) and Serbia and Montenegro (2002).

COUNTRY/CAPITAL	MAIN LANGUAGES	CURRENCY
Afghanistan/Kabul	Pushtu, Dari Persian, Turkic languages	Afghani
Albania/Tiranë	Albanian, Greek	Lek
Algeria/Algiers	Arabic, French, Berber dialects	Dinar
Andorra/Andorra la Vella	Catalan, French, Spanish	Euro
Angola/Luanda	Bantu, Portuguese	Kwanza
Antigua and Barbuda/Saint John's	English	East Caribbean dollar
Argentina/Buenos Aires	Spanish, English, Italian, German	Peso
Armenia/Yerevan	Armenian, Russian	Dram
Australia/Canberra	English	Australian dollar
Austria/Vienna	German	Euro
Azerbaijan/Baku	Azerbaijani Turkic, Russian, Armenian	Manat
Bahamas/Nassau	English, Creole	Bahamian dollar
Bahrain/Manama	Arabic, English, Farsi, Urdu	Bahrain dinar
Bangladesh/Dhaka	Bangla, English	Taka
Barbados/Bridgetown	English	Barbados dollar
Belarus/Minsk	Belorussian	Belorussian ruble
Belgium/Brussels	Dutch, French, German	Euro
Belize/Belmopan	English, Creole, Spanish, Garifuna	Belize dollar
Benin/Porto-Norvo	French	Franc CFA
Bhutan/Thimphu	Dzongkha	Ngultrum
Bolivia/La Paz, Sucre	Spanish, Quechua, Aymara, Guarani	Boliviano
Bosnia and Herzegovina/Sarajevo	Serbian, Croatian	Dinar
Botswana/Gaborone	English, Setswana	Pula
Brazil/Brasília	Portuguese	Real
Brunei/Bandar Seri Begawan	Malay, English, Chinese	Brunei dollar
Bulgaria/Sofia	Bulgarian	Lev
Burkina Faso/Ouagadougou	French, tribal languages	Franc
Burundi/Bujumbura	Kirundi, French, Swahili	Burundi franc

of the World

COUNTRY/CAPITAL	MAIN LANGUAGES	CURRENCY
Cambodia/Phnom Penh	Khmer, French, English	Rial
Cameroon/Yaoundé	French, English, tribal languages	Franc CFA
Canada/Ottawa	English, French	Canadian dollar
Cape Verde/Praia	Portuguese, Crioulo	Cape Verdean escudo
Central African Republic/Bangui	French, Sangho, Arabic, Swahili	Franc CFA
Chad/N'Djamena	French, Arabic	Franc CFA
Chile/Santiago	Spanish	Peso
China/Beijing	Chinese, Mandarin	Yuan
Colombia/Bogotá	Spanish	Peso
Comoros/Moroni	French, Arabic	Franc CFA
Congo, Dem. Rep. of the/Kinshasa	French, Swahili, Ishiluba, Kikongo	Congolese franc
Congo, Republic of the/Brazzaville	French, Lingala, Kikongo	Franc CFA
Costa Rica/San José	Spanish	Colón
Croatia/Zagreb	Serbian, Croatian	Kuna
Cuba/Havana	Spanish	Peso
Cyprus/Lefkosia (Nicosia)	Greek, Turkish, English	Cyprus pound
Czech Republic/Prague	Czech, Slovak	Koruna
Denmark/Copenhagen	Danish, Faeroese, Greenlandic	Krone
Djibouti/Djibouti	Arabic, French, Somali, Afar	Djibouti franc
Dominica/Roseau	English, French patois	East Caribbean dollar
Dominican Republic/Santo Domingo	Spanish, English	Peso
East Timor/Dili	Portuguese, Indonesian, Tetum	Egyptian pound
Ecuador/Quito	Spanish, Quechua	U.S. dollar
Egypt/Cairo	Arabic, English, French	Egyptian pound
El Salvador/San Salvador	Spanish, Nahua	Colón
Equatorial Guinea/Malabo	Spanish, pidgin English, Fang, Bubi	Franc CFA
Eritrea/Asmara	Afar, Bilen, Tigre, Kunama, Nara	Nakfa
Estonia/Tallinn	Estonian, Russian, Finnish, English	Kroon
Ethiopia/Addis Ababa	Amharic, English, Tigrigna, Orominga	Birr
Fiji/Suva	Fijian, English, Hindustani	Fiji dollar
Finland/Helsinki	Finnish, Swedish, Lapp, Russian	Euro
France/Paris	French	Euro

Countries of the World, continued

COUNTRY/CAPITAL	MAIN LANGUAGES	CURRENCY
Gabon/Libreville	French, Myene	Franc CFA
Gambia/Banjul	English	Dalasi
Georgia/Tbilisi	Georgian, Russian	Lari
Germany/Berlin	German	Euro
Ghana/Accra	English	Cedi
Greece/Athens	Greek	Drachma
Grenada/St. George's	English, French patois	East Caribbean dollar
Guatemala/Guatemala City	Spanish, Indian languages	Quetzal
Guinea/Conakry	French, African languages	Francs
Guinea-Bissau/Bissau	Portuguese, Criolo	Guinea-Bissau peso
Guyana/Georgetown	English, Amerindian languages	Guyana dollar
Haiti/Port-au-Prince	Creole, French	Gourde
Honduras/Tegucigalpa	Spanish, English	Lempira
Hungary/Budapest	Hungarian	Forint
Iceland/Reykjavik	Icelandic	Icelandic krona
India/New Delhi	Hindi, English	Rupee
Indonesia/Jakarta	Bahasa Indonesian, Dutch, English	Rupiah
Iran/Tehran	Persian, Asari, Kurdish, Arabic	Rial
Iraq/Baghdad	Arabic, Kurdish	Iraqi dinar
Ireland/Dublin	English, Irish	Euro
Israel/Jerusalem	Hebrew, Arabic, English	Shekel
Italy/Rome	Italian	Euro
Ivory Coast/Yamoussoukro	French, African languages	Franc CFA
Jamaica/Kingston	English, Jamaican, Creole	Jamaican dollar
Japan/Tokyo	Japanese	Yen
Jordan/Amman	Arabic, English	Jordanian dinar
Kazakhstan/Astana	Kazak, Russian	Tenge
Kenya/Nairobi	English, Swahili	Kenyan shilling
Kiribati/Tarawa	English, Gilbertese	Australian dollar
Korea, North/Pyongyang	Korean	Won
Korea, South/Seoul	Korean, English	Won
Kuwait/Kuwait	Arabic, English	Kuwaiti dinar
Kyrgyzstan/Bishkek	Kyrgyz, Russian	Som
Laos/Vientiane	Lao, French, English	Kip

COUNTRY/CAPITAL	MAIN LANGUAGES	CURRENCY
Latvia/Riga	Latvian	Lats
Lebanon/Beirut	Arabic, French, English	Lebanese pound
Lesotho/Maseru	Sesotho, English, Zulu, Xhosa	Loti
Liberia/Monrovia	English	Liberian dollar
Libya/Tripoli	Arabic, Italian, English	Libyan dinar
Liechtenstein/Vaduz	German, Alemannic dialect	Swiss franc
Lithuania/Vilnius	Lithuanian, Polish, Russian	Litas
Luxembourg/Luxembourg	Luxembourgisch, German, French	Euro
Macedonia/Skopje	Macedonian, Albanian, Turkish	Denar
Madagascar/Antananarivo	French, Malagasy	Malagasy franc
Malawi/Lilongwe	English, Chichewa	Kwacha
Malaysia/Kuala Lumpur	Malay, English, Chinese, Tamil	Ringgit
Maldives/Male	Dhivehi, Arabic, Hindi, English	Maldivian rufiyaa
Mali/Bamako	French, African languages	Franc CFA
Malta/Valletta	Maltese, English	Maltese lira
Marshall Islands/Majuro	English	U.S. dollar
Mauritania/Nouakchott	Arabic, French	Ouguiya
Mauritius/Port Louis	English, French	Rupee
Mexico/Mexico City	Spanish, Indian Languages	Peso
Micronesia/Palikir	English	U.S. dollar
Moldova/Chişnău	Moldovan, Russian	Moldovan leu
Monaco/Monaco	French, English, Italian, Monegasque	French franc
Mongolia/Ulaanbaatar	Mongolian, Turkic, Russian, Chinese	Tugrik
Morocco/Rabat	Arabic, Berber, French, Spanish	Dirham
Mozambique/Maputo	Portuguese, Bantu	Metical
Myanmar/Rangoon	Burmese	Kyat
Namibia/Windhoek	Afrikaans, German, English	Namibian dollar
Nauru/Yaren District	Nauruan, English	Australian dollar
Nepal/Kathmandu	Nepali, Newari, Bhutia	Nepalese rupee
Netherlands/Amsterdam	Dutch, Frisian	Euro
New Zealand/Wellington	English, Maori	New Zealand dollar
Nicaragua/Managua	Spanish	Córdoba
Niger/Niamey	French, Hausa, Songhai, Arabic	Franc CFA
Nigeria/Abuja	English, Hausa, Yoruba, Ib	Naira
Norway/Oslo	Norwegian	Krone

Countries of the World, continued

COUNTRY/CAPITAL	MAIN LANGUAGES	CURRENCY
Oman/Muscat	Arabic, English	Rial
Pakistan/Islamabad	Punjabi, Sindhi, Pashtu, English	Rupee
Palau/Koror	Palauan, English	U.S. dollar
Panama/Panama City	Spanish, English	Balboa
Papua New Guinea/Port Moresby	English, Tok Pisin	Kina
Paraguay/Asunción	Spanish, Guarani	Guarani
Peru/Lima	Spanish, Quechua, Aymara	Nuevo sol
Philippines/Manila	Philippino, English	Peso
Poland/Warsaw	Polish	Zloty
Portugal/Lisbon	Portuguese	Euro
Qatar/Doha	Arabic, English	Riyal
Romania/Bucharest	Romanian, Hungarian, German	Leu
Russia/Moscow	Russian	Ruble
Rwanda/Kigali	Kinyarwanda, French, English	Franc
Saint Kitts-Nevis/Basseterre	English	East Caribbean dollar
Saint Lucia/Castries	English, French patois	East Caribbean dollar
St.Vincent & the Grenadines/Kingstown	English, French patois	East Caribbean dollar
Samoa/Apia	Samoan, English	Tala
San Marino/San Marino	Italian	Lira
São Tomé & Príncipe/São Tomé	Portuguese	Dobra
Saudi Arabia/Riyadh	Arabic, English	Riyal
Senegal/Dakar	French, Wolof, Serer	Franc CFA
Serbia and Montenegro/Belgrade	Serbian	New dinar
Seychelles/Victoria	English, French	Rupee
Sierra Leone/Freetown	English, Krio, Mende, Temne	Leone
Singapore/Singapore	Chinese, Malay, Tamil, English	Singapore dollar
Slovakia/Bratislava	Slovak, Hungarian	Koruna
Slovenia/Ljubljana	Slovenian, Serbo-Croatian	Tolar
Solomon Islands/Honiara	Solomon pidgin, English	Solomon Islands dollar
Somalia/Mogadishu	Somali, Arabic, Italian, English	Somalia shilling
South Africa/Pretoria	English, Afrikaans, Zulu, Xhosa	Rand
Spain/Madrid	Spanish, Catalan, Galician, Basque	Euro
Sri Lanka/Colombo	Sinhala, Tamil, English	Sri Lanka rupee
Sudan/Khartoum	Arabic, English	Sudanese pound

COUNTRY/CAPITAL	MAIN LANGUAGES	CURRENCY
Suriname/Paramaribo	Dutch, English, Surinamese	Guilder
Swaziland/Mbabane	English, Swazi	Lilangeni
Sweden/Stockholm	Swedish	Krona
Switzerland/Bern	German, French, Italian, Romansch	Swiss franc
Syria/Damascus	Arabic, French, English	Syrian pound
Taiwan/Taipei	Mandarin Chinese	New Taiwan dollar
Tajikistan/Dushanbe	Tajik	Tajik ruble
Tanzania/Dar es Salaam	Swahili, English	Tanzanian shilling
Thailand/Bangkok	Thai, Chinese, English	Baht
Togo/Lomé	French, Ewé, Mina, Kabye	Franc CFA
Tonga/Nuku'alofa	Tongan, English	Pa'anga
Trinidad and Tobago/Port of Spain	English, Hindi, French, Spanish	Trinidad & Tobago dollar
Tunisia/Tunis	Arabic, French	Tunisian dinar
Turkey/Ankara	Turkish	Turkish lira
Turkmenistan/Ashgabat	Turkmen, Russian, Uzbek	Manat
Tuvalu/Funafuti	Tuvaluan, English	Tuvaluan dollar
Uganda/Kampala	English, Luganda, Swahili, Ateso	Ugandan shilling
Ukraine/Kyiv (Kiev)	Ukrainian	Hryvnia
United Arab Emirates/Abu Dhabi	Arabic, English	U.A.E. dirham
United Kingdom/London	English, Welsh, Scots Gaelic	Pound sterling
United States of America/Washington, D.C.	English	U.S. dollar
Uruguay/Montevideo	Spanish	Peso
Uzbekistan/Tashkent	Uzbek, Russian, Tajik	Uzbekistani som
Vanuatu/Port Vila	English, French, Bislama	Vatu
Vatican City/Vatican City	Italian, Latin	Euro
Venezuela/Caracas	Spanish	Bolivar
Vietnam/Hanoi	Vietnamese, French, English, Chinese	Dong
Yemen/Sanaa	Arabic	Rial
Yugoslavia/Belgrade	Serbian, Albanian	Yugoslav new dinar
Zambia/Lusaka	English	Kwacha
Zimbabwe/Harare	English, Shona, Ndebele	Zimbabwe dollar

What are the world's biggest and smallest countries in terms of their land areas?

Answer: The biggest is still Russia, even after the breakup of the Soviet Union. The smallest is Vatican City, which is just over 100 acres (44 hectares).

Ancient Gods

People in many cultures created stories about supreme beings to explain the events in their lives. This list gives the names of some of those gods and goddesses. Deities from Greece, Egypt, Rome, and Scandinavian countries often changed roles and names, so you will sometimes see different spellings and responsibilities for many of them.

RESPONSIBILITY	GREEK	EGYPTIAN	NORSE	ROMAN
Supreme god	Zeus	Ammon	Odin	Jupiter
Marriage, fertility	Hera	Isis	Frigg	Juno
Thunder, lightning	Zeus	none	Thor	Jupiter
Water, sea	Poseidon	Sebek	Njørd	Neptune
Sun, sky	Helios	Ra, Horus	Sol	Apollo
Moon	Artemis	Khonsu	Moon	Diana
Fire	Hephaestus	none	Loki	Vulcan
Wisdom	Athena	Thoth	Mimir	Minerva
Love, beauty	Aphrodite	Hathor	Balder	Venus
Earth, agriculture	Demeter	Geb	Jørd	Ceres
War, destruction	Ares	Seth	Tyr	Mars
Wine, fertility	Dionysus	Min	Freya	Bacchus
Underworld	Hades	Osiris	Hel	Pluto
Messenger	Hermes	none	none	Mercury
Peace	Irene	Ma'at	Frey	Pax

The ancient Egyptians believed that their pharaohs were both people and gods. While ruling, the pharaoh was Ra, and when he died he was Osiris. Anubis, the god with the head of a jackal, supposedly told Egyptians about embalming and creating mummies.

World Religions

Many religious groups do not keep accurate or up-to-date records, so the numbers of reported believers change all the time. Looking at percentages is another way to discover what people believe. The percentages on this list are based on a world population of 6,157,000,000.

RELIGIOUS GROUP	NUMBER OF BELIEVERS (PERCENTAGE)	
Baha'is	6,000,000	*
Buddhists	359,981,000	6%
Christians	2,000,000,000	32%
Orthodox	220,000,000	4%
Others	375,000,000	5%
Protestants	495,000,000	6%
Roman Catholics	1,100,000,000	17%
Hindus	900,000,000	15%
Jains	4,218,000	*
Jews	14,433,000	*
Muslims	1,300,000,000	22%
Shintoists	4,000,000	*
Sikhs	23,000,000	*
Spiritists	14,000,000	*
Zoroastrians	1,500,000	*

* Less than 1 percent.

Nonreligious people (those who do not follow any faith) total about **768** million. Atheists, people who deny the existence of a god, have worldwide numbers of **150** million.

Forms of Government

When a group of people live together, they organize themselves using a government. You probably have one at your school. The type of government depends on the will of the people, or the military force of a leader. The settlers in the American colonies had lived under a monarchy, so they set up a new government ruled by the people — a representative democracy.

Anarchy	No organized rule, confusion
Autocracy	One person governs with unlimited power
Communism	One-party system, state controls economy
Democracy	Government ruled by the people, usually the majority
Direct democracy	All people make their laws and vote on them
Representative democracy	People elect representatives to make the laws
Dictatorship	Rule by one person, often through military force
Matriarchy	Rule by a female or group of females
Military junta	Takeover and rule of government by military forces
Monarchy	Rule by a king or queen
Absolute monarchy	Ruler has unlimited power
Constitutional monarchy	Ruler's power is limited by the constitution
Parliamentary monarchy	Ruler is usually a symbol and has little power
Oligarchy	Government ruled by a few powerful people
Plutocracy	Government ruled by wealthy people
Republic	Rule by a chief of state, citizens elect officials
Socialism	Rule by shared ownership of government and goods
Theocracy	Rule by organized religion or religious leaders
Totalitarianism	Rule of the people by the state

PsSST

Humans are not the only ones who organize their lives with a system of government. Animals sometimes choose a leader to head their group. For example, canines will choose an "alpha dog" to lead their pack.

Biggest Cities

Cities in the United States list are ranked according to the total population of the city. In the world list, cities are ranked according to the population of the city and its suburbs. Just two U.S. cities make it onto the world list.

UNITED STATES		WORLD	
CITY	POP. IN MILLIONS	CITY	POP. IN MILLIONS
New York, New York	8.0	Tokyo, Japan	31.2
Los Angeles, California	3.8	Mexico City, Mexico	21.5
Chicago, Illinois	2.9	São Paulo, Brazil	19.9
Houston, Texas	2.0	New York, U.S.A.	18.0
Philadelphia, Penn.	1.5	Mumbai (Bombay), India	17.3
Phoenix, Arizona	1.4	Los Angeles, U.S.A.	16.7
San Diego, California	1.2	Kolkata (Calcutta), India	14.3
San Antonio, Texas	1.2	Shanghai, China	13.9
Dallas, Texas	1.2	Lagos, Nigeria	13.4
Detroit, Michigan	.9	Buenos Aires, Argentina	13.2

PsSST

It is estimated that the New York City area will fall to eighth on the world list by the year 2015, pushed aside by Lagos, Nigeria; Dhaka, Bangladesh; and Karachi, Pakistan.

U.S. Government Agencies
Alphabet Soup

On the menu for today — USA Alphabet Soup! The federal government seems to have an endless supply of agencies and departments. Many go by their initials. You'll recognize some, but others might be a bit obscure.

ACF	Administration for Children and Families
BIA	Bureau of Indian Affairs
BLM	Bureau of Land Management
CDC	Centers for Disease Control and Prevention
CIA	Central Intelligence Agency
HHA	Department of Health and Human Services
HUD	Department of Housing and Urban Development
VA	Department of Veterans Affairs
EPA	Environmental Protection Agency
FAA	Federal Aviation Administration
FCC	Federal Communications Commission
FEMA	Federal Emergency Management Agency
FDA	Food and Drug Administration
HHS	Health and Human Services Department
INS	Immigration and Naturalization Service
NASA	National Aeronautics and Space Administration
NOAA	National Oceanic and Atmospheric Administration
OSHA	Occupational Safety & Health Administration
OMB	Office of Management and Budget
SEC	Securities and Exchange Commission
SBA	Small Business Administration
SSA	Social Security Administration

See if you know the names that go with these initials: DOD, FBI, USDA, ZAW.

Answers: Department of Defense; Federal Bureau of Investigation; U.S. Department of Agriculture; and we put in ZAW just to trick you. It doesn't mean anything!

The U.S. Government

By order of the Constitution, the U.S. government is split into three separate, but equal, parts. These "branches" each control different parts of the nation's government. Here are some of the offices in each branch of government.

EXECUTIVE BRANCH

President

Vice President

Executive Office of the President

White House Office

Office of the Vice President

Council of Economic Advisers

Council on Environmental Quality

National Security Council

Office of Management and Budget

Office of National Drug Control Policy

Office of Policy Development

Office of Science and Technology Policy

Office of the U.S. Trade Representative

LEGISLATIVE BRANCH

Senate

House of Representatives

Architect of the Capitol

U.S. Botanic Garden

LEGISLATIVE BRANCH CONTINUED

General Accounting Office

Government Printing Office

Library of Congress

Congressional Budget Office

Tax Court

JUDICIAL BRANCH

Supreme Court of the United States

Courts of Appeals

District Courts

Territorial Courts

Court of International Trade

Court of Federal Claims

Court of Appeals for the Armed Forces

Court of Veterans Appeals

Administrative Office of the Courts

Federal Judicial Center

Sentencing Commission

A person cannot serve in more than one branch at a time; that is, a person can't be a judge and president at the same time.

Land and People

Two things many people often want to know about the world are: What is the biggest country, in terms of land area; and what country has the most people? These two lists answer those burning questions. The statistics are through the middle of 2005. With the world's population growing every day, the population list will change slightly over time. As for size, well, most countries can't grow any bigger!

WORLD'S LARGEST COUNTRIES: AREA

COUNTRY	SQ MI*	SQ KM*
Russia	6.59	17.06
Canada	3.85	9.97
United States	3.71	9.60
China	3.70	9.58
Brazil	3.28	8.49
Australia	2.96	7.66
India	1.27	3.28
Argentina	1.07	2.77
Kazakhstan	1.05	2.71
Sudan	.97	2.51

* in millions

WORLD'S LARGEST COUNTRIES: POPULATION

COUNTRY	POPULATION
China	1,306,000,000
India	1,080,000,000
United States	295,000,000
Indonesia	241,000,000
Brazil	186,000,000
Pakistan	162,000,000
Bangladesh	144,000,000
Russia	143,000,000
Nigeria	128,000,000
Japan	127,000,000

According to an online calculator called the **POPClock**, the world population through the summer of 2005 was more than 6,540,000,000 (that's 6.5 billion with a "b"!). The calculator estimates that in 30 years, the world population, at current growth rates, will be more than 8.5 billion. Everybody move over. . . . There are more people coming!

United Nations Organizations

Start throwing letters around and sooner or later you will end up with one of the many organizations sponsored by the United Nations. Here is a partial listing of those organizations, which can be found all around the globe, working hard to make life better for millions of people.

IAEA	International Atomic Energy Agency
IBRD	International Bank for Reconstruction and Development (World Bank)
ICAO	International Civil Aviation Organization
ICC	International Computing Center
ICJ	International Court of Justice
ICS	International Center for Science and High Technology
IFAD	International Fund for Agricultural Development
ILI	International Law Institute
IMF	International Monetary Fund
ODCCP	Office for Drug Control and Crime Prevention
OOSA	Office for Outer Space Affairs
POPIN	United Nations Population Information Network
UNESCO	United Nations Educational, Scientific, and Cultural Organization
UNEP	United Nations Environment Program
UNICEF	United Nations Children's Fund
UNIS	United Nations International School
UNU	United Nations University
WHO	World Health Organization
WFP	World Food Program
WMO	World Meteorological Organization

The United Nations employs more than 61,000 people around the world. Its headquarters is in New York City. The leader of the U.N. is called the Secretary-General.

Seven Wonders of the
Ancient World

Scholars in the Middle Ages created a famous list of Seven Wonders of the Ancient World that existed between 3000 B.C. and A.D. 476. The list was based on structures known to the ancient Greek world.

WONDER/LOCATION	DATE BUILT
Great Pyramid Giza, Egypt	2613–2494 B.C.
Hanging Gardens of Babylon Babylon (near today's Baghdad, Iraq)	604–564 B.C.
Temple of Artemis Ephesus (now Selcuk, Turkey)	550 B.C.
Statue of Zeus Olympia, Greece	435 B.C.
Mausoleum at Halicarnassus Halicarnassus (now Bodrum, Turkey)	350 B.C.
Colossus of Rhodes Rhodes, Greece	282 B.C.
Lighthouse of Alexandria Island of Pharos (now Alexandria, Egypt)	283–246 B.C.

The first of the Seven Wonders of the Ancient World to be built was the Great Pyramid in Giza, Egypt. The Great Pyramid served as Pharaoh Khufu's tomb, and is the only one of the Seven Ancient Wonders still in existence.

Wonders of the
Modern World

Unlike the Seven Wonders of the Ancient World, the Wonders of the Modern World have never been officially listed. No one can agree on just seven! Here is a list of the human-made structures that would top many experts' lists.

WONDER/LOCATION

Abu Simbel Temple/Egypt

Angkor Wat/Cambodia

Aswan High Dam/Egypt

Aztec Temple in Tenochtitlán/Mexico

Banaue Rice Terraces/Philippines

Big Ben/England

Borobudur Temple/Indonesia

Channel Tunnel/England—France

CN Tower/Canada

Colosseum/Italy

Dneproges Dam/Russia

Eiffel Tower/France

Empire State Building/New York, U.S.A.

Gateway Arch/Missouri, U.S.A.

Great Wall of China/China

Great Sphinx/Egypt

Golden Gate Bridge/California, U.S.A.

Hoover Dam/Arizona—Nevada, U.S.A.

WONDER/LOCATION

Itaipu Dam/Brazil—Paraguay

Leaning Tower of Pisa/Italy

Machu Picchu/Peru

Mayan Temples of Tikal/Guatemala

Moai Statues on Easter Island/Chile

Mont-Saint-Michel/France

Mount Rushmore/South Dakota, U.S.A.

Panama Canal/Panama

Parthenon/Greece

Persepolis Throne Hall/Iran

Petronas Towers/Malaysia

Shwedaung Pagoda/Myanmar

Statue of Liberty/New York, U.S.A.

Stonehenge/England

Suez Canal/Egypt

Sydney Opera House/Australia

Taj Mahal/India

Considered by many to be the most beautiful building in the world, the Taj Mahal in Agra, India, is often mistaken for a palace. Emperor Shah Jahan actually had the structure built in 1650 as a tomb for his wife, Mumtaz Mahal.

Medals of Freedom

The president of the United States gets to do a lot of cool stuff — ride helicopters, get into baseball games for free, eat whatever he wants, meet world leaders, stuff like that. He also gets to give out medals. The Presidential Medals of Freedom were first awarded in 1945, but then not again until 1962, when President John Kennedy began annual presentations. Nearly 400 people have received the medal, considered America's highest nonmilitary honor. The people selected come from all walks of life and all parts of America. Here is a list of some of the honorees.

HONOREE/YEAR	HONORED AS . . .
Hank Aaron/2002	Baseball's all-time home-run champ
Arthur Ashe/1993	Tennis pro; first black player to win the U.S. Open
Lucille Ball/1989	Comedienne and TV star
Count Basie/1985	Musician, bandleader, songwriter
Edgar Bronfman, Jr./1999	Leader of the World Jewish Congress
Bear Bryant/1983	Legendary college football coach
César Chávez/1994	Hispanic-American labor leader
Julia Child/2004	Cookbook author and TV host
Roberto Clemente/2003	Baseball star and Puerto Rican hero
Joan Ganz Cooney/1995	Helped create *Sesame Street*
Bill Cosby/2002	Entertainer and educator
Justin Dart, Jr./1998	Created the Americans with Disabilities Act
Walt Disney/1964	Animator, founder of Walt Disney Co.
Marian W. Edelman/2000	President of the Children's Defense Fund
Ella Fitzgerald/1992	Jazz singer
Frances Hesselbein/1998	Former leader of the Girl Scouts USA

HONOREE/YEAR	HONORED AS . . .
Rev. Jesse Jackson/2000	Civil rights activist
Rev. Martin Luther King, Jr./1977	Civil rights leader
Mathilde Krim/2000	AIDS researcher
Estée Lauder/2004	Cosmetics industry entrepreneur
Wilma Mankiller/1998	Former leader of the Cherokee Nation
Georgia O'Keefe/1976	Artist
Jesse Owens/1977	Track-and-field star, civil rights leader
Rosa Parks/1996	Civil rights activist
Richard Petty/1992	NASCAR's all-time winningest driver
Colin Powell/1993	U.S. military leader and former secretary of state
Jackie Robinson/1983	Baseball hero and civil rights leader
Fred Rogers/2002	"Mr. Rogers," host of a kids' TV show
Frank Sinatra/1985	Singer
Sam Walton/1992	Founder of Wal-Mart stores
John Wayne/1980	Actor
Ted Williams/1991	Baseball Hall of Fame legend
Tennessee Williams/1980	Playwright

You don't have to be an American to earn the Medal of Freedom. Among the international honorees are Nelson Mandela of South Africa, Mario Obledo of Mexico, Aung San Suu Kyi of Myanmar, Anwar el-Sadat of Egypt, Margaret Thatcher of Great Britain, and Mother Teresa, an Albanian who worked in India. U.S. presidents Jimmy Carter, Ronald Reagan, and Gerald Ford have also received the honor.

Makin' the Law!

Our government uses a series of checks and balances to make sure that when a law is passed, everyone has had a chance to consider it carefully. Here are the steps that Congress and the president go through to turn a bill into the law of the land.

STEP 1
- A bill is introduced by a senator or a representative.
- The bill is assigned a number and title and is sent to the appropriate committee. This is called the first reading.

STEP 2
- The committee can reject the bill, put the bill aside, or hold hearings.
- A rejected or "tabled" bill ends the process and the bill dies.
- If the bill receives a favorable committee vote, it returns to the Senate or House for debate.

STEP 3
- The bill is read to congressional members; this is called the second reading.
- The Senate and House both debate the bill separately.
- The bill is read by title only; this is called the third reading. A vote is taken.
- If either the Senate or House rejects the bill, the bill dies.
- A joint Senate and House committee can meet to iron out differences; amendments can be added.

STEP 4
- A new version of the bill is sent to the House of Representatives and the Senate for a vote.
- If approved, the bill is sent to the president for his signature.

STEP 5
- The president has ten days to sign the bill; if he does, the bill becomes law.
- If the president vetoes (rejects) the bill, Congress can still pass the bill with a two-thirds majority vote.

STEP 6
- Bills become law on January 1 of the year following the president's signing of the bill or Congress's voting an override of his veto.

The president can pass a bill into law without signing it. He holds on to the bill for ten days without signing or vetoing. After ten days — Sundays don't count — the bill becomes law.

The Bill of Rights

There are 27 amendments, or added parts, to the U.S. Constitution. These changes were made after the Constitution was adopted in 1789. The first ten amendments, known as the Bill of Rights, are briefly described here.

Amendment I
Freedom of speech, freedom of the press, freedom of religion, freedom to assemble peaceably

Amendment II
Right of the people to keep and bear arms

Amendment III
Soldiers can't be housed in private homes without permission

Amendment IV
Right of the people to be free from unreasonable searches and seizures

Amendment V
A person cannot be made to testify against himself or herself

Amendment VI
Right to a speedy and public trial

Amendment VII
Provides the right to a trial by an impartial jury

Amendment VIII
Prohibits "cruel and unusual" punishment by government

Amendment IX
Any rights not spelled out in the Constitution remain with the people

Amendment X
Any powers not given to the federal government are reserved for the states

One of the later amendments to the Constitution (XXVI in 1971) set a minimum age for voters. Thanks to that amendment, how old does a person now have to be to vote?

Answer: 18 years old. Hang in there . . . that's just a few years away!

U.S. Monuments

The United States is packed with great places to visit. Some are part of nature, while others are human-made. History plays a big part in making many of these landmarks and monuments famous.

SITE	STATE
Alamo	Texas
Cabrillo National Monument	California
Cape Krusenstern	Alaska
Castillo de San Marco	Florida
Castle Clinton	New York
Craters of the Moon	Idaho
Custer Battlefield	Montana
Death Valley	California–Nevada
Ellis Island	New York–New Jersey
Empire State Building	New York
Ford's Theatre	Washington, D.C.
Fort Laramie	Wyoming
Fort McHenry	Maryland
Fort Sumter	South Carolina
Gateway Arch	Missouri
Gila Cliff Dwellings	New Mexico
Golden Gate Bridge	California

and Landmarks

SITE	STATE
Hoover Dam	Arizona
Independence Hall	Pennsylvania
Jefferson Memorial	Washington, D.C.
Korean War Veterans Memorial	Washington, D.C.
Liberty Bell	Pennsylvania
Lincoln Memorial	Washington, D.C.
Little Big Horn National Monument	Montana
Montezuma Castle	Arizona
Mount Rushmore	South Dakota
Muir Woods National Monument	California
Niagara Falls	New York
Statue of Liberty	New York
Vietnam Veterans Memorial	Washington, D.C.
Washington Monument	Washington, D.C.
Wright Brothers Memorial	North Carolina

Why is the Washington Monument two shades of white? Check it out — the color of the marble changes as the Washington Monument climbs higher. The original construction stopped in 1854. Construction resumed in 1880, but with slightly darker marble, resulting in a two-tone monument.

Great Inventions

Many of the world's most important inventions can't be tied to any one person or date. Among these are paper from China, the wheel from Mesopotamia, and printing from Japan. Other inventions came about because of need. For instance, 33 years after canned food was invented, someone had to invent the can opener. Wonder what took them so long?

INVENTION	INVENTOR	YEAR
Airplane	Orville and Wilbur Wright	1903
Camera, handheld	George Eastman	1888
Canned food	Nicolas Appert	1811
Can opener	Robert Yeates	1844
Chocolate chips	Ruth Wakefield	1930
Computer language (COBOL)	Grace Hopper	1959
Disposable diapers	Marion Donovan	1951
Elevator	Elisha Graves Otis	1854
Game Boy™	Nintendo Company	1989
Helicopter	Igor Sikorsky	1938
Ice-cream freezer	Beulah Henry	1912
Kevlar™ fabric	Stephanie Kwolek	1971
Lightbulb	Thomas Edison	1879
Liquid Paper™	Bette Nesmith Graham	1951
Peanut butter	George Washington Carver	1890
Radio	Guglielmo Marconi	1895
School desk	Anna Breadin	1889
Telephone	Alexander Graham Bell	1876
Velcro	George D. Mestral	1955
Videotape	Alexander M. Pontiatoff	1956
Virtual reality	Ivan Sutherland	1965

Some inventions are claimed by multiple inventors. The inventor of the automobile could be considered to be Karl Benz in 1885, or Henry Ford in 1896. It depends on your definition of automobile.

Kid Inventors

Kids make great inventors (but you probably knew that). They see a need for a better product, or a better way to do something, and find new and unique ways to solve the problem. We use some of these inventions every day. Young inventors also get involved in invention competitions at their schools. Here are a few inventive kids, their ages, and their creations.

INVENTOR, AGE	INVENTION
Alexia Abernathy, 11	No-spill pet feeding bowl
Eric Brunnelle, 12	Remote-control fish feeder
Frank Epperson, 11	Popsicles
Kevin Germino, 15	Biodegradable fishing lure
Suzanna Goodin, 6	Edible pet spoon
Chester Greenwood, 15	Earmuffs
Charles Johnson, 13	Train detecting device
Jeannie Low, 5	Foldaway kiddie stool
Ivy Summer Lumpkin, 9	Lighted address mailbox
Daniel McKay, 13	Glow Glass — lighted drinking glass
Austin Meggett, 12	Baseball glove and bat carrier
Jessica Peach, 12	Adjustable jump-rope belt
Albert Sadacca, 15	Electric Christmas lights
Brian Schreyer, 17	Emergency traffic signal
Rishi Vasudeva, 17	Biodegradable disposable diaper
Larry Villella, 11	Circular conservation sprinkler

Jeannie Low, the inventor of the Kiddie Stool, thought of her invention in kindergarten! She wanted to be able to reach the bathroom sink and invented foldaway steps.

O Canada!

"A tip of the Mountie hat in greeting from your neighbors to the north, the great nation of Canada! While you down south have 50 states, we up here in Canada have what we call 'provinces,' created by our constitution. There are also three 'territories,' which have been added since our confederation was formed in 1867. Come visit us up here in the Great White North!"

PROVINCE	CAPITAL
Alberta	**Edmonton**
British Columbia	**Victoria**
Manitoba	**Winnipeg**
New Brunswick	**Fredericton**
Newfoundland and Labrador	**St. John's**
Nova Scotia	**Halifax**
Ontario	**Toronto**
Prince Edward Island	**Charlottetown**
Québec	**Québec**
Saskatchewan	**Regina**

TERRITORY	CAPITAL
Northwest Territories	**Yellowknife**
Nunavut	**Iqaluit**
Yukon	**Whitehorse**

Which Canadian territory is the newest part of the nation? And what is unique about it?

Nunavut became an official territory in 1999; it is the only part of Canada that is occupied by a majority of Native peoples, most of whom are the Inuit, who have lived in this frozen land for more than 4,000 years!

Next!

Who Takes Over If the President Can't Work?

Everyone knows that if the president passes away while in office — or can't do the job for some other reason — the vice president takes over. But who is in charge if the vice president cannot fulfill the presidential duties? The 20th and 25th amendments to the Constitution and the Presidential Succession Act of 1947 answer the question. In case of a vacancy, the office of president will be filled in this order:

1. **Vice President**
2. **Speaker of the House**
3. **President Pro Tempore of the Senate**
4. **Secretary of State**
5. **Secretary of the Treasury**
6. **Secretary of Defense**
7. **Attorney General**
8. **Secretary of the Interior**
9. **Secretary of Agriculture**
10. **Secretary of Commerce**
11. **Secretary of Labor**
12. **Secretary of Health and Human Services**
13. **Secretary of Housing and Urban Development**
14. **Secretary of Transportation**
15. **Secretary of Energy**
16. **Secretary of Education**
17. **Secretary of Veterans Affairs**

No one other than a vice president has ever taken over for a president. One close call came in 1973 when there was no vice president for more than six weeks after Vice President Spiro Agnew resigned.

Army Ranks

Whom Do I Salute?

These are the ranks, listed from highest to lowest, of members of the U.S. Army.

General of the Army
General
Lieutenant General
Major General
Brigadier General
Colonel
Lieutenant Colonel
Major
Captain
First Lieutenant
Second Lieutenant
Chief Warrant Officer
Warrant Officer
Sergeant Major
First or Master Sergeant
Sergeant First Class
Staff Sergeant
Sergeant
Corporal
Private First Class
Private

There have been only nine men who have reached the rank of General of the Army. The most recent to earn the fifth star that the rank receives was General Omar Bradley in 1950.

Weird Laws

You always obey the law, right? You follow the rules and respect police officers. They enforce all the laws of the land, whether those laws are made by federal, state, or local governments. However, there are quite a few old, outdated, or unusual laws that are still on the books in various states. Here is a sampling of America's weirdest laws.

Alaska
You can't wake up a sleeping bear to take its picture.

Florida
Unmarried women may not parachute on Sundays.

Hawaii
No placing coins in your ears.

Idaho
You can't fish from the back of a camel.

Oklahoma
Whaling is illegal.*

You can't sleep on a refrigerator outdoors.

Baldwin Park, California
No riding bicycles in swimming pools.

Houston, Texas
You can't sell Limburger cheese on Sunday.

Lexington, Kentucky
You can't carry an ice-cream cone in your pocket.

Marion, Ohio
You can't eat a donut and walk backward on a city street.

Myrtle Creek, Oregon
No boxing with kangaroos.

Nashville, Tennessee
You must be 18 years old to play pinball.

New Orleans, Louisiana
You may not tie an alligator to a fire hydrant.

Whitehall, Montana
You can't drive a car with ice picks attached to the wheels.

Wynona, Oklahoma
You can't wash your clothes in a birdbath.

* This is a weird law because there aren't any oceans, let alone any whales, in Oklahoma!

Most odd laws are just old laws that haven't been repealed (which means taken off the law books). For instance, some cities have laws that say hotels should have hitching posts and water buckets out front. This is from the days when people rode on horses, not in cars!

Look! Up in the Sky!

Well, not exactly *in* the sky, but these tallest buildings in the world are certainly skyscrapers. Thanks to advances in engineering and construction materials, buildings have been going higher and higher. This list includes buildings that people live and work in, not radio towers or antennas.

BUILDING	SITE	BUILT IN	HEIGHT (FT/M)
Taipei 101 Tower	Taipei, Taiwan	2004	1,670/509
Petronas Tower I	Kuala Lumpur, Malaysia	1998	1,483/452
Petronas Tower II	Kuala Lumpur, Malaysia	1998	1,483/452
Sears Tower	Chicago, Illinois	1974	1,450/442
Jin Mao Building	Shanghai, China	1999	1,381/421
Two Intl. Finance Center	Hong Kong	2003	1,362/415
Sky Central Plaza	Guanzhou, China	1997	1,283/391
Shun Hing Square	Shenzhen, China	1996	1,260/384
Empire State Building	New York, New York	1931	1,250/381
Central Plaza	Hong Kong	1992	1,227/374
Bank of China Tower	Hong Kong	1989	1,209/369
T&C Tower	Kaoshiung, Taiwan	1997	1,140/348
Amoco Building	Chicago, Illinois	1973	1,136/346
Central Station	Hong Kong	1998	1,135/346
John Hancock Center	Chicago, Illinois	1969	1,127/344

This list will certainly change in the years to come. Among the enormous buildings either under construction or being planned are Burj Dubai in the United Arab Emirates (2,313/705), the Tower of Russia in Moscow (2,129/649), and Freedom Tower at the World Trade Center site in New York City (1,776/551).

Mythical Places

Ever heard of the lost continent of Atlantis? This list shows places that may or may not be real. Many of them have become legends and myths based on stories from many cultures and ancient civilizations.

Asgard Home of Norse gods and goddesses

Atlantis Lost continent, destroyed by volcanoes and earthquakes

Avalon Mythical western land, home of Great Britain's King Arthur after he died

Bermuda Triangle Section of the Atlantic Ocean, site of many ship/airplane disappearances

Camelot Home of King Arthur of Great Britain and the Knights of the Round Table

Easter Island Real Pacific island, home of massive, unexplained stone statues of heads

Fountain of Youth Spring of water that restores youth, sought in Florida by Spanish explorer Ponce de León

Gog/Magog Mythical nations of heathens and barbarians

Lemuria Lost sunken continent, near Africa, Madagascar, and India

Mount Olympus Home of the Greek gods and goddesses

Mu Lost continent under the Pacific Ocean near Polynesia

Shangri-la Fictional paradise in a region of Tibet

Stonehenge Real stone formation in Great Britain, purpose and origins unexplained

Valhalla Norse hall, home to warriors who had been slain in battle

Pssst

Theories about lost continents linking cultures and regions are used to explain how customs and traditions traveled around the world. Did the lost continent of Lemuria connect Africa with India? Did Mu link islands in the Pacific Ocean with South America? No one knows.

Real or Folk?

As our country opened up and people began to explore the unknown lands, brave pioneers and frontier people became the objects of tales both true and tall. This list includes both real-life heroes and storybook legends.

REAL

Johnny Appleseed (1774–1845)
Frontiersman John Chapman planted apple seeds for pioneers

Daniel Boone (1734–1820)
Pioneer and frontiersman who explored the West

Buffalo Bill (1846–1917)
Frontiersman who shot buffaloes for the railroads and had a western show

Kit Carson (1809–1868)
Frontiersman who explored between the Mississippi River and California

Davy Crockett (1786–1836)
Trapper, explorer, frontiersman, soldier, statesman

Mike Fink (1770–1823)
Famous captain of river craft known as keelboats

Casey Jones (1864–1900)
Engineer who saved his passengers, but was killed while stopping the train

Pocahontas (1595–1617)
Native American in early Virginia who may have saved Captain John Smith

Sacagawea (1788–1812)
Native American guide for the Lewis and Clark expedition

FOLK

Pecos Bill
Cowboy legend with super-cowboy strength

Paul Bunyan and Babe the Ox
Larger-than-life lumberjack, accompanied by his pet blue ox, Babe

John Henry
African-American railroad worker, pitted himself against machines

Uncle Sam
Patriotic symbol for the United States

Which of these real or folk heroes appears on the only current gold-colored U.S. coin?

Answer: Sacagawea and her son are on the front of the gold-colored $1 coin.

Show Us the Money!

United States coins and paper money ("currency") have changed slightly in recent years. Most of the changes are to prevent counterfeiting, or illegal copying of money. But some of the changes are to celebrate our nation's history. Here's a list that shows who is on the front of coins and currency.

CURRENCY

$1	George Washington
$2	Thomas Jefferson
$5	Abraham Lincoln
$10	Alexander Hamilton
$20	Andrew Jackson
$50	Ulysses Grant
$100	Benjamin Franklin
$500	William McKinley
$1,000	Grover Cleveland
$10,000	Salmon P. Chase
$100,000	Woodrow Wilson

COINS

1¢	Abraham Lincoln
5¢	Thomas Jefferson
10¢	Franklin Roosevelt
25¢	George Washington
50¢	John F. Kennedy
$1	Sacagawea*

* Older one-dollar coins featuring Susan B. Anthony or Dwight D. Eisenhower are also in circulation.

PSSST A $10,000 bill?! Don't count on finding one in your next birthday envelope. Bills above $100 are only used by banks and large businesses. You won't find them in the cash register of the 7-Eleven.

Our Fifty States

From the first state of Delaware in 1787 to the last states of Alaska and Hawaii in 1959, the United States of America has admitted 50 states to the Union. Each state has its own identity, often reflected in the state's nickname.

STATE	CAPITAL	NICKNAME	YEAR ADMITTED
Alabama	Montgomery	Yellowhammer State	1819
Alaska	Juneau	The Last Frontier	1959
Arizona	Phoenix	Grand Canyon State	1912
Arkansas	Little Rock	Land of Opportunity	1836
California	Sacramento	Golden State	1850
Colorado	Denver	Centennial State	1876
Connecticut	Hartford	Constitution State	1788
Delaware	Dover	Diamond State	1787
Florida	Tallahassee	Sunshine State	1845
Georgia	Atlanta	Peach State	1788
Hawaii	Honolulu	Aloha State	1959
Idaho	Boise	Gem State	1890
Illinois	Springfield	Prairie State	1818
Indiana	Indianapolis	Hoosier State	1816
Iowa	Des Moines	Hawkeye State	1846
Kansas	Topeka	Sunflower State	1861
Kentucky	Frankfort	Bluegrass State	1792
Louisiana	Baton Rouge	Pelican State	1812
Maine	Augusta	Pine Tree State	1820
Maryland	Annapolis	Free State	1788
Massachusetts	Boston	Bay State	1788
Michigan	Lansing	Wolverine State	1837
Minnesota	St. Paul	North Star State	1858
Mississippi	Jackson	Magnolia State	1817
Missouri	Jefferson City	Show Me State	1821

STATE	CAPITAL	NICKNAME	YEAR ADMITTED
Montana	Helena	Treasure State	1889
Nebraska	Lincoln	Cornhusker State	1867
Nevada	Carson City	Silver State	1864
New Hampshire	Concord	Granite State	1788
New Jersey	Trenton	Garden State	1787
New Mexico	Santa Fe	Land of Enchantment	1912
New York	Albany	Empire State	1788
North Carolina	Raleigh	Tar Heel State	1789
North Dakota	Bismarck	Sioux State	1889
Ohio	Columbus	Buckeye State	1803
Oklahoma	Oklahoma City	Sooner State	1907
Oregon	Salem	Beaver State	1859
Pennsylvania	Harrisburg	Keystone State	1787
Rhode Island	Providence	Ocean State	1790
South Carolina	Columbia	Palmetto State	1788
South Dakota	Pierre	Mount Rushmore State	1889
Tennessee	Nashville	Volunteer State	1796
Texas	Austin	Lone Star State	1845
Utah	Salt Lake City	Beehive State	1896
Vermont	Montpelier	Green Mountain State	1791
Virginia	Richmond	The Old Dominion	1788
Washington	Olympia	Evergreen State	1889
West Virginia	Charleston	Mountain State	1863
Wisconsin	Madison	Badger State	1848
Wyoming	Cheyenne	Equality State	1890

Although not one of the 50 states, Washington, D.C. (District of Columbia), is often mentioned with lists of states. George Washington chose the site for our nation's capital in 1790. Congress moved there from Philadelphia in 1800.

All About My State

Several of the lists in this chapter deal with the United States. On this list, it's time to find out more about your own state. You might have to do a little research (no, it's not more homework . . . and some of the answers are on page 76–77!), but as you do, you'll learn more about the place that you live in. Not all states will have all of these "official" things, but if your state doesn't have one, write to your governor and let him or her know what you think it should be!

My state _____

My state's capital _____

My state's nickname(s) _____

My state's official flower _____

My state's official animal _____

My state's official bird _____

My state's official rock _____

The biggest city in my state _____

My state is bordered by these states and/or countries

_____

The best thing about my state is _____

Do your best to draw your state flag in this box.

CHAPTER THREE

The World and The Weather

It's a big world . . . but you've got plenty of time to see it all. In here, we've got lists of rivers, mountains, oceans, and more. Check out the weather info so you know what to wear!

Hot Enough for You?

Think it's hot in your classroom on a steamy day in June with the windows closed? That's nothin'. Here are the highest-ever temperatures in the United States. What's the hottest temperature ever? See the box below.

FAHRENHEIT	CELSIUS	LOCATION	DATE
134°	56.6°	Greenland Ranch, California	July 10, 1913
128°	53.3°	Lake Havasu City, Arizona	June 29, 1994
125°	51.6°	Laughlin, Nevada	June 29, 1994
122°	50.0°	Waste Isolat, New Mexico	June 27, 1994
121°	49.4°	Alton, Kansas	July 24, 1936
121°	49.4°	Steele, North Dakota	July 6, 1936
120°	48.9°	Ozark, Arkansas	August 10, 1936
120°	48.9°	Tipton, Oklahoma	June 27, 1994
120°	48.9°	Gannvalley, South Dakota	July 5, 1936
120°	48.9°	Seymour, Texas	August 12, 1936
119°	48.3°	Pendleton, Oregon	August 10, 1898
118°	47.8°	Bennett, Colorado	July 11, 1888
118°	47.8°	Orofino, Idaho	July 28, 1934
118°	47.8°	Keokuk, Iowa	July 20, 1934
118°	47.8°	Warsaw, Missouri	July 14, 1954
118°	47.8°	Minden, Nebraska	July 24, 1936
118°	47.8°	Ice Harbor Dam, Washington	August 5, 1961

Hottest place of all time? That would be the little town of Al Aziziyah in the African nation of Libya. On September 13, 1922, it was a pleasant 136° F (57.7° C).

Coldest Places in the U.S.

Looking for a cold state? Here are the temperature records for the top ten coldest states. Coldest temperature ever? Try Vostok Base in Antarctica. On July 21, 1983, they recorded a temperature of –128.6° F (–89.2° C). Brrrr!

FAHRENHEIT	CELSIUS	STATE	DATE
−80°	−62°	Alaska	January 23, 1971
−70°	−57°	Montana	January 20, 1954
−69°	−56°	Utah	February 1, 1985
−66°	−54°	Wyoming	February 9, 1933
−61°	−52°	Colorado	February 1, 1985
−60°	−51°	Idaho	January 18, 1943
−60°	−51°	Minnesota	February 2, 1996
−60°	−51°	North Dakota	February 15, 1936
−58°	−50°	South Dakota	February 17, 1936
−54°	−48°	Oregon	February 10, 1933
−54°	−48°	Wisconsin	January 24, 1922
−52°	−47°	New York	February 18, 1979
−51°	−46°	Michigan	February 9, 1934

Forty-nine of the 50 states have recorded a temperature below zero. Even Florida had a temperature of -2° F (-18° C) on February 13, 1899. Only Hawaii has escaped negative Farenheit temperatures. It had a low of 12° F (-11° C) on May 17, 1979.

Highest Mountain Peaks

The world's highest mountain peaks are located in the Himalayan Mountains in Asia. In fact, the 60-plus highest mountain peaks in the world are all found there. This list names the highest peaks on each continent.

MOUNTAIN/COUNTRY	HEIGHT IN FEET	HEIGHT IN METERS
ASIA		
Mt. Everest/Nepal	29,035	8,849
K2/Nepal	28,250	8,610
AFRICA		
Mt. Kilimanjaro/Tanzania	19,340	5,895
Mt. Kenya/Kenya	17,058	5,199
OCEANIA (AUSTRALASIA)		
Mt. Wilhelm/Papua New Guinea	14,793	4,492
Mt. Giluwe/Papua New Guinea	14,330	4,367
ANTARCTICA		
Vinson Massif	16,066	4,897
Mt. Markham	14,049	4,282
EUROPE		
Mt. Elbrus/Russia	18,510	5,642
Mont Blanc/France–Italy	15,771	4,807
NORTH AMERICA		
Mt. McKinley/United States	20,320	6,193
Mt. Logan/Canada	19,524	5,951
SOUTH AMERICA		
Aconcagua/Argentina	22,834	6,960
Ojos del Salado/Argentina	22,664	6,908

Although Mount Everest is the world's highest mountain, you could also give that award to Hawaii's Mauna Kea. If you measure Mauna Kea from the ocean floor (instead of from sea level), it rises 32,000 feet (9,753 m)!

Volcanoes!

Would you want to be a volcanologist? Volcanologists study volcanoes from the air, using airplanes and satellites. They also visit volcanoes in person to monitor their scientific equipment and collect data.

VOLCANO	LOCATION	DATE	VEI*
Tambora	Indonesia	1815	7
Krakatau	Indonesia	1883	6
Novarupta	Alaska	1912	6
Pinatubo	Philippines	1991	6
Santa Maria	Guatemala	1902	6
Santorini	Greece	1645 B.C.	6
Taupo	New Zealand	186	6
El Chichon	Mexico	1982	5
Mt. St. Helens	Washington	1980	5
Tarawera	New Zealand	1886	5
Vesuvius (Mount)	Italy	79	5
Galunggung	Indonesia	1982	4
Laki	Iceland	1783	4
Pelée	Martinique	1902	4
Etna	Italy	1669	3

* VEI stands for volcano explosion intensity, a way of measuring eruptions. The higher the number, the more powerful the eruption and more terrible the damage.

The word *volcano* comes from the name of the Roman fire god, Vulcan. There were supposedly a lot of volcanoes on the planet Vulcan in *Star Trek*.

Largest Lakes

Lakes are usually defined as bodies of water completely surrounded by land. Lakes are generally freshwater, but you will find some lakes with salt water in them. Since the Caspian Sea is a saltwater lake, Lake Superior is the world's largest freshwater lake.

LAKE	BORDERING COUNTRIES	SQ. MI.	SQ. KM
Caspian Sea	Azerbaijan, Iran, Kazakhstan, Russia, Turkmenistan	143,244	371,002
Lake Superior	Canada, United States	31,700	82,103
Lake Victoria	Kenya, Tanzania, Uganda	26,828	69,484
Lake Huron	Canada, United States	23,000	59,570
Lake Michigan	Canada, United States	22,300	57,757
Aral Sea	Kazakhstan, Uzbekistan	13,000	33,670
Lake Tanganyika	Burundi, Tanzania, Zaire, Zambia	12,350	31,986
Lake Baikal	Russia	12,200	31,598
Great Bear Lake	Canada	12,162	31,499
Lake Nyasa	Malawi, Mozambique, Tanzania	11,150	28,875
Great Slave Lake	Canada	11,030	28,567
Lake Erie	Canada, United States	9,910	25,667
Lake Winnipeg	Canada	9,417	24,390
Lake Ontario	Canada, United States	7,340	19,011

What lake has dropped on this list? At 24,700 square miles (63,973 sq. km), the Aral Sea was once the the world's fourth largest lake. However, the lake has changed size dramatically as rivers that feed into it have been diverted, dropping it to sixth place.

Biggest Deserts

The deserts of the world (some of which are listed by continent below) do not all have the same temperatures. A subtropical desert has a hot climate year-round. A cold winter desert has a range of temperatures. A desert area receives less than 10 inches (22 cm) of precipitation per year.

DESERT	SQ. MI.	SQ. KM
AFRICA		
Sahara Desert	3.3 million	8.5 million
Kalahari Desert	1 million	2.6 million
Namib Desert	80,300	207,977
ASIA		
Gobi Desert	500,000	1.3 million
Chang Tang Desert	309,000	800,310
Rub al-Khali Desert	250,000	647,500
OCEANIA (AUSTRALASIA)		
Great Sandy Desert	150,000	388,500
Great Victoria Desert	125,000	323,750
Gibson Desert	85,000	220,150
NORTH AMERICA		
Chihuahuan Desert	200,000	518,000
Great Basin Desert	190,000	492,100
Sonoran Desert	120,000	310,800
SOUTH AMERICA		
Patagonian Desert	260,000	673,400
Peruvian Desert	98,000	253,820
Atacama Desert	70,000	181,300

Today's spelling tip: Remember, a desert is sandy (one *s*), a dessert is sweet and sticky (two *s*'s).

What? No Gilligan?

The size of an island can change. Some islands are covered with ice and snow and are hard to measure. Other islands suffer beach erosion and shrink. This list contains the world's 20 largest islands, but be warned that the order may change.

NAME	OCEAN	SQ. MI.	SQ. KM
Greenland	Atlantic	839,999	2.2 million
New Guinea	Pacific	316,615	820,033
Borneo	Pacific	286,914	742,333
Madagascar	Indian	226,657	587,042
Baffin	Atlantic	183,810	476,068
Sumatra	Indian	182,859	473,605
Honshu	Pacific	88,925	230,316
Great Britain	Atlantic	88,758	229,883
Ellesmere	Arctic	82,119	212,688
Victoria	Arctic	81,930	212,199
Sulawesi	Pacific	72,986	189,034
South Island	Pacific	58,093	150,461
Java	Indian	48,990	126,884
North Island	Pacific	44,281	114,688
Cuba	Atlantic	44,218	114,525
Newfoundland	Atlantic	42,734	110,681
Luzon	Pacific	40,420	104,688
Iceland	Atlantic	39,768	102,999
Mindanao	Pacific	36,537	94,631
Ireland	Atlantic	32,597	84,426

PsSST

Perhaps the largest island ever was called Pangaea. Many geographers believe that the continents began as one huge landmass. As this landmass, called Pangaea, drifted apart, the continents and oceans were formed.

How Deep Is the Ocean?

The ocean depths are among our planet's last unexplored areas. Some trenches on ocean bottoms are so deep that unmanned probes must be used to explore and chart them. In those deep places, sea creatures have adapted to live in cold and darkness, and under tremendous pressure. This list shows the deepest trenches and their depths in feet and meters.

NAME	OCEAN	FEET	METERS
Mariana Trench	Pacific	35,837	10,923
Tonga Trench	Pacific	35,433	10,800
Kermadec Trench	Pacific	32,963	10,047
Philippine Trench	Pacific	32,955	10,045
Bonin Trench	Pacific	32,788	9,994
Kuril Trench	Pacific	31,988	9,753
Izu Trench	Pacific	31,808	9,695
New Britain Trench	Pacific	29,331	8,940
Puerto Rico Trench	Atlantic	28,232	8,605
Yap Trench	Pacific	27,976	8,527
Japan Trench	Pacific	27,599	8,412
South Sandwich Trench	Atlantic	27,313	8,325
Peru–Chile Trench	Pacific	26,457	8,064
Palau Trench	Pacific	26,424	8,054
Romanche Gap	Atlantic	25,354	7,728
Aleutian Trench	Pacific	25,194	7,679

Here are the average depths of the world's major oceans, in feet/meters: Arctic, 3,407/1,038; Atlantic, 11,730/3,575; Indian, 12,598/3,839; Pacific, 12,925/3,939.

World Rivers

Rollin', rollin', rollin' in the rivers of the world. Many of the world's first civilizations were formed next to rivers. Now, billions of people depend on the water from rivers to supply irrigation for farming. Without the rivers, farmers wouldn't be able to provide enough food to feed the world.

RIVER/CONTINENT	LENGTH (MI.)	(KM)
Nile/Africa	4,160	6,943
Amazon/S.America	4,000	6,676
Yangtze/Asia	3,960	6,609
Huang Ho/Asia	3,400	5,675
Ob-Irtysh/Asia	3,360	5,608
Amur/Asia	2,740	4,573
Lena/Asia	2,730	4,393
Congo/Africa	2,720	4,377
Mackenzie/N. America	2,640	4,250
Mekong/Asia	2,600	4,239
Niger/Africa	2,590	4,233
Yenisey/Asia	2,540	4,205
Parana/S. America	2,480	4,139
Mississippi/N. America	2,340	3,905
Missouri/N. America	2,320	3,872
Volga/Europe	2,290	3,822
Purus/S. America	2,100	3,505
Madeira/S. America	2,010	3,355
Sao Francisco/S. America	1,990	3,321
Yukon/N. America	1,980	3,304

Although the Amazon River is shorter than the Nile River, the Amazon has a greater flow of water at its mouth, which is the place where it empties into the Atlantic Ocean.

What Time Is It, Sarge?

People in the military do all sorts of things differently from regular folks. One difference is how they tell time. Military units use a 24-hour clock. This list shows what time it is if you're in the Army, Navy, or Air Force.

REGULAR TIME	MILITARY TIME	REGULAR TIME	MILITARY TIME
1 A.M.	0100	1 P.M.	1300
2 A.M.	0200	2 P.M.	1400
3 A.M.	0300	3 P.M.	1500
4 A.M.	0400	4 P.M.	1600
5 A.M.	0500	5 P.M.	1700
6 A.M.	0600	6 P.M.	1800
7 A.M.	0700	7 P.M.	1900
8 A.M.	0800	8 P.M.	2000
9 A.M.	0900	9 P.M.	2100
10 A.M.	1000	10 P.M.	2200
11 A.M.	1100	11 P.M.	2300
12 noon	1200	12 midnight	2400

Times before 10 A.M., such as 6 A.M., are pronounced "oh-six-hundred hours." For times such as 2 P.M., you'd say "14-hundred hours," and times such as 9:30 P.M. as "21-30 hours."

Name That Hurricane

Storms that reach wind speeds of greater than 74 miles (119 km) per hour achieve hurricane status and are given specific names. Each year, 21 names wait to be assigned to a hurricane. Several lists of names rotate, though the letters Q, U, X, Y, and Z are not used. Here are the names for hurricanes for the next four years. Can you find your name on these lists?

2006	2007	2008	2009
Alberto	Andrea	Arthur	Ana
Beryl	Barry	Bertha	Bill
Chris	Chantal	Cristobal	Claudette
Debby	Dean	Dolly	Danny
Ernesto	Erin	Edouard	Erika
Florence	Felix	Fay	Fred
Gordon	Gabrielle	Gustav	Grace
Helene	Humberto	Hanna	Henri
Isaac	Ingrid	Ike	Ida
Joyce	Jerry	Josephine	Joaquin
Kirk	Karen	Kyle	Kate
Leslie	Lorenzo	Laura	Larry
Michael	Melissa	Marco	Mindy
Nadine	Noel	Nana	Nicholas
Oscar	Olga	Omar	Odette
Patty	Pablo	Paloma	Peter
Rafael	Rebekah	Rene	Rose
Sandy	Sebastien	Sally	Sam
Tony	Tanya	Teddy	Teresa
Valerie	Van	Vicky	Victor
William	Wendy	Wilfred	Wanda

PsSST

You can tell how far away a thunderstorm is by timing the difference between seeing lightning flash and hearing a thunderclap. The shorter the time, the closer the storm.

Hurricanes Gone,
but Names Not Forgotten

Up until 1979, Hurricanes only had female names, as chosen by national hurricane trackers. Now the lists alternate between girls' and boys' names. Some hurricanes are so severe, and the damage from them so extensive, that people don't want to be reminded. The terrible hurricanes of 2005, Katrina and Rita, are the latest to make this list. The names on this list will never be used to name hurricanes again.

Name	Year	Name	Year	Name	Year
Agnes	1972	Diane	1955	Ione	1955
Alicia	1983	Donna	1960	Iris	2001
Allen	1980	Dora	1964	Isabel	2003
Allison	2001	Edna	1968	Isidore	2002
Andrew	1992	Elena	1985	Ivan	2004
Anita	1977	Eloise	1975	Janet	1955
Audrey	1957	Fabian	2003	Jeanne	2004
Betsy	1965	Fifi	1974	Joan	1988
Beulah	1967	Flora	1963	Juan	2003
Bob	1991	Floyd	1999	Katrina	2005
Camille	1969	Fran	1996	Keith	2000
Carla	1961	Frances	2004	Klaus	1990
Carmen	1974	Frederic	1979	Lenny	1999
Carol	1954	Georges	1998	Lili	2002
Celia	1970	Gloria	1985	Luis	1995
Cesar	1996	Hattie	1961	Marilyn	1995
Charley	2004	Hazel	1954	Michelle	2001
Cleo	1964	Hilda	1964	Mitch	1998
Connie	1955	Hortense	1996	Opal	1995
David	1979	Hugo	1989	Rita	2005
Diana	1990	Inez	1966	Roxanne	1995

Notice that only a few of the names on this list go past M? That actually is a good thing as storms receive their names alphabetically as they occur each year. According to this list, the third storm of each year might be the one that is most often a terrible one: Nine C names have been retired, the most of any letter.

Rain Forest Facts

To be considered a tropical rain forest, the forest area must be located between the Tropic of Cancer and the Tropic of Capricorn (two bands of latitude around Earth) and annually receive 40 inches (101 cm) or more of rain. Although they originally covered about 12 percent of Earth's surface, tropical rain forests now cover about half that.

LAYERS OF THE RAIN FOREST, FROM THE GROUND UP:

Ground Layer
Lower Layer
Middle Layer
(also called Understory)
Canopy Layer
Emergent Layer

THREE MAIN REGIONS OF TROPICAL RAIN FORESTS:

Central and South America
West and Central Africa
Southeast Asia

FOODS ORIGINATING IN RAIN FORESTS:

Avocado
Banana
Black pepper
Brazil nuts
Cayenne pepper
Cassava
Cashews
Cocoa
Cinnamon
Cloves

Coconut
Coffee
Cola
Corn
Eggplant
Fig
Ginger
Guava
Lemon
Orange

Papaya
Paprika
Peanut
Pineapple
Rice
Sugar
Sweet pepper
Tomato
Vanilla
Winter squash

Tropical rain forests in South America are called the Amazon Basin forest, and can be found in nine countries. About 40 percent of the world's tropical rain forests are contained in this Amazon Basin region.

Brrrr!
Some Very Snowy Spots

The U.S. Army Corps of Engineers has identified some of the snowiest spots in the world over different periods of time. Some of the snowfalls listed below accumulated in a matter of hours, while others took months.

LOCATION	INCHES	CM	DATE/TIME SPAN
Mt. Baker, Washington	1,140	2,895	1998–1999/one season
Thompson Pass, Alaska	974	2,474	1952–1953/one season
British Columbia, Canada	964	2,448	1971–1972/one season
Tamarack, California	390	990	Jan. 1911/one month
Mt. Shasta, California	189	480	Feb. 13–19, 1959/one storm
Thompson Pass, Alaska	175	444	Dec. 26–31, 1955/one storm
Montague, New York	127	322	Dec. 24, 2001– Jan. 1, 2002/one storm
Buffalo, New York	81	207	Dec. 24–28, 2001/one storm
Silver Lake, Colorado	76	193	April 14–15, 1921/24 hours
Bessans, France	68	173	April 4–5, 1969/19 hours
Thompson Pass, Alaska	62	157	Dec. 29, 1955/24 hours

The language spoken by the Aleuts, who are Native Americans in Alaska, at one time included more than 30 different words describing snow in various forms.

Terrible Tornadoes

Tornadoes are terrible swirling windstorms that usually appear in their classic funnel shape. Touching down to earth, they can cause a huge amount of damage to buildings, property, and, sadly, people. Here is a list of the worst tornadoes in U.S. history, ranked by the number of casualties.

DATE	STATES AFFECTED	NUMBER OF DEATHS
March 18, 1925	Illinois, Indiana, Missouri	695
May 7, 1840	Mississippi	317
May 27, 1896	Missouri	255
April 5, 1936	Mississippi	216
April 6, 1936	Georgia	203
April 9, 1947	Oklahoma	181
April 24, 1908	Mississippi	143
June 12, 1899	Wisconsin	117
June 8, 1953	Michigan	115
May 11, 1953	Texas	114
May 18, 1902	Texas	114
March 23, 1913	Nebraska	103
May 26, 1917	Illinois	101
June 23, 1944	West Virginia	100
April 18, 1880	Missouri	99
June 1, 1903	Georgia	98
May 9, 1927	Missouri	98
May 10, 1905	Oklahoma	97
April 24, 1908	Mississippi	91

In an average year, more than 800 tornadoes touch down in the United States, more than in any other country. Scientists use the Fujita Scale to rank them. F0 on the scale is for winds from 40–72 mph. The scale goes up to F5 for winds above 261 mph (420 kph).

Quake, Rattle, and Roll

If you've ever felt an earthquake, you know how a bowl of Jell-O® feels. But how do scientists measure how strong earthquakes are? They use the Richter scale, developed by Charles Richter in 1935. Using mathematical formulas, seismographs record the vibrations of the quake as they travel through the ground. The resulting numbers (below) tell people how bad the earthquake was. The distances listed are from the epicenter, which is the spot where the earthquake originates.

Magnitude 1, 2 Very minor

Magnitude 3
Minor; recorded on local seismographs, but generally not felt

Magnitude 4 Light; often felt, no damage

Magnitude 5 Moderate; felt widely, slight damage

Magnitude 6
Strong; damage to structures within 6.2 miles (10 km)

Magnitude 7
Major; causes serious damage up to 62 miles (100 km)

Magnitude 8
Great; much destruction, loss of life beyond 62 miles (100 km)

Magnitude 9
Rare and huge; major damage beyond 620 miles (1,000 km)

The largest recorded earthquake occurred on May 22, 1960, in Chile, a 9.5 magnitude on the Richter scale. The largest recorded earthquake in the United States occurred on March 28, 1964, in Prince William Sound, Alaska, a 9.2-magnitude earthquake.

Geographical Terms

In geography, you can't really read a map or talk the talk without knowing the right words and terms. Here are the words that will make you sound like a real geographer.

Bay
An opening in the coastline where water reaches into the land.

Continent
One of the seven large landmasses on Earth surrounded by water.

Desert
Dry, almost rainless region of land.

Glacier
A large body of ice that slowly moves over the land.

Gulf
An opening in the coastline larger than a bay.

Hill
Land that is higher than the land around it.

Iceberg
Large section of mostly submerged ice, floating in the water.

Island
Land completely surrounded by water.

Lake
Water completely surrounded by land, usually freshwater.

Mountain
A high piece of land, usually with a pointed or rounded top.

Ocean
One of the four large bodies of salt water on Earth.

Peninsula
Land with water on three sides.

Plain
Flatland.

Prairie
Flatland covered with grass.

River
A large stream of running water through the land.

Sea
Large body of water partly surrounded by land.

Source
The place where a river begins, usually in the mountains.

Swamp
Land that is soaked with water, also referred to as a marsh.

Tributary
A body of water that flows into a larger body of water.

Valley
Lowland between hills or mountains.

What do you call the place where a river empties into a larger body of water, such as an ocean or bay? Throat, ear, or mouth?

Answer: It's the mouth of the river.

What State Is That?

The U.S. Postal Service uses this list of official abbreviations for U.S. states and possessions. There are a lot of *M*s and *N*s and it can get confusing, so keep this list handy next time you're sending out holiday cards.

Alabama	AL	Hawaii	HI	Missouri	MO	Pennsylvania	PA
Alaska	AK	Idaho	ID	Montana	MT	Puerto Rico	PR
American Samoa	AS	Illinois	IL	Nebraska	NE	Rhode Island	RI
Arizona	AZ	Indiana	IN	Nevada	NV	South Carolina	SC
Arkansas	AR	Iowa	IA	New Hampshire	NH	South Dakota	SD
California	CA	Kansas	KS	New Jersey	NJ	Tennessee	TN
Colorado	CO	Kentucky	KY	New Mexico	NM	Texas	TX
Connecticut	CT	Louisiana	LA	New York	NY	Utah	UT
Delaware	DE	Maine	ME	North Carolina	NC	Vermont	VT
District of Columbia	DC	Marshall Islands	MH	North Dakota	ND	Virgin Islands	VI
Federated States of Micronesia	FM	Maryland	MD	Northern Mariana Islands	MP	Virginia	VA
		Massachusetts	MA	Ohio	OH	Washington	WA
Florida	FL	Michigan	MI	Oklahoma	OK	West Virginia	WV
Georgia	GA	Minnesota	MN	Oregon	OR	Wisconsin	WI
Guam	GU	Mississippi	MS	Palau	PW	Wyoming	WY

American Samoa, Guam, Micronesia, the Marshalls, the Marianas, and Palau are all islands in the South Pacific that are United States "possessions." The Virgin Islands in the Caribbean are the same. The people in these places are U.S. citizens and can vote in elections. The Caribbean island of Puerto Rico is called a commonwealth, and has more independence than the other islands.

Our National Parks

The National Park Service is in charge of America's 55 national parks, which range from a rain forest in American Samoa to vast mountain ranges in the Alaskan wilderness to islands around the nation. The parks are protected from development and filled with many animals and attractions to see.

NATIONAL PARK	STATE(S)	NATIONAL PARK	STATE(S)
Acadia	Maine	Death Valley	California, Nevada
American Samoa	Am. Samoa*	Denali	Alaska
Arches	Utah	Dry Tortugas	Florida
Badlands	South Dakota	Everglades	Florida
Big Bend	Texas	Gates of the Arctic	Alaska
Biscayne	Florida	Glacier	Montana
Black Canyon of Gunnison	Colorado	Glacier Bay	Alaska
Bryce Canyon	Utah	Grand Canyon	Arizona
Canyonlands	Utah	Grand Teton	Wyoming
Capitol Reef	Utah	Great Basin	Nevada
Carlsbad Caverns	New Mexico	Great Smoky Mts.	Tennessee, North Carolina
Channel Islands	California	Guadalupe Mts.	Texas
Crater Lake	Oregon	Haleakala	Hawaii

NATIONAL PARK	STATE(S)	NATIONAL PARK	STATE(S)
Hawaii Volcanoes	Hawaii	Petrified Forest	Arizona
Hot Springs	Arkansas	Redwood	California
Isle Royal	Michigan	Rocky Mountain	Colorado
Joshua Tree	California	Saguaro	Arizona
Katmai	Alaska	Sequoia	California
Kenai Fjords	Alaska	Shenandoah	Virginia
Kings Canyon	California	Theodore Roosevelt	N. Dakota
Kobuk Valley	Alaska	Virgin Islands	Virgin Islands*
Lake Clark	Alaska	Voyageurs	Minnesota
Lassen Volcanic	California	Wind Cave	South Dakota
Mammoth Cave	Kentucky	Wrangell-Saint Elias	Alaska
Mesa Verde	Colorado	Yellowstone	Idaho, Montana, Wyoming
Mount Rainier	Washington	Yosemite	California
North Cascades	Washington	Zion	Utah
Olympic	Washington		

* Not states, but U.S. territories

The biggest national park? It's Gates of the Arctic, at more than 8.4 million acres (3.4 million hectares). The smallest? Hot Springs, at only 5,549 acres (2,427 hectares).

Longest Tunnels

Tunnels around the world go under bodies of water or through mountains. In some cases, a tunnel begins in one country and ends in another. As this list shows, tunnels can go for miles. Most of these tunnels are just for trains; car tunnels are marked with an asterisk (*).

TUNNEL/LOCATION	LENGTH (MI.)	(KM)
Seikan/Japan	33.5	55.9
Channel Tunnel/England–France	31.1	51.9
Laerdal*/Norway	15.2	25.4
Simplon (I, II)/Switzerland–Italy	12.3	20.5
Apennine/Italy	11.5	19.1
St. Gotthard*/Switzerland	10.2	17.0
St. Gotthard/Switzerland	9.3	15.5
Lotschberg/Switzerland	9.1	15.1
Mont Cenis/France	8.5	14.1
New Cascade/Washington	7.8	13.0
Vosges/France	7.0	11.7
Flathead/Montana	7.0	11.7
Mt. Blanc*/France–Italy	7.0	11.7
Arlberg/Austria	6.3	10.5
Moffat/Colorado	6.2	10.3
Shimizu/Japan	6.1	10.1

PSSST

The Seikan Tunnel was built without using the huge tunnel-boring machines used in most places. The soil beneath Japan's Tsugaru Strait was too soft. Miners used blasting and hand tools to do the job.

Longest Bridges

A log over a stream was probably the first bridge. Most likely, a tree fell across the span, and people used it as a bridge. There are many types of bridges in use now: suspension, beam, cantilever, arch, and truss. This list shows the world's longest suspension bridges.

BRIDGE/LOCATION	LENGTH (FT.)	(M)
Akashi Kaikyo/Japan	6,529	1,990
Izmit Bay/Turkey	5,472	1,668
Storebaelt/Denmark	5,328	1,624
Humber/England	4,626	1,410
Jiangyin Yangtze/China	4,543	1,385
Tsing Ma/Hong Kong	4,518	1,377
Verrazano-Narrows/New York	4,260	1,298
Golden Gate/California	4,200	1,280
Höga Kusten Bridge/Sweden	3,969	1,210
Mackinac/Michigan	3,800	1,158
Minami Bisan-Seto/Japan	3,609	1,100
Second Bosporus/Turkey	3,576	1,090
First Bosporus/Turkey	3,524	1,074
George Washington/New York	3,500	1,067

A few readers of the first edition of this book wrote to say that the Pontchartrain Causeway (24 miles/38.6 km) near New Orleans should have been number one — but it's officially a causeway, not a bridge.

Weird U.S. City Names

Do you like the name of your village, town, or city? Imagine having to use Worstville or Ding Dong as your address! If you think your town's name belongs on this list, go ahead and add it!

Chicken, Alaska

Show Low, Arizona

Hercules, California

Prunedale, California

Gunbarrel, Colorado

Chicken Head, Florida

Frostproof, Florida

Fruitville, Florida

Two Egg, Florida

Big Foot, Illinois

Goofy Ridge, Illinois

Roachtown, Illinois

Bald Head, Maine

Grosse Pointe, Michigan

Inkster, Michigan

Yazoo City, Mississippi

Frankenstein, Missouri

Lizard Lick, North Carolina

Kill Devil Hills, North Carolina

Pepper Pike, Ohio

Worstville, Ohio

Frogtown, Pennsylvania

Mars, Pennsylvania

Dentsville, South Carolina

Ding Dong, Texas

Lollipop, Texas

Sugar Land, Texas

Food provides great names for cities. Here's an entire meal of cities: Orange, Connecticut; Strawberry, California; Mango, Florida; Sandwich, Illinois.

Unusual Roadside Attractions

Across America, there are a wide variety of things that people have created just to get their towns on lists like this one. Most of these things are just big — really big. Folks figure the bigger something is, the easier it will be to spot from the highway! And if you spot it, they hope you'll stop and visit.

LARGEST WHAT	WHERE
Artichoke	Castroville, California
Ball of twine	Darwin, Minnesota
Basket	Newark, Ohio
Breakfast table	Battle Creek, Michigan
Buffalo	Jamestown, North Dakota
Catsup bottle	Collinsville, Illinois
Chest of drawers	High Point, North Carolina
Covered wagon	Milford, Nebraska
Egg	Mentone, Ind.; Winlock, Wash.
Holstein cow	New Salem, North Dakota
Illuminated star	Roanoke, Virginia
Loon	Virginia, Minnesota
Office chair	Anniston, Alabama
Peanut	Ashburn, Georgia
Prairie chicken	Rothsay, Minnesota
Stump	Kokomo, Indiana
Talking cow	Neillsville, Wisconsin
Tire	Dearborn, Michigan
Turkey	Frazee, Minnesota
Turtle	Bottineau, North Dakota
Wheel of cheese	Berlin, Ohio

Many of the big "attractions" that people make are foods, which are assembled each year and eaten. For a list of some of these big foods, see page 262.

A Zoo Full of Cities

Many towns and cities in the United States are named for other places in the world (New Orleans), their founders (Johnson City), or for a natural feature nearby (Riverdale). But these places were named after animals, none of whom, we assume, were the founders of the cities.

Alligator, Mississippi

Anaconda, New Mexico

Bear, Delaware

Bee, Virginia

Buffalo, New York

Bullfrog, Utah

Butterfly, Kentucky

Caribou, Maine

Chicken, Alaska

Chinchilla, Pennsylvania

Deer, Arkansas

Dolphin, Virginia

Duck, North Carolina

Elk, New Mexico

Fox, Montana

Moose, Wyoming

Oyster, Virginia

Parrot, Kentucky

Pigeon, Michigan

Salmon, Idaho

Squirrel, Idaho

Sturgeon, Missouri

Swan, Texas

Tiger, Georgia

Trout, Louisiana

Whitefish, Montana

Wolf, Ohio

Yellow Jacket, Colorado

Maybe it's because he is so active (busy as a beaver . . . get it?) that the beaver has many places named after him. You can find a city or town called Beaver in 13 states from Alaska to West Virginia.

Z Cities

These zippy and zany names add a zing to cities in the United States. There are still some good *Z* words available for city names — you could name your new town Zombie, Zit, or Zebu, for instance. Or not . . .

Zachow	WI	Zieglerville	PA
Zaleski	OH	Zigzag	WA
Zanesville	IN, OH	Zillah	WA
Zanoni	VA	Zilwaukee	MI
Zap	ND	Zimmerman	MN
Zapata	TX	Zion	AL, GA, IL
Zarephath	NJ	Zion City	LA
Zearing	IA	Zionhill	PA
Zebulon	GA, NC	Zoar	AL, OH
Zeeland	MI	Zoe	OK
Zeigler	IL	Zolfo Springs	FL
Zelienople	PA	Zucks Corner	PA
Zella	TX	Zumbro Falls	MN
Zellwood	FL	Zumbrota	MN
Zenda	WI	Zuni Pueblo	NM
Zeona	SD	Zwolle	LA
Zephyrhills	FL	Zylks	LA

Check it out! Almost all of these *Z* city names have a vowel for the second letter. All of the vowels are used, with the letters *A* and *E* coming in as the most popular. The one exception to the rule is easy to find — it's Zwolle, located in Louisiana.

My Travel Almanac

This chapter talked about some of the most amazing natural and human-made places in the world. This list will give you space to see which of these features you've experienced in person. Talk to your parents and family and look back on your various trips together. Then fill in as much of this list as you can. Remember, even though you might not have visited a lake or been to a mountain yet . . . doesn't mean you won't someday soon!

I've been to these places. . . .

RIVERS

1. _____
2. _____
3. _____
4. _____

LAKES

1. _____
2. _____
3. _____
4. _____

OCEANS

1. _____
2. _____
3. _____
4. _____

MOUNTAINS

1. _____
2. _____
3. _____
4. _____

NATIONAL PARKS

1. _____
2. _____
3. _____
4. _____

TUNNELS

1. _____
2. _____
3. _____
4. _____

BRIDGES

1. _____
2. _____
3. _____
4. _____

ISLANDS

1. _____
2. _____
3. _____
4. _____

Numbers

From counting your change at the candy store
to keeping track of the score at recess,
you use numbers dozens of times a day.
This chapter gives you even more ways
to use numbers, including measuring things,
playing games, and even cooking!

Metric vs.

America's system of measurement goes by many names: customary, English, or traditional. In the late 18th century, the metric system was created by French scientists. Most of the world outside the United States uses the metric system, so it's a good thing to know about. This list shows how to convert measurements from one system to the other.

FROM	TO	MULTIPLY BY
Inches	Millimeters	25.4
Millimeters	Inches	0.04
Inches	Centimeters	2.54
Centimeters	Inches	0.4
Feet	Meters	0.305
Meters	Feet	0.33
Square feet	Square meters	0.09
Square meters	Square feet	1.2
Yards	Meters	0.914
Meters	Yards	1.1
Miles	Kilometers	1.669
Kilometers	Miles	0.62

"English"

For your information, the metric system is also called the international measurement system. Its basic length — a meter — was first measured as 1/10,000,000 of the distance between the Equator and the North Pole. Today, one meter is 1/299,792,548 of the distance light travels for one second in a vacuum. Thank goodness we don't have to calculate that every day!

FROM	TO	MULTIPLY BY
Fluid ounces	Milliliters	29.57
Milliliters	Fluid ounces	0.034
Quarts	Liters	0.95
Liters	Quarts	1.06
Gallons	Liters	3.785
Liters	Gallons	0.26
Pounds	Kilograms	0.453
Kilograms	Pounds	2.2

How long is long? For many years, standard measurements varied from culture to culture. For instance, a cubit is a measurement from the elbow to the fingertip. In ancient Egypt, a cubit was the equivalent of 20.6 inches (52.4 cm). A Hebrew cubit was 17.7 inches (45 cm). The foot varied also. A foot in Rome was 11.66 inches (29.6 cm). In old England, the modern equivalent of a foot was 13.9 inches (33.5 cm).

Ways of Counting

Our number system uses Arabic numerals, since they were first drawn that way in Arabia in the Middle Ages. Cardinal numbers are the counting numbers, while ordinal numbers give the order of things. Roman numerals were used in ancient Rome and can still be found today in some places, often as a way of stating the year. The year 2003 would be written as MMIII, 2004 as MMIV, and 2005 as MMV.

CARDINAL	CARDINAL	ORDINAL	ORDINAL	ROMAN
One	1	First	1st	I
Two	2	Second	2nd	II
Three	3	Third	3rd	III
Four	4	Fourth	4th	IV
Five	5	Fifth	5th	V
Six	6	Sixth	6th	VI
Seven	7	Seventh	7th	VII
Eight	8	Eighth	8th	VIII
Nine	9	Ninth	9th	IX
Ten	10	Tenth	10th	X
Eleven	11	Eleventh	11th	XI
Twelve	12	Twelfth	12th	XII
Thirteen	13	Thirteenth	13th	XIII
Fourteen	14	Fourteenth	14th	XIV

CARDINAL	CARDINAL	ORDINAL	ORDINAL	ROMAN
Fifteen	15	Fifteenth	15th	XV
Sixteen	16	Sixteenth	16th	XVI
Seventeen	17	Seventeenth	17th	XVII
Eighteen	18	Eighteenth	18th	XVIII
Nineteen	19	Nineteenth	19th	XIX
Twenty	20	Twentieth	20th	XX
Thirty	30	Thirtieth	30th	XXX
Forty	40	Fortieth	40th	XL
Fifty	50	Fiftieth	50th	L
Sixty	60	Sixtieth	60th	LX
Seventy	70	Seventieth	70th	LXX
Eighty	80	Eightieth	80th	LXXX
Ninety	90	Nintieth	90th	XC
One Hundred	100	One Hundredth	100th	C
Five Hundred	500	Five Hundredth	500th	D
One Thousand	1,000	One Thousandth	1000th	M

To write Roman numerals higher than M, you place a bar on top of a letter. A bar on top of the letter increases the value by 1,000. So a bar above an M (M̄) would mean 1,000,000.

Prime Numbers

A prime number is any number that can be divided only by itself and one, without a remainder. That automatically leaves out the even numbers and any numbers ending in five (with the exceptions of 2 and 5, which are considered prime numbers). Non-prime numbers are called composite numbers. Here is a list of all the prime numbers between 1 and 1,000.

2	3	5	7	11	13	17	19	23	29	31	37
41	43	47	53	59	61	67	71	73	79	83	89
97	101	103	107	109	113	127	131	137	139	149	151
157	163	167	173	179	181	191	193	197	199	211	223
227	229	233	239	241	251	257	263	269	271	277	281
283	293	307	311	313	317	331	337	347	349	353	359
367	373	379	383	389	397	401	409	419	421	431	433
439	443	449	457	461	463	467	479	487	491	499	503
509	521	523	541	547	557	563	569	571	577	587	593
599	601	607	613	617	619	631	641	643	647	653	659
661	673	677	683	691	701	709	719	727	733	739	743
751	757	761	769	773	787	797	809	811	821	823	827
829	839	853	857	859	863	877	881	883	887	907	911
919	929	937	941	947	953	967	971	977	983	991	997

You may be thinking, what's the big deal about prime numbers? Well, the big deal is that many important math problems you'll run into use prime numbers. It's also good to know prime numbers as you continue doing long division. Knowing prime numbers (or how to find them) will make division easier.

Square Roots

When you "square" a number, you don't put a box around it. You multiply it by itself. For example, the square of 6 is 36 (6 x 6). A number's square root is the number you "square" to equal your original number. So, the square root of 9 is 3 (since 3 x 3 = 9). Get it? Square roots can come in handy when solving all sorts of equations. Here is a list of the square roots of numbers from 2 to 25. (The square root of 1 is . . . 1!) As you can see, they're not always simple numbers. These are decimal approximations in some cases.

$$\sqrt{2} = 1.414$$
$$\sqrt{3} = 1.732$$
$$\sqrt{4} = 2$$
$$\sqrt{5} = 2.236$$
$$\sqrt{6} = 2.449$$
$$\sqrt{7} = 2.645$$
$$\sqrt{8} = 2.828$$
$$\sqrt{9} = 3$$
$$\sqrt{10} = 3.162$$
$$\sqrt{11} = 3.316$$
$$\sqrt{12} = 3.464$$
$$\sqrt{13} = 3.605$$

$$\sqrt{14} = 3.741$$
$$\sqrt{15} = 3.872$$
$$\sqrt{16} = 4$$
$$\sqrt{17} = 4.123$$
$$\sqrt{18} = 4.242$$
$$\sqrt{19} = 4.358$$
$$\sqrt{20} = 4.472$$
$$\sqrt{21} = 4.582$$
$$\sqrt{22} = 4.690$$
$$\sqrt{23} = 4.795$$
$$\sqrt{24} = 4.898$$
$$\sqrt{25} = 5$$

Look for more squares of numbers on the times tables on pages 118–119.

Look for this symbol $\sqrt{}$ to tell you when you will need the square root of a number.

Geometric Shapes

A polygon is a flat, two-dimensional shape that has three or more sides. In other words, polygons have length and width but not depth; a square is a polygon but a cube is not. Here are the names of a wide variety of polygon shapes, named after their number of sides. Check out all the different kinds of triangles!

NAME/
SIDES OR DESCRIPTION

Triangle
three sides

Equilateral triangle
has equal sides and angles

Scalene triangle
all three sides have different lengths

Isosceles triangle
two sides of equal length

Right triangle
two sides meet at a 90-degree angle

Quadrilateral
four sides

Trapezoid
four sides with one pair of parallel sides

Rhombus
four equal sides, but without any right angles

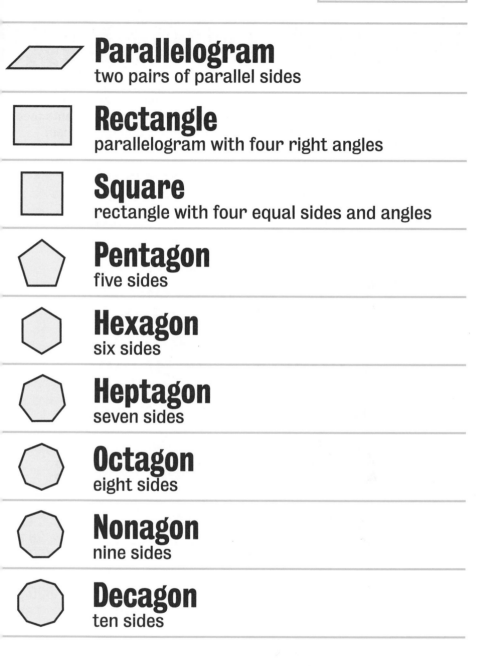

Parallelogram
two pairs of parallel sides

Rectangle
parallelogram with four right angles

Square
rectangle with four equal sides and angles

Pentagon
five sides

Hexagon
six sides

Heptagon
seven sides

Octagon
eight sides

Nonagon
nine sides

Decagon
ten sides

A circle, of course, has no sides and is not a polygon. The official definition of a circle is a set of points on a line, all at an equal distance from the center of the shape.

What's Cooking?

Teaspoons and ounces and cups — oh my! Cooking has its own world of measurements and numbers that can sometimes be a bit confusing. Plus, sometimes you have to switch from English to metric measurements (see page 108). Here's a handy list of terms you might need in the kitchen.

3 teaspoons = 1 tablespoon
16 tablespoons = 1 cup
8 tablespoons = ¹/₂ cup
4 tablespoons = ¹/₄ cup
1 tablespoon = ¹/₁₆ cup
1 cup = 8 fluid ounces
2 cups = 1 pint
2 pints = 1 quart
2 quarts = ¹/₂ gallon
4 quarts = 1 gallon
48 teaspoons = 1 cup

Kitchen Switchin': English to Metric

LIQUID		DRY	
1 tsp.	5 ml*	0.35 oz.	1 g
1 tbs.	13 ml	1 oz.	28 g
1 fluid oz.	30 ml	3.4 oz.	100 g
1 cup	237 ml	1 lb.	454 g
1 pint	473 ml	1.10 lbs.	500 g
1 quart	0.95 l	2.205 lb., 35 oz.	1 kg
1 gallon	3.8 l		
34 fluid oz.	1 l		

* (ml=milliliter, l=liter, tsp.=teaspoon, tbs.=tablespoon, g=grams, oz.=ounces, lb.=pounds, kg=kilograms)

Because many food products are sold around the world, look for both English and metric measurements listed on the labels of the foods you eat.

Ewww! Fractions!

Come on, they're not that bad. Without fractions, how could you have a slice (⅛) of pizza? Without fractions, how could you get quarters for the video game? (That's right — money is fractions.) Of course, fractions are also written as decimal numbers. This chart lists three ways of writing many of the fractions that you might run across.

FRACTIONS	WORDS	DECIMALS	FRACTIONS	WORDS	DECIMALS
$1/2$	one-half	0.5	$1/64$	one-sixty-fourth	0.0156
$1/3$	one-third	0.3333	$2/3$	two-thirds	0.6667
$1/4$	one-fourth	0.25	$2/5$	two-fifths	0.4
$1/5$	one-fifth	0.2	$3/4$	three-fourths	0.75
$1/6$	one-sixth	0.1667	$3/5$	three-fifths	0.6
$1/7$	one-seventh	0.1429	$3/8$	three-eighths	0.375
$1/8$	one-eighth	0.125	$3/10$	three-tenths	0.3
$1/9$	one-ninth	0.1111	$4/5$	four-fifths	0.8
$1/10$	one-tenth	0.1	$5/6$	five-sixths	0.8333
$1/11$	one-eleventh	0.09	$5/8$	five-eighths	0.625
$1/16$	one-sixteenth	0.0625	$7/8$	seven-eighths	0.875
$1/25$	one-twenty-fifth	0.04	$7/10$	seven-tenths	0.7
$1/32$	one-thirty-second	0.0313	$9/10$	nine-tenths	0.9

PSSST

The quick way to find the decimal number for any fraction is to divide the top number by the bottom number. For example, in ⅝, divide 5 by 8 to get .625. Pick a fraction that's not on our list and try it out.

Multiplication Tables

X	0	1	2	3	4	5
1	0	1	2	3	4	5
2	0	2	4	6	8	10
3	0	3	6	9	12	15
4	0	4	8	12	16	20
5	0	5	10	15	20	25
6	0	6	12	18	24	30
7	0	7	14	21	28	35
8	0	8	16	24	32	40
9	0	9	18	27	36	45
10	0	10	20	30	40	50
11	0	11	22	33	44	55
12	0	12	24	36	48	60

You can use this handy-dandy times-table chart to help you memorize the multiplication tables up through the number 12. Here's an example of how to use it: To figure the answer to 8x5, locate the 8 on the top horizontal row of numbers. Then move down the column below the 8 to the place where it crosses the horizontal row that starts with 5 (over on the left-hand side of page 118). Where the column for 8 and the row for 5 meet, you'll find your answer: 40.

6	7	8	9	10	11	12
6	7	8	9	10	11	12
12	14	16	18	20	22	24
18	21	24	27	30	33	36
24	28	32	36	40	44	48
30	35	40	45	50	55	60
36	42	48	54	60	66	72
42	49	56	63	70	77	84
48	56	64	72	80	88	96
54	63	72	81	90	99	108
60	70	80	90	100	110	120
66	77	88	99	110	121	132
72	84	96	108	120	132	144

Ahoy, Matey!

When sailing or going anywhere on the water, such as a lake or an ocean (though probably not your bathtub), you need to know terms that measure distances and depths. Who knows? This might make a sailor out of you!

Furlong
220 yards (201.17 m)

Cable*
120 fathoms or 720 feet (219.46 m)

* Can be used to measure distance across water or depth of the water.

International Nautical Mile
6,076 feet or 8.44 cables or 1.15 miles (1,852.96 m)

League
3.11 miles (5 km)

Knot
Measure of speed on water

One knot
1 nautical mile per hour

Sounding
Taking a measurement of the depth of water

Fathom
6 feet (1.82 m); usually used to measure depth

Mark
6 feet (1.82 m); a riverboat term for depth

The pen name of the famous American author Samuel Clemens is a water measurement. "Mark" is 6 feet (1.82 m); "Mark Twain" is twice that, or 12 feet (3.65 m).

Math Symbols

Do you speak more than one language? Of course you do; everyone who does math of any kind uses a special language made up of numbers and symbols. Here are the meanings of important symbols you can use in "speaking" this international language.

+	add (plus)	**%**	percentage
—	subtract (minus)	**:**	ratio
		π	pi*
✗ or •	multiply	**X^2**	a number squared, or multiplied by itself
/ or ÷	divide		
=	equal to		
≠	not equal to	**X^3**	a number cubed, or multiplied by itself and then by itself again
>	is greater than		
<	is less than		
≥	is greater than or equal to	**√**	square root (see page 113)
≤	is less than or equal to	**$**	dollars
		¢	cents

*The measurement called pi (pronounced like pie that you eat) is named for the sixteenth letter of the Greek alphabet. Pi is a number used to help measure the circumference of a circle (the distance around it), as well as the circle's area (the space inside). Pi is about 3.1415.

Cool Math Tricks

Math and magic go together in this list of cool math tricks. Try them on your friends and amaze them with your mathematical mind-reading ability. Just be sure that you do your math correctly!

Back to the Beginning

- Pick any number between 1 and 10 and write it down. Write down the next four consecutive numbers following your first number.
- Add these five numbers and divide the sum by 5.
- Subtract 2.
- You now have your original number back!

Math Magic for Class

To find out if any number can be evenly divided by:

2 If the number ends in 0, 2, 4, 6, or 8, it is divisible by 2.

3 Add together the digits of the number. If necessary, repeat until you have a one-digit sum. If the sum is evenly divisible by 3, then so is the original number.

4 If the number's last two digits are 00 or they form a two-digit number evenly divisible by 4, the number is divisible by 4.

5 If the number ends in a 0 or 5, it can be evenly divided by 5.

6 For even numbers only, add the digits. If the sum is evenly divisible by 3, the number can be evenly divided by 6.

9 Add together the digits of the number. If necessary, repeat until you have a one-digit sum. If the sum is evenly divisible by 9, the original number is divisible by 9.

10 If the number ends in 0, it can be divided by 10.

Guess Their Age*

- Ask the person to multiply the first number of his/her age by 5.
- Add 3.
- Double this figure.
- Tell the person to add the second number of his/her age to the figure and have them tell you their answer. Deduct 6 and you will have their age!
  (* For kids under 10, their age is the first digit of the result.)

Age Over and Over

- Take your age.
- Multiply it by 7.
- Multiply that product by 1,443.
- Your age shows up over and over in the answer.

Always 18

- Select three different numbers between 1 and 9.
- Write the three numbers down next to one another, largest first, forming a three-digit number.
- Reverse the digits, putting the smallest first, and write this number underneath the first number.
- Subtract the lower three-digit number from the upper three-digit number to get a result.
- The sum of the three digits of the result is always 18!

Here's another trick: To easily multiply double-digit numbers by 11, split the digits of the number. Put the sum of those two digits in the middle. The new number is the answer. Example: 24 x 11. Split 2 and 4; add them and put the resulting 6 in the middle: 264.

My Numbers

You're probably just about numbered-out by this point. Don't worry, just one more list and we promise that you'll know all the answers (or at least you should!). Here is a list of the important numbers in your life.

My favorite number _____

My lucky number _____

My age in years _____

My age in months _____
(years x 12 — see page 118!)

My homeroom or classroom number _____

My phone number _____

My school's phone number _____

My ZIP code _____

The number of teeth I've lost _____

The number of kids at my school _____

The number of times I am told to clean my room before I actually do it _____

My highest score ever on a video or computer game _____

Don't write it down here, but you should also memorize your Social Security number. Your parents can tell you what it is. It's an important way that you can identify yourself. It's also used by the government to keep track of information and services you may need.

Phone numbers were not always seven digits. When phones were first used, people didn't have numbers; an operator connected each call. The first phone numbers were different lengths in different parts of the United States. Seven digits became standard in the 1950s.

CHAPTER FIVE

Science

From the stars in the sky to the rocks in the
earth and everything in between, science
studies the way the universe works.
In this chapter, see how science works!

Sciences and Scientists

Scientists are everywhere! A baker uses science to make a cake rise, and science is used every time someone balances the chemicals in a swimming pool. More important, without science there would be no video games, no e-mail, no bizarrely colored candy, no hair gel or shampoo, and no skateboard wheels. Here is a list of some of the many types of scientists, the name of their sciences, and what they study.

SCIENTIST/SCIENCE	STUDY OF
Aerospace engineer/Aerospace engineering	aircraft and spacecraft
Anthropologist/Anthropology	human origin
Archaeologist/Archaeology	past people and cultures
Astronomer/Astronomy	heavenly bodies
Bacteriologist/Bacteriology	bacteria
Biologist/Biology	plants and animals
Botanist/Botany	plants
Chemist/Chemistry	relationships between substances
Ecologist/Ecology	plants, animals, and the environment
Endocrinologist/Endocrinology	human glands and hormones
Entomologist/Entomology	insects
Environmentalist/Environment	relationships between all living things
Forensic scientist/Forensic science	science involved in solving crimes
Geneticist/Genetics	genes and hereditary characteristics

SCIENTIST/SCIENCE	STUDY OF
Geologist/Geology	Earth's composition, structure, and changes
Mathematician/Mathematics	relationship of numbers
Marine biologist/Marine biology	life in and surrounding water
Mechanical engineer/Mechanics	interaction of forces and objects
Meteorologist/Meteorology	weather
Metallurgist/Metallurgy	metals
Microbiologist/Microbiology	microscopic organisms
Mineralogist/Mineralogy	minerals
Oceanographer/Oceanography	oceans and ocean life
Paleontologist/Paleontology	fossils
Pharmacist/Pharmacology	drugs to help people
Psychologist/Psychology	human and animal behavior
Physicist/Physics	matter and energy
Sociologist/Sociology	individuals and groups
Zoologist/Zoology	animals

Most of the names of these sciences end in "-ology." This is from a Greek word *logos*, which means knowledge. The suffix means "the study of."

Planets

Nine planets revolve around our sun: Mercury, Venus, Earth, Mars, Jupiter, Saturn, Uranus, Neptune, and Pluto. To remember all of them in their order, use a sentence like: **My Very Eager Mother Just Served Us Nine Pizzas.** Or, make up your own sentence. This memory device is called a "mnemonic" [ni-MAHN-ik]. The period of revolution is the amount of time as measured on Earth that it takes a planet to complete one orbit around the sun.

PLANET	DIAMETER OF PLANET	GRAVITATIONAL PULL	PERIOD OF REVOLUTION
Mercury	3,032 miles/4,880 km	0.38	87.97 days
Venus	7,519 miles/12,100 km	0.91	224.70 days
Earth	7,926 miles/12,756 km	1	1 year
Mars	4,194 miles/6,750 km	0.38	1.88 years
Jupiter	88,736 miles/142,806 km	2.54	11.9 years
Saturn	74,978 miles/120,665 km	0.93	29.5 years
Uranus	32,193 miles/51,810 km	0.8	84 years
Neptune	30,775 miles/49,528 km	1.2	164.8 years
Pluto	1,423 miles/2,290 km	0.1	248.5 years

Figure out how much you weigh on another planet! Multiply your weight by the "gravitational pull" factors. If you weigh 97 pounds (43.9 kg) on Earth and want to compare that to your weight on Mars, multiply 97 by .38. You would weigh about 37 pounds (16.7 kg).

Constellations

By looking up at the night sky you can see star patterns that remind people of the shapes of animals and other objects. These patterns are called constellations. Here is a list of some of the constellations you can see at various times of the year. Check with your science teacher to get a star chart for your home area, and see how many you can spot.

CONSTELLATION	COMMON NAME	CONSTELLATION	COMMON NAME
Andromeda	Princess	Leo	Lion
Aquarius	Water-bearer	Leo Minor	Little Lion
Aries	Ram	Lepus	Hare
Auriga	Charioteer	Libra	Scales
Cancer	Crab	Lupus	Wolf
Canes Venatici	Hunting Dogs	Monoceros	Unicorn
Canis Major	Great Dog	Orion	Hunter
Canis Minor	Little Dog	Pegasus	Flying Horse
Capricornus	Sea-goat	Phoenix	Phoenix
Cassiopeia	Queen	Pisces	Fishes
Centaurus	Centaur	Pyxis	Compass
Crater	Cup	Sagittarius	Archer
Cygnus	Swan	Scorpius	Scorpion
Gemini	Twins	Serpens	Serpent
Grus	Crane	Taurus	Bull
Hercules	Hercules	Vela	Sails
Lacerta	Lizard	Vulpecula	Fox

Most of the names of constellations come from the shapes that can be drawn using the stars as points in the shape.

Star Light, Star Bright

It is estimated that there are more than 200 billion stars in the universe. The sun, of course, is the closest star to Earth, and it forms the center of our solar system. This list of the brightest stars and the constellations in which they can be located begins with the brightest star seen from Earth; the stars get dimmer as you move down the list. Ask your teachers or check the library for a star chart of your area to help you find these stars and the constellations listed here and on page 129.

STAR NAME	CONSTELLATION	STAR NAME	CONSTELLATION
Sirius	Canis Major	Beta Centauri	Centaurus
Canopus	Carina	Altair	Aquila
Alpha Centauri	Centaurus	Aldebaran	Taurus
Arcturus	Boötes	Spica	Virgo
Vega	Lyra	Pollux	Gemini
Capella	Auriga	Antares	Scorpius
Rigel	Orion	Fomalhaut	Piscis Austrinus
Procyon	Canis Minor	Deneb	Cygnus
Achernar	Eridanus	Regulus	Leo
Betelgeuse	Orion	Beta Crucis	Crux

Our sun is considered a yellow dwarf star and is estimated to have enough fuel to last another five billion years. At the end of its life, our sun will become a white dwarf, as it collapses under its own weight. Don't worry — scientists don't think that will happen for billions of years.

Crowded Space

Stars like those listed on page 130 fill the night sky above Earth, but those twinkling lights are not alone. This list describes other types of heavenly bodies (and other things) found in our sky.

Asteroids
Bodies of rock and metal that orbit the sun

Comets
Bodies of ice and dirt that orbit the sun

Galaxies
Groupings of stars in four types: spiral, barred spiral, elliptical, and irregular

Human-made Space Objects
These include rocket parts, space stations, and probes.

Meteors
Meteoroids falling into Earth's atmosphere

Meteorites
Meteors that reach Earth's surface

Meteoroids
Space debris in the solar system

Moons
Satellites of rock, ice, and/or liquid that orbit around planets. Earth has one moon; Saturn has 18. Other planets have between one and 28 moons.

Planets
Nine heavenly bodies that orbit the sun (See page 128 and note below.)

Stars
Huge bodies of burning gasses; types include blue-white, white, yellow, orange, and red

Like a mystery? There may be a tenth planet, beyond Pluto. Called Planet X, it has yet to be discovered, but is thought to exist because of an unexplained pull on Uranus and Neptune. But then, some astronomers now believe that Pluto is not really a planet at all. Stay tuned!

Classification of Living Things

In order to study life on Earth, scientists have divided all living things into five categories called kingdoms. In order to name a specific organism, seven categories are used. However, we just use common names most of the time.

FIVE KINGDOMS

Animalia
animals

Plantae
plants

Fungi
yeast, mushrooms, mildew, mold

Protista
one-celled organisms

Monera
bacteria, blue-green algae

SEVEN CLASSIFICATIONS

Kingdom
Phylum (animals)
Division (plants)
Class
Order
Family
Genus
Species

EXAMPLES OF CLASSIFICATIONS

COMMON NAME	HUMAN	LION	SWEET BAY
KINGDOM	Animalia	Animalia	Plantae
PHYLUM*	Chordata	Chordata	Magnoliophyta
CLASS	Mammalia	Mammalia	Magnoliopsida
ORDER	Primate	Carnivora	Magnoliales
FAMILY	Hominidae	Felidae	Magnoliaceae
GENUS	Homo	Panthera	Magnolia
SPECIES	Homo sapiens	Leo	M. virginiana

* This category is called a "Division" for plants, such as sweet bay in this example.

The classification of organisms is called taxonomy. Not all taxonomists believe that there are only five kingdoms. Some add a sixth kingdom, Archaebacteria — single-celled organisms that create methane gas.

Food Chain

All living beings take part in the food chain. It works something like this: Grass uses photosynthesis to make its own food and grow. A mouse eats the grass. A snake eats the mouse. A hawk eats the snake. The hawk dies and is broken down by bacteria, becoming part of the soil, which helps more grass grow, and bingo, we're back at the beginning. To borrow a popular phrase, it's the "circle of life."

Step 1. PRODUCERS

Autotrophs: Plants that produce their own food.
EXAMPLES: trees, grass, grains

Step 2. CONSUMERS

Heterotrophs: Organisms that cannot produce their own food.

Primary consumers: Animals that eat plants, called herbivores. EXAMPLES: mice, cows, sheep, rabbits

Secondary consumers: Animals that eat primary consumers. They are usually called carnivores — animals that eat meat. EXAMPLES: snakes, frogs, birds of prey

Tertiary* consumers: Animals that eat secondary consumers. They are called omnivores because they eat both plants and animals. EXAMPLES: squirrels, bears, turtles

Step 3. DECOMPOSERS

Bacteria: Organisms that break down dead plants and animals. This provides nutrients for autotrophs and begins the cycle all over again.

* Tertiary means "third."

What about us? Humans can be either primary, secondary, or tertiary consumers. Whether you enjoy hamburgers, avoid meat, or are even a strict vegan, you're a heterotroph, because you can't produce your own food without help.

What Makes a Plant?

What makes a plant? The answer is cells, lots of them! When cells arrange themselves into specialized tissues they form the different parts of the plant. All plants have all or most of the parts on this list.

Roots

Roots anchor and hold the plant in the ground or water, while absorbing water and minerals.

Stems

Stems support the plant and hold leaves up to the light. Inside stems, xylem tissue transports water and minerals up from the roots, while phloem tissue takes the leaf-produced food throughout the plant.

Leaves

Leaves are the areas of a plant that produce food for the plant. Plants use light energy, water, and carbon dioxide to produce food, releasing oxygen. Green stuff called chlorophyll gathers the energy from the sun.

Seeds

Seeds are the part of the plant that reproduces.

Flowers

Seeds are made in the flowering part of the plants. Flower parts include stamens, anthers, stylem, fruit, and petals.

Plants that contain both male and female parts of the reproductive system in one flower are known as perfect flowers.

Inside the Animal Kingdom

The animal kingdom consists of many-celled organisms. They are divided into classes (see page 132). Here are the animal classes, some of the characteristics that animals in each class share, and examples of each class.

INVERTEBRATES

Multicelled organisms without backbones

Annelida
soft, segmented body, two body openings (earthworms, leeches)

Arthropoda
jointed legs, segmented body: arachnids (spiders, ticks); crustaceans (crabs, shrimp); insects (fleas, crickets)

Coelenterata
tentacles, stinger cells, primitive nervous systems (corals, jellyfish, sea anemones)

Echinodermata
tube feet, no head, can regenerate body parts, aquatic (sand dollars, sea urchins, starfish)

Mollusca
soft body, usually a hard shell, head, sense organs, aquatic (clams, octopuses, snails)

Nematoda
smooth outer skin, pointed ends, usually microscopic (nematodes, pinworms)

Platyhelminthes
head, simple nervous system, lives in wet environments (tapeworms, flukes)

Porifera
live in colonies, attach to underwater rocks (sponges)

VERTEBRATES

Animals with backbones

Amphibia
lay eggs, live in water and on land, true legs, gills grow into lungs (frogs, salamanders)

Aves (Birds)
warm-blooded, feathers, wings, bills, lay eggs, most fly (owls, ostriches, robins)

Fish
scales, aquatic, gills, fins, lay eggs (rays, sharks, goldfish)

Mammalia
hair, bear their young live, produce milk, warm-blooded (mice, humans, whales)

Reptilia
lay eggs, scales, lungs, most cold-blooded (crocodiles, alligators, turtles, snakes)

The category of Arthropoda has more than 80 percent of the animals in the world. In other words, insects rule the planet!

Don't Eat That Plant!

We can eat many parts of the plants we have around our homes and in our gardens. Some plants, however, can make you feel mildly uncomfortable or lead to severe pain or death. When in doubt, don't taste it! Beware of these plants and their specific parts:

Azalea
All parts

Buttercup
All parts

Daffodil
Bulbs

Elderberry
Roots

English Holly
Berries

Foxglove
Leaves, seeds, flowers

Hyacinth
Bulbs

Hydrangea
Buds, leaves, branches

Jack-in-the-pulpit
All parts

Laurel
All parts

Lily of the Valley
Leaves, flowers

Mistletoe
All parts

Morning Glory
Seeds

Mushroom
All parts of many wild varieties

Poinsettia
All parts

Poison Hemlock
All parts

Poison Ivy
All parts

Poison Oak
All parts

Poison Sumac
All parts

Rhododendron
All parts

Wisteria
Seeds, pods

During December many families decorate their homes with poinsettia plants, hang mistletoe above the doors, and use holly and ivy in many pretty arrangements. All of these plants made it on the list of poisonous plants. So when your parents tell you not to eat the decorations, it's for a good reason!

Medicines from Plants

Besides providing beauty and food, plants can help cure our aches and pains. We still have many plants to examine for their medicinal properties, and it is important to discover them before they disappear from our planet. This list provides a small sample of the hundreds of ways in which plants help us. **Do not**, however, try any of these remedies unless you have checked with your doctor first.

PLANT	HELPS WITH . . .
Aloe	easing sunburns
Chili pepper	reducing pain
Eucalyptus	killing germs
Garlic	infections
Ginger	digestion
Mint	nausea, indigestion
Pacific yew	fighting cancer
Purple coneflower	resisting infection
Rose	vitamin C
St. John's wort	nervous system
Willow	headaches, fevers
Wormwood	parasitic worms
Yarrow	nosebleeds

Psst

Found in Asia, the Neem tree (*Azadirachta indica*) can be used in many ways: to get rid of athlete's foot, ringworm, and lice; to treat malaria and fever; to prevent viral diseases; and even as a toothpaste!

A Fossil Time Line

The remains of plants and animals in rocks, or outlines of them, are called fossils. A fossil can be a small part of a leaf, a shark's tooth, an insect, or part of an early human. Fossils give us the history of plants and animals that no longer exist. Here are some key moments in the history of fossils.

1780
First fossils of dinosaur bones found in England.

1811
First ichthyosaur* fossil found in England.

1856
Hominid (early human) skull fragment fossil found in Germany.

1860
Earliest known bird fossil found.

1974
Complete skeleton of early human (*Australopithecus afarensis*) found in Ethiopia; named "Lucy."

1976
Footprints of *Australopithecus afarensis* found in Tanzania.

1987
Oldest known fossil dinosaur egg embryo (more than 230 million years old) found.

1991
Body of a 5,000-year-old man, preserved in ice, found in the Italian Alps.

"Lucy's Grandson," *Australopithecus afarensis*, male skull found in Ethiopia.

2002
"Toumai," 7-million-year-old hominid fossil, found in Africa.

2004
Fossils of tiny pygmy-like hominids found in a cave in Indonesia.

* A flying dinosaur; found by a explorer named Mary Annin

Coelacanth (SEEL-uh-kanth) fossils have been found that date this fish to 400 million years ago. In 1938, and again in 1998, live coelacanths were caught. This fish, once thought extinct, is known as a "living fossil"!

Earth's Eras

Earth's history is divided into four eras, or very long time periods. We use fossil and geological records to discover in what era various livings things existed. Each era is broken up into periods. All numbers below (except the first) are in "millions of years ago."

ERA/PERIOD	MILLIONS OF YEARS AGO	LIVING THINGS
Precambrian Era	**4.5 billion–600**	
		one-celled organisms
Paleozoic Era	**600–245**	
Cambrian	600–510	fossil records of hard-shell animals
Ordovician	510–439	animal life in the oceans
Silurian	439–408	first land plants evolve, reefs build up
Devonian	408–360	land plants and amphibians evolve
Carboniferous	360–290	amphibians and reptiles evolve
Permian	290–245	cone-bearing plants and reptiles evolve
Mesozoic Era	**245–65**	
Triassic	245–208	mammals
Jurassic	208–144.2	dinosaurs
Cretaceous	144.2–65	more dinosaurs
Cenozoic Era	**65–today**	
Tertiary	65–1.64	apes and humanoids
Quaternary	1.64–today	finally — people!

Most scientists now agree that a massive meteor that struck Earth near Mexico about 65 million years ago was one of the main reasons dinosaurs suddenly disappeared.

It's Element–ary

We're not talking elementary school here. Science has figured out that all substances on Earth are made of the same basic elements. That is, they are made of substances that cannot be broken down any further. So far, chemists have discovered 113 elements. They're listed here alphabetically, but they are also sometimes arranged according to their atomic number in the periodic table of the elements.

NAME	SYMBOL	ATOMIC NUMBER	NAME	SYMBOL	ATOMIC NUMBER
Actinium	Ac	89	Erbium	Er	68
Aluminum	Al	13	Europium	Eu	63
Americium	Am	95	Fermium	Fm	100
Antimony	Sb	51	Fluorine	F	9
Argon	Ar	18	Francium	Fr	87
Arsenic	As	33	Gadolinium	Gd	64
Astatine	At	85	Gallium	Ga	3
Barium	Ba	56	Germanium	Ge	32
Berkelium	Bk	97	Gold	Au	79
Beryllium	Be	4	Hafnium	Hf	72
Bismuth	Bi	83	Hassium*	Mt	101
Bohrium*	Bh	107	Helium	He	2
Boron	B	5	Holmium	Ho	6
Bromine	Br	35	Hydrogen	H	
Cadmium	Cd	48	Indium	In	49
Calcium	Ca	20	Iodine	I	53
Californium	Cf	98	Iridium	Ir	7
Carbon	C	6	Iron	Fe	26
Cerium	Ce	58	Krypton	Kr	36
Cesium	Cs	55	Lanthanum	La	5
Chlorine	Cl	17	Lawrencium	Lr	103
Chromium	Cr	24	Lead	Pb	82
Cobalt	Co	27	Lithium	Li	
Copper	Cu	29	Lutetium	Lu	7
Curium	Cm	96	Magnesium	Mg	12
Dubnium*	Db	105	Manganese	Mn	25
Dysprosium	Dy	66	Meitnerium*	Mt	109
Einsteinium	Es	99	Mendelevium	Md	10

NAME	SYMBOL	ATOMIC NUMBER
Mercury	Hg	80
Molybdenum	Mo	42
Neodymium	Nd	60
Neon	Ne	10
Neptunium	Np	93
Nickel	Ni	28
Niobium	Nb	41
Nitrogen	N	7
Nobelium	No	102
Osmium	Os	76
Oxygen	O	8
Palladium	Pd	46
Phosphorus	P	15
Platinum	Pt	78
Plutonium	Pu	94
Polonium	Po	84
Potassium	K	19
Praseodymium	Pr	59
Promethium	Pm	61
Protactinium	Pa	91
Radium	Ra	88
Radon	Rn	86
Rhenium	Re	75
Rhodium	Rh	45
Rubidium	Rb	37
Ruthenium	Ru	44
Rutherfordium*	Rf	104
Samarium	Sm	62
Scandium	Sc	21
Seaborgium*	Sg	106

NAME	SYMBOL	ATOMIC NUMBER
Selenium	Se	34
Silicon	Si	14
Silver	Ag	47
Sodium	Na	11
Strontium	Sr	38
Sulfur	S	16
Tantalum	Ta	73
Technetium	Tc	43
Tellurium	Te	52
Terbium	Tb	65
Thallium	Tl	81
Thorium	Th	90
Thulium	Tm	69
Tin	Sn	50
Titanium	Ti	22
Tungsten	W	74
Ununbium	Uub	112
Ununhexium	Uuh	116
Ununium	Uuu	111
Ununnilium	Uun	110
Ununoctium	Uuo	118
Ununquadium	Uuq	114
Uranium	U	92
Vanadium	V	23
Xenon	Xe	54
Ytterbium	Yb	70
Yttrium	Y	39
Zinc	Zn	30
Zirconium	Zr	40

* You might see these elements called by other names; scientists can't agree on which names to use.

Dmitry Mendeleyev organized the elements into what is called the periodic table of the elements. Forty-five years later, in 1914, Henry G. J. Moseley rearranged the table using the atomic numbers of the elements.

Famous Robots

Baseball players have a hall of fame. So do hoopsters and gridiron greats. So why not robots? That's what the brainy and creative folks at Carnegie Mellon University in Pennsylvania thought. They started the Robot Hall of Fame in 2003 to honor robots from real life and from science fiction. Here is the list of those robots inducted into the hall so far. Maybe you can invent one someday that will earn a spot there, too!

Astro Boy
Japanese cartoon character

C-3PO
Star Wars' android of six million languages

HAL 9000
A computer that wanted to live, from the movie *2001: A Space Odyssey*

Mars Pathfinder Sojourner Rover
The wheeled robot that explored Mars

R2-D2
The spunky rolling 'droid from *Star Wars* movies

Robby the Robot
From the movie *Forbidden Planet*

Shakey
First robot able to navigate by itself (1966)

Unimate
First robot arm to be used in an assembly line

 Some movie fans might point out that **HAL 9000** is not actually a robot, but a computer. But he was enough of a machine with human-like qualities to earn a spot in the hall of fame.

Machines

Machines are more than just big, metal things that manufacture cars, clean streets, or make concrete. A machine is any device that makes work easier by using energy to overcome or change the direction of a force, and give a mechanical advantage. Scientists created these categories of machines.

Simple Machines

These basic machines are used to accomplish different types of work. All six machines involve a load and an effort, that is, taking something and moving it in a particular direction.

Incline plane
Surface raised in an inclined position, a ramp

Lever
Different ways of lifting things, such as crowbars, wheelbarrows, or a lifting arm

Pulley
Rope or chain placed over a wheel or track in a wheel

Screw
An inclined plane twisting around an axis, such as a blender or a ship's propeller

Wheel and axle
Round frame on central rod, such as a bicycle tire or car wheels

Wedge
Two or more sloping surfaces tapering to a thin edge, such as an ax

Complex Machines

Any combination of simple machines that work together to perform their job. Among the millions of different types of complex machines are:

airplanes, automobiles, cameras, computers, telephones, televisions

Can machines think? Some scientists are working on ways to make computers do more than just what we tell them to. The science of "artificial intelligence" is trying to build computers that can have original thoughts.

Systems of the Human Body

Twenty-four hours a day, seven days a week, your body systems function, enabling you to move, eat, play video games, and do your homework. Some systems and organs do their jobs without your permission, such as your heart. Other systems wait for your directions, such as muscles that make you walk. Here are the systems that keep your body humming, along with some of their key organs.

Circulatory carries blood throughout the body
PARTS: heart, veins, arteries

Digestive breaks down food into nutrients
PARTS: mouth, stomach, intestines

Excretory removes waste products
PARTS: kidneys, colon

Muscular helps with movement
PARTS: muscles

Nervous nerves that control the responses of the body
PARTS: brain, spinal cord

Reproductive system used to create offspring
PARTS: ovaries (female); testes (male)

Respiratory takes in oxygen and nitrogen from the air and supplies those to the blood PARTS: mouth, nose, lungs

Skeletal bones that provide framework and support
PARTS: 206 bones, cartilage, ligaments

Immune provides protection from disease and infection PARTS: lymph nodes, skin

What's missing here? Your senses.
Your ears, eyes, tongue, skin, and nose all do specific jobs and are also considered part of the nervous system.

Boning Up on Bones

You have 206 bones in your body. Most of them make up your arms, hands, legs, and toes. Check out the number of bones it takes to have working ankles and wrists — no wonder it takes so long for them to heal! Here are the number of bones in various parts of your body. Add 'em up and you'll get 206.

BODY SECTION	NO. OF BONES
Cranium (skull)	**22**
Ears	**6**
Spine	**26**
Ribs	**24**
Sternum (breastbone)	**1**
Throat (hyoid bone)	**1**
Shoulders	**4**
Forearms	**6**
Wrists (carpus)	**26**
Fingers (phalanges)	**28**
Hips	**2**
Legs	**8**
Ankles (tarsus)	**24**
Toes (phalanges)	**28**
TOTAL	**206**

Without your hammer, anvil, and stirrups, you couldn't hear someone read out loud. These three bones in the ear are the tiniest bones in your body, but they have a vital function in helping you hear.

Mighty Muscles

You have three types of muscles: heart, smooth, and striped. Of course, the heart muscles are found in your heart. Smooth muscles are found in your organs, such as your stomach. Striped muscles make up your skeletal, or voluntary, muscles. On this list are the muscles that you may have heard about; they're the muscles you use to move around in the world.

Biceps
bends your arm

Brachioradialis
bends your elbow

Deltoid
moves your shoulder

Flexor
moves your hand

Gastrocnemius
used to walk and jump

Gracilis
bends and twists your leg

Pectoralis major
used to breathe and move your shoulders

Quadriceps
straightens your leg

Rectus femoris
moves your thigh

Sartorius
bends your leg

Soleus
used to stand

Tibialis anterior
used to walk

Trapezius
keeps your shoulders straight

Triceps
straightens your arm

Vastus lateralis
extends your knee

Vastus medialis
bends and extends your knee

How many muscles does your face need to help you smile, frown, show surprise, show fear, or display other emotions? A. 10 B. 40 C. 80.

Answer: Forty. In all, that's all the muscles in your face, working together to show whatever emotion you're feeling.

My Gooey Body

Everyone tells you that your body is mostly water, but there are many types of fluid running through and out of your body. Some of these fluids can be quite messy, but they are all necessary to keep you healthy, lubricated, and moving.

Bile
made by the liver, used to break down fats

Blood
transports food and oxygen to the body cells

Chyme
in the stomach, breaks down food into liquid form

Diarrhea
watery solid waste

Gastric juice
stomach fluids, enzymes, and acids

Inner-ear fluid
in the inner ear, used to help keep balance

Lymph
found in the lymphatic system

Mucus
protective fluid of membrane linings, such as those in the nose

Pus
dead bacteria and cells

Rhinorrhea
fluid running from your nose

Saliva
in the mouth, used to begin digestive process

Synovial fluid
lubricates cartilage, movable joints

Tears
produced to wash dust out of eyes

Urine
produced by the kidneys, then eliminated from the body

Vomit
stomach fluid ejected from body through the esophagus and the mouth

Rhinorrhea and mucus come flying out of your nose at more than 60 miles per hour (100 kph) when you sneeze. It's impossible to keep your eyes open when you sneeze — probably to keep rhinorrhea out of your eyes!

10 Cool Things About Feet

We use and misuse them every day, but do we know much about our hardworking feet? They may be at the end of our bodies, tend to be a bit smelly and sweaty, and even look kind of funny, but we sure do need them. So look down at your footsies and say, "Thanks!"

1. The world's tallest man, Robert Pershing Wadlow (8'11.1"/2.13 m), wore size 37 shoes.

2. In many Asian countries it is considered the height of rudeness to let the soles of your feet face another person.

3. Your foot and ankle together contain 26 bones.

4. The Achilles tendon is the longest and strongest tendon in your foot. The tendon is named after the Greek warrior who was killed when he was hit there with an arrow.

5. The skin on the soles of your feet is 0.2 inches (5 mm) thick.

6. Athlete's foot can cause intense itching and pain. It is a fungus that grows between your toes because it likes the dark, moist conditions found there.

7. It takes 20 muscles to hold each of your feet together and allow them to move (and dance and run and skip . . .).

8. Getting "cold feet" means you want to back down or walk away from something you had planned to do.

9. Your toes can get into lots of trouble. You can have hammer toes, claw toes, and overlapping toes, not to mention ingrown toenails.

10. If you have fallen arches, the arch of your foot has flattened. The entire sole of your foot is on the ground, so you don't have a natural shock-absorber system as you walk.

A person's "Achilles' heel" is the one thing that can always defeat or frustrate them. The Greek warrior Achilles was made invulnerable when dipped into a special river. But he was held by his heel when being dipped, so his heel was his weak point. An enemy hit him there with an arrow and killed him.

Stuff in Your Mouth

You need your mouth for a lot of stuff. You use it to breathe, chew, whistle, sing, talk, yell, kiss, cough, spit, and vomit. Your mouth and its parts are mighty important, so take good care of yours — you only get one.

Jaw bony structure that supports teeth, helps open and close the mouth, protects soft mouth tissue

Cheeks soft tissue, fleshy sides of mouth

Palate roof of your mouth; two sections — soft and hard

Lips outer folds of the mouth

Teeth bonelike structures in the jaw that help with chewing; hardest substance in the body

Gums tissue that surrounds and holds the teeth

Tongue organ that helps with speaking and digestion process of tasting, chewing, and swallowing

Papillae bumpy surface of the tongue

Taste buds cells on the surface of the tongue used to taste

Taste hairs tiny hairs on top of the taste buds

Tongue nerves three: two for taste, one for movement

Tonsils part of the throat; thought to protect against infections

Saliva fluid in the mouth consisting of enzymes that begin the digestive process

Uvula fleshy knob that hangs from the back of the roof of your mouth

You can make a map of your tongue. Use different foods to find four tastes. Look for the sweet taste at the tip of your tongue, the salty along the sides in the front, the sour along the sides near the rear, and the bitter toward the back of your tongue.

Seeing into Your Eye

Your eyes are among the most amazing structures ever invented — or evolved, or created, or whatever. Eyes actually need many moving, complicated parts to take in light and reveal to our brains just what it says on the chalkboard at the front of class — among other things. Here are all the parts of your eyes.

Blood vessels
carry blood to and from the eye, taking nutrients to cells

Cones
cells that are part of the retina, used to see colors and clear images

Cornea
transparent outside of your eye; covers iris and pupil

Iris
colored part of the eye that opens and closes, allowing light to enter

Lens
clear part of the eye that focuses the images

Optic nerve
nerve that takes signals from the retina to the brain

Pupil
opening in the iris through which light enters the eye

Retina
lining in the back of the eye, contains cones and rods

Rods
cells that are part of the retina; used to see in dim light

Sclera
outer covering of the eyeball, the "whites" of your eyes

Vitreous humor
clear jellylike fluid contained in the eyeball

You see the world upside down. The image your retina transfers to your brain through the optic nerve is upside down. Your retina uses more than 125 million cones and rods to accomplish this feat. Your brain interprets and flips the image around so you see the world in a normal position.

Rocks and Minerals

Although we often use the terms "rocks" and "minerals" together, they are different. Minerals (marked with * on this list) consist of one or more elements (see page 140), while rocks consist of one or more minerals. Here are some examples of rocks and minerals you may have run across.

Agate
Aquamarine
Basalt
Borax*
Corundum*
Diamond*
Emerald*
Garnet*
Gold*
Granite
Graphite*
Gypsum*
Limestone

Nickel-iron*
Obsidian
Opal
Platinum*
Pyrite*
Quartz
Ruby*
Sandstone
Shale
Silver*
Sulfur*
Turquoise
Zircon

Rocks are classified by how they were formed. IGNEOUS rocks are formed from magma or lava. Examples: granite, obsidian, pumice. SEDIMENTARY rocks are formed over long periods of time by the buildup of layers of rock fragments, dirt, sand, mud, or clay. Examples: limestone, sandstone, shale. METAMORPHIC rocks are formed from other rocks that have been subjected to heat and pressure. Examples: coal, marble, slate.

To test the hardness of minerals, geologists use Mohs scale, with a range from 1 to 10 (softest to hardest). Here are examples of all the levels on Mohs scale: Talc 1; Gypsum 2; Calcite 3; Fluorite 4; Apatite 5; Orthoclase 6; Quartz 7; Topaz 8; Corundum 9; Diamond 10.

Living with Rocks

Believe it or not, we use all kinds of rocks and minerals every day. We write with them (lead pencils), build our homes with them (gypsum walls), brush our teeth with them (fluoride toothpaste), and even wear them on our bodies (silver and gold jewelry). Some of the other uses might surprise you.

ROCK OR MINERAL/USED IN OR AS . . .

Aluminum   cans, planes, automobiles, sports equipment

Coal   energy source

Copper   wire, brass, bronze, coins, jewelry, cooking utensils

Gold   jewelry, dentistry, medicine, coins, computers, electronics

Graphite   pencils

Gypsum   Sheetrock™

Iron   steel for cars, cans, construction, appliances

Lead   batteries, radiation shielding, pencils

Limestone   cement, antacid medicine

Marble   construction, household items

Salt   food, food preservation, to melt ice, water treatment

Silica   food products, computer chips, glass, ceramics

Silver   photography, jewelry, coins, mirrors, dentistry

Slate   roofs, gardens, billiard tables

Sulfur   fertilizers, paints, detergents, explosives, matches

Talc   powder, paint, rubber, paper

Titanium   metal products, whitener in paints, toothpaste

Trona   baking soda, baking powder, toothpaste, cleaning agents

Tungsten   metal products, lightbulb filaments, dyes

Zinc   rust inhibitor for steel used in cars, buildings, bridges

We give the rocks and minerals that we wear unique names. Some gemstones you can wear are dust pearls, flash opals, green starstones, Montana jets, pigeon blood agates, volcanic glass, and zebra stones.

Talking Temperatures

How hot is it outside? How cold is the water in the pool? The answer might depend on where you live. In the United States, most people use the Fahrenheit scale to measure temperature. In Europe, Asia, and most of the rest of the world, people use the Celsius (or centigrade) scale. In the World and Weather section of this book, we gave temperature readings in both scales. Here's the scoop on these two important ways for your mom to find out just how much to insist on your wearing a sweater to school.

FAHRENHEIT

Invented by: Gabriel Daniel Fahrenheit of Germany in 1720

Freezing: 32°

Body temperature: 98.6°

Water boils: 212°

CELSIUS

Invented by: Anders Celsius of Sweden in the 1740s

Freezing: 0°

Body temperature: 37°

Water boils: 100°

TEMPERATURE CONVERSIONS

To convert X° Fahrenheit to the Celsius scale:

Subtract 32 from X; multiply by 5; then divide by 9.

To convert X° Celsius to the Fahrenheit scale:

Multiply X by 9; divide by 5; then add 32.

Celsius was actually an astronomer, not a chemist or physicist. He gained great fame in his day for his many observations about the world and the heavens. He was involved with determining the real shape of Earth and with discovering the magnetic causes of the aurora borealis, the famous "northern lights."

How Loud Is Loud?

Turn down the music, do you want to go deaf? How many times have you heard (or should we say, not heard) that demand? Now you have some research to back you up when you crank the tunes. Sounds are measured using decibels, or "db" for short. Hearing noise of 100 dbs or more over several hours can hurt your ears, so wear ear protection in those cases.

Barely Audible

Breathing	10
Rustling leaves	20
Whispering	20

Very Quiet

Quiet conversation	30
Phone conversation	50

Quiet

Restaurant conversation	60

Loud

Noisy office	70
Vacuum cleaner	70

Possible Hearing Damage

Garbage disposal	80

Hearing Damage
After Eight Hours

Busy urban street	90
Food blender	90

Extremely Loud

Jackhammer	100
Power lawn mower	100
Motorcycle	100
Car horn	110
Live rock music	120

Threshold of Pain

Jet takeoff *	130
Aircraft carrier deck	140

Physical Pain

Jet takeoff **	150
Rocket engine	180

* from 110 yards (100 m)   ** from 27.5 yards (25 m)

Though it's not spelled the same way, the term *decibel* is actually named after Alexander Graham Bell, the inventor of the telephone. The term means one-tenth ("deci") of one bel, a measurement of sound intensity.

Women in Science

For centuries women were not encouraged or allowed to take part in the study of science. Hypatia and St. Hildegard, below, are two early exceptions. This list features women who made key contributions to science. Imagine what we might have learned if women had been in the labs sooner!

SCIENTIST/LIFE SPAN	WORK
Elizabeth Blackwell/1821–1910	First woman medical doctor in the United States
Rachel Carson/1907–1964	Leader in public awareness of environmental issues
Marie Curie/1867–1934	Researched radioactive elements and compounds
Anna Freud/1895–1982	Psychoanalyst who worked with her father, Sigmund Freud
Jane Goodall/1934–	Studies chimpanzee behavior
Alice Hamilton/1869–1970	First woman professor at Harvard Medical School
Caroline Herschel/1750–1848	Astronomer and first woman to discover a comet
St. Hildegard of Bingen/1098–1179	Wrote about using plants and animals in medicine
Dorothy Crowfoot Hodgkin/1910–1994	Biochemist who worked with penicillin and insulin
Grace Hopper/1906–1992	Invented the computer language COBOL
Hypatia/370–415	Egyptian who was first woman mathematician
Katherine G. Johnson/1918–	Did pioneer work for NASA in navigation
Sister Elizabeth Kenny/1886–1952	Developed new treatments for polio
Ruth Ella Moore/1903–1994	Biochemist, did research in blood grouping
Agnes Fay Morgan/1884–1968	Researched vitamins and nutrition
Ann Haven Morgan/1928–	Zoologist who researches human and animal behavior
Florence Nightingale/1820–1910	Nurse and founder of modern nursing
Edith Hinckley Quimby/1891–1982	Discovered how to use radiation for cancer treatments
Florence Rena Sabin/1871–1953	Worked to cure tuberculosis and to improve sanitation
Roger Arliner Young/1889–1964	A biologist, first black woman scientist to publish research

Marie Curie is one of the few people — and the only woman — to win two Nobel Prizes. She won in 1903 for physics and in 1911 for chemistry. She discovered the radioactive element radium in 1898.

Famous Hoaxes

A hoax is something created to fool people. Over the years, many people have "discovered" things that thrilled and excited the scientific community — until those things were proven to be hoaxes. Here are some of the most well-known hoaxes in science history.

The Feejee Mermaid, 1842
Fake: A man showed up in New York with a "mermaid." Famous showman P. T. Barnum put the mermaid on display for thousands of visitors.
Fact: Barnum had hired the man to create the mermaid, which appeared to be the dead body of a monkey attached to the tail of a fish.

The Cardiff Giant, 1869
Fake: The fossilized body of an ancient man more than 10 feet (3 m) tall was found on a farm in Wales, in Great Britain.
Fact: The "man" was really a stone statue buried by pranksters.

The Piltdown Man, 1911
Fake: A half-million-year-old skull was found in Piltdown, England.
Fact: The skull was 50,000 years old, but the jawbone was only about a decade old. Forgers had built the "prehistoric" skull to fool the public.

The Human Clone, 1978
Fake: A well-known science writer's book revealed that a millionaire had successfully made a clone of himself.
Fact: No such cloning took place; in fact, no human has ever been cloned.

The Piltdown Chicken, 1999
Fake: A "missing link" fossil between birds and dinosaurs is found.
Fact: Two fossils had been patched together to form the "new" one.

Shinichi Fujimara's Rocks, 2000
Fake: The famous archaeologist "discovered" stone tools he said were more than 600,000 years old.
Fact: Fujimara later admitted burying the tools himself.

The Monster Cat, 2000
Fake: A photo showed a man holding Snowball, a cat the size of a sheep.
Fact: The photo had been digitally changed to look real.

People often want to believe amazing stories. When Barnum could not buy the Cardiff Giant and put it on display, he built his own. Amazingly, thousands of people came to see this fake version of a fake "man."

Who's on the Net?

The Internet has literally changed the way that billions of people live. Whether that means searching the World Wide Web for information, sending e-mail, or transferring vast sums of money instantly, the Internet is the first communications system to link the whole world tightly together. Not surprisingly, among the countries that use the Internet (and pretty much all of them do in some way), the United States has the most Internet users, as this list shows. After all, the Internet was mostly invented here.

COUNTRY	RANK	COUNTRY	RANK
United States	1	France	9
China	2	Canada	10
Japan	3	Brazil	11
Germany	4	Taiwan	12
United Kingdom	5	Spain	13
India	6	Australia	14
South Korea	7	Mexico	15
Italy	8	Netherlands	16

Everyone has a computer, right? Not quite. A survey in 2004 showed that only 61 percent of U.S. households own computers, but that number is up from 36 percent in 1997.

More Science of Me

In the first edition of the *Scholastic Book of Lists*, this page was the place where you could list all sorts of measurements about you and your body. We came up with a few more, so get out your tape measure (and a friend to help) and see what you're made of!

My birthday _____

My age in years_____   **My age in months** _____

My age in days _____

My foot is _____ **inches (**_____ **cm) long**

and _____ **inches (**_____ **cm) wide at its widest point.**

My head is _____ **inches (**_____ **cm) around.**

My right arm is _____ **inches (**_____ **cm) long.**

My left arm is _____ **inches (**_____ **cm) long.**

(Measure from the top of your shoulder to the tip of your longest finger.)

I've lost _____ **baby teeth.**

I have _____ **teeth now.**

I have _____ **freckles.** (You can estimate this one!)

I have broken _____ **bones.** (Here's hoping the answer is zero!)

The oddest thing about my body is _____.

Here's a cool one: The scientific name for freckles is *ephelides*. Your genes determine whether you have freckles or not, but exposure to sunlight can make freckles appear darker and more numerous.

CHAPTER SIX

Words

Without words, this would be nothing but a book of pictures. Of course, that might not be a bad thing, but it would make the lists harder to figure out. This chapter is all about the words we use to communicate.

World Languages

Language is what humans use to communicate. It allows people to talk to one another and share thoughts and ideas. A common language allows human beings to work together and made possible the development of civilization. Without language for communication, this sentence might read like this: "   ."

LANGUAGE	PRIMARY COUNTRIES	SPEAKERS (IN MILLIONS)
Mandarin Chinese	China	885
English	United States, U.K.*	355
Spanish	Spain, Mexico	332
Bengali	Bangladesh	189
Hindi	India	182
Portuguese	Portugal, Brazil	170
Russian	Russia	170
Japanese	Japan	125
German	Germany	98
Wu Chinese	China	77
Javanese	Indonesia, Java, Bali	75
Korean	North and South Korea	75
French	France	72
Vietnamese	Vietnam	67
Telugu	India	60
Cantonese Chinese	China	60

* United Kingdom (Great Britain)

The United States is also home to many Spanish-speaking people. More than 20 million adults in America speak Spanish, about 10 percent of the population.

Spoken in America

What is the official language of the United States? Surprise — we don't have one! You might think it's English, but there actually is no "official" language. However, twenty states have adopted English as their official state language and three states are officially bilingual. Over 336 languages are spoken in our country. This list, from the U.S. Census Bureau, shows the percentage of the population that reports these languages spoken at home:

LANGUAGE	PERCENTAGE
1. English (only)	82.00
2. Spanish	11.00
3. Chinese	0.77
4. French	0.63
5. German	0.53
6. Tagalog	0.47
7. Vietnamese	0.39
8. Italian	0.38
9. Korean	0.34
10. Russian	0.27
11. Polish	0.25
12. Arabic	0.23
13. Portuguese	0.22
14. Japanese	0.18
15. French Creole	0.17
16. African languages	0.16
17. Other Asian languages	0.15
18. Greek	0.14
19. Hindi	0.12
20. Persian	0.12

One popular language that is not included is American Sign Language, which might actually be in the top 10, according to some estimates. Check out the hand gestures used in ASL on page 165.

How to Count in Other Languages

Uno to Shi

Here's a handy chart for the numbers 1 to 10 in six major languages. Check out how similar the sounds are for some numbers (7, for instance) even though the languages are very different and come from all over the world.

NO.	SPANISH	FRENCH	GERMAN	ARABIC#	SWAHILI	CHINESE**
1	uno	un	eins	wahid	moia	yi
2	dos	deux	zwei	ithnin	mbili	er
3	tres	trois	drei	thalatha	tatu	san
4	quatro	quatre	vier	arba	nne	si
5	cinco	cinq	fünf	khamsa	tano	wu
6	seis	six	sechs	sitta	sita	liu
7	siete	sept	sieben	saba	saba	qi
8	ocho	huit	acht	thamania	nane	ba
9	nueve	neuf	neun	tisa	tisa	jiu
10	diez	dix	zehn	ashra	kumi	shi

\# These languages use non-Western characters that are pronounced with these sounds.
* Mandarin Chinese

French and Spanish are part of the "Romance" language family, meaning they came from Latin the language of ancient Rome. Latin also gave us the names of some months of the year, based on how the Romans counted months. In the Roman calendar, September, October, November, and December were months 7 through 10. Take off the "ber" and you've got the Latin numbers for 7 through 10.

Thanks, World

It is one of the most polite things you can say. Your parent or teacher probably reminds you to say it 20 times a day. You can use it in almost any situation. Next time you have to say thank you, try one of these on for size.

PHRASE	LANGUAGE	HOW TO SAY IT
Asante	Swahili	ah-SANT-ay
Danke	German	DAHNK-uh
Domo arigato	Japanese	DOH-moh ar-ee-GAHT-oh
Dziekuje	Polish	zeh-KOOJ-uh
Efcharisto	Greek	ef-har-EES-toh
Gracias	Spanish	GRA-see-ahs
Grazie	Italian	GRA-tzee
Kiitos	Finnish	KIH-tos
Köszönöm	Hungarian	KEHS-seh-nem
Mahalo	Hawaiian	mah-HAH-low
Merci	French	mare-SEE
Obrigado	Portuguese	oh-bree-GAH-doh
Salamat	Tagalog	sah-LAH-maht
Shoukran	Arabic	show-KROHN
Spasibo	Russian	spahs-EE-boh
Tack	Swedish	TOK
Tesekkur	Turkish	tehs-eh-KUR
Todah	Hebrew	TOE-dah

On the TV show and movie series *Star Trek*, how do the characters from the planet Vulcan and Klingon say thank you? (The show's producers created vocabularies for these imaginary planets, and many fans learned to speak the "languages.")

Answer: Vulcan: Nemaye; Klingon: Tlho'.

Dots and Hands

Letters, words, and speech are just a few of the many ways we communicate with other people. Here are two systems of communication that you can use. On this page is Morse code, invented by Samuel Morse in 1840 when he perfected the telegraph. This system transmitted electronic sounds — called dots and dashes, that is, a short click for a dot and a longer click for dash — over long distances across wires. On the opposite page are the hand signals used in American Sign Language to form letters. ASL is often used by hearing-impaired people. These letters are joined by hundreds of other hand signals to form a complete language.

LETTER	MORSE CODE	LETTER	MORSE CODE
A	· —	O	— — —
B	— · · ·	P	· — — ·
C	— · — ·	Q	— — · —
D	— · ·	R	· — ·
E	·	S	· · ·
F	· · — ·	T	—
G	— — ·	U	· · —
H	· · · ·	V	· · · —
I	· ·	W	· — —
J	· — — —	X	— · · —
K	— · —	Y	— · — —
L	· — · ·	Z	— — · ·
M	— —	Period	· — · — · —
N	— ·	Comma	— — · · — —

AMERICAN SIGN LANGUAGE

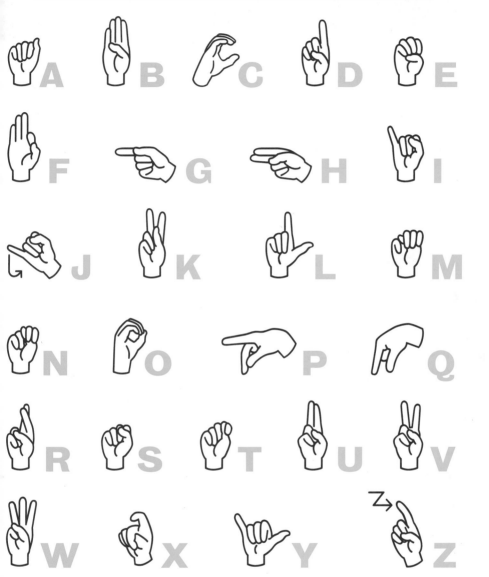

Along with these letters, hearing impaired people have a wide range of other hand signals that stand for words or phrases. Using a combination of these hand movements, people trained in sign language can "talk" as quickly as people who use their voices.

Parts of Speech

The parts of speech are the classification of words according to how they are used in a sentence. In English, there are eight parts of speech. But, of course, you know that already since you've paid so much attention in English class, right?

Adjectives descriptive words; usually modify nouns.
EXAMPLES: big, sweet, beautiful

Adverbs words that modify verbs or adjectives, often end in "ly." EXAMPLES: wildly, brightly, beautifully

Conjunctions connecting words that link sentences and phrases. EXAMPLES: and, but, because, as

Interjections either stand-alone words or words thrown into a sentence without becoming a part of the structure of the sentence. They express surprise, excitement, or some other strong emotion or feeling.
EXAMPLES: hello! yikes! ouch! oh, my!

Nouns word used to name a person, place, thing, idea, or action. EXAMPLES: book, rocket, science, call (as in "make a call")

Prepositions connecting words that show the relationship or position of one word or thing to another.
EXAMPLES: of, over, under, beside, for

Pronouns words that take the place of nouns.
EXAMPLES: he, she, it, they, himself

Verbs words that express action.
EXAMPLES: run, eat, poke, spit, scream

Can you think of some sentences that have only one word in them? Here's a hint: You always need a verb to make a sentence . . . but you don't need a noun or pronoun.

Answers: Some choices are "Go," "Eat," "Wait," and "Run!" You probably thought of others, too.

Punctuation Marks

Just as traffic signs govern the rules of the road, punctuation marks help you follow the rules of writing. For example, all drivers stop at a red light, and all readers stop at a period. Look, here comes one now. A yellow blinking light means slow down, much like a comma, like that one or this one, which serves as a breather for the reader.

' **Apostrophe** shows possession (or missing letters)

[ ] **Brackets** enclose a category or group of thoughts

: **Colon** indicates a list that follows

, **Comma** marks separation within the sentence

— **Dash** indicates a break in thought

... **Ellipsis** shows a thought continues or words are missing

! **Exclamation point** shows emphasis and strong feeling

- **Hyphen** joins words

( ) **Parentheses** provide added information or an aside

. **Period** ends a sentence

? **Question mark** asks a direct question

" " **Quotation marks** identify speech or special words

; **Semicolon** links major elements of a sentence

___ **Underline** adds emphasis to words or phrases

PsSST You can also use punctuation to create little sideways "faces" on your computer. They're called emoticons. Some examples: :) [happy] and :([sad] and ;-) [winking face] and :-o [surprised]. What others can you create?

Forms of Poetry

Usually, poetry is thought of as a written art, but poetry began before writing, in prehistoric times. People used a kind of poetic language in songs, prayers, and magic spells. The rhyming patterns helped storytellers and others to remember the words. Lyric poetry usually deals with feelings, emotions, and the senses. Narrative poems are more focused on telling stories.

LYRIC POETRY

Haiku a Japanese form with 17 syllables — five syllables in the first line, seven in the second, and five in the third

Ode a form that marks a serious event, gives high praise, or is about noble feelings

Elegy a meditation on life and death

Sonnet a 14-line love poem

Limerick a five-line form of humorous verse (see below)

NARRATIVE POETRY

Epic a lengthy poem that describes an historic and/or heroic event

Ballad a shorter story about a particular person

DRAMATIC POETRY

Dramatic poets tell stories through many characters, much like a playwright. If a play's dialogue has many rhymes, the play is considered to be dramatic poetry. English playwright William Shakespeare is the most famous dramatic poet.

There once was a book made of lists.
'Twas so heavy I 'bout broke my wrists.
But I read it all through
'Til I knew what to do,
And I had more good grades in my fists.

Forms of Prose

Prose (rhymes with *nose*) is any writing that is not poetry. Newspapers are prose. This book is filled with prose. Most of the books you read are in some form of prose. There are many types of prose, however, and here are some of the ones you might run into.

FICTION

Fable uses characters to convey a simple message
Fairy tale adventure in which heroes win over evil
Fantasy set in an imaginary world with imaginary characters
Historical fiction story based on history, with fictional main characters
Horror stories about scary things
Mystery stories, often involving crime, in which the characters search for something
Myth a story made up to explain real events or about gods and godesses of ancient cultures
Romance stories in which the characters look for love
Science fiction futuristic stories that use elements of modern science
Tall tales humorous stories that are full of exaggeration

NONFICTION

Autobiography a story of the author's life
Biography a story of a person's life written by someone else
Essay nonfiction story that discusses one topic
History an account of a past event or era
Journal a diary or record of day-to-day events
News stories reports about events of the recent past
Reference a collection of useful facts and information

This is an easy one. What form of prose is the *Scholastic Book of Lists*?

Answer: Fantasy! No, just kidding. It's reference.

A Writer's Toolbox

Writers have many ways to express their thoughts. Without knowing it, you probably use some of these popular tools in your own writing. Work with your teacher to try out one or two of these that you haven't used before.

Alliteration repetition of the same sound at the beginning of two or more words

Allusion something talked about through hints

Assonance words that have the same vowel sound

Characters the people or creatures in a story

Climax the high point of a story, usually just before the ending

Dialogue conversation between two or more characters

Hyperbole extreme exaggeration used to express an idea or opinion

Imagery words that help form pictures in readers' minds

Irony says one thing but has a second, usually opposite, meaning

Metaphor comparison of different things to show likeness

Mood the feeling of a story; can be sad, happy, gloomy, scary, etc.

Onomatopoeia invented words that imitate real sounds

Plot the actions or events that drive a story forward

Setting the time and location in which the story takes place

Simile a figure of speech that compares two unlike things

Without onomatopoeia (on-ah-maht-ah-PEA-ah), comic-book characters could not go "POW!" "ZAP!" "WHAM!" or "ZING!" See if you can make up a word to describe a real sound.

You Can Look It Up

Believe it or not, the Internet is not always the fastest way to find what you need. Reference books come in many varieties, from ones with general information to those with a very narrow focus. You may not have all of these, but your classroom, school library, or community library may have exactly what you need.

Almanacs
Tables, charts, graphs, short descriptions, facts

Atlases
Maps, locations, names of geographic land and water forms

Biographical resources
Information about specific people or collections of people

Chronologies
Historical events arranged by date and/or year order

Cookbooks
Specific information on food, recipes, and cooking

Dictionaries
Origins, pronunciations, and definitions of specific words

Directories
Information about specific people and/or organizations

Encyclopedias, general
Facts on a general range of topics

Encyclopedias, subject
Facts on specific topics

Handbooks
Information and facts usually related to one topic

Guidebooks
Dictionary of geographic places

Indexes
Alphabetical information in periodicals and newspapers

Quotations
Famous sayings from literature and history

Rhyming dictionaries
Words that rhyme with one another

Thesauruses
Words that are similar in meaning, synonyms

PSSST

The authors of this book would like to take a moment to thank you for reading their reference book. We'd like to say we invented such books, but they have been around for some time. We like to think that our reference book, though, is one of your favorites!

Homonyms

English can be a puzzling language. It's filled with many confusing words, such as homonyms. These are words that sound the same but have different meanings. A dictionary can help you sort out the meanings of each of these word pairs. Here are some homonyms that you might trip over.

allowed	aloud	meat	meet
bare	bear	pair	pear
blew	blue	peace	piece
brake	break	plain	plane
colonel	kernel	pray	prey
dear	deer	right	write
fair	fare	role	roll
feat	feet	sail	sale
flour	flower	soar	sore
hear	here	son	sun
heard	herd	stair	stare
hole	whole	tail	tale
hour	our	threw	through
know	no	waist	waste
loan	lone	wait	weight
mail	male	way	weigh
main	mane	weak	week

There are even some "triple" homonyms. Some examples of these are *to, too, two; their, there, they're; rain, rein, reign; cent, sent, scent.*

Contractions

A contraction is a word made up of two words combined into one by leaving out one or more letters. An apostrophe appears in place of the missing letters. Here is a list of common contractions and their meanings.

CONTRACTION	MEANING	CONTRACTION	MEANING
aren't	are not	she'll	she will
can't	cannot	she's	she is, she has
couldn't	could not	shouldn't	should not
could've	could have	should've	should have
didn't	did not	there'll	there will
doesn't	does not	there's	there is
don't	do not	they'll	they will
hadn't	had not	they're	they are
hasn't	has not	they've	they have
haven't	have not	'twas	it was
he'd	he would	wasn't	was not
he'll	he will	we'd	we would
he's	he is, he has	we'll	we will
I'd	I would	we're	we are
I'll	I will	weren't	were not
I'm	I am	we've	we have
isn't	is not	what's	what is
it'll	it will	won't	will not
it's	it is	wouldn't	would not
I've	I have	would've	would have
let's	let us	you'll	you will
mightn't	might not	you're	you are
might've	might have	you've	you have
mustn't	must not		

The contraction "ain't" means "have not" or "has not" or "is not" or "am not." And no matter what you hear on TV, "ain't" isn't proper to use in speech or writing.

Abbreviations

Abbreviations make words shorter by leaving out letters. The letters that are left mean the same thing that the longer original word did. Periods are sometimes used to show an abbreviation.

A.I.	artificial intelligence
aka	also known as
A.M.	morning (Latin: *ante meridien*)
ASAP	as soon as possible
asst.	assistant
ave.	avenue
blvd.	boulevard
co.	company
CPR	cardiopulmonary resuscitation
dept.	department
Dr.	doctor
DVD	digital video disc
e.g.	for example (Latin: *exempli gratia*)
ESP	extrasensory perception
ETA	estimated time of arrival
et al.	and others (Latin: *et alia*)
etc.	and so forth (Latin: *et cetera*)

FYI	for your information
i.e.	that is (Latin: *id est*)
IQ	Intelligence Quotient
Jr.	Junior
lb.	pound (from the Latin *libra*, for scale)
M.D.	medical doctor
Messrs.	plural of Mr.
m.p.h.	miles per hour
oz.	ounce (from the Italian word *onza*)
PC	politically correct
P.M.	afternoon (Latin: *post meridien*)
PS	postscript, at end of a letter
Sr.	Senior
TBA	to be announced
TBD	to be determined
TLC	tender loving care
UFO	unidentified flying object
VCR	video cassette recorder

PSSST

RSVP is an abbreviation you've probably seen. It stands for the French phrase *répondez s'il vous plaît*, which means "please reply" in English.

Palindromes—semordnilaP

A palindrome is a word or phrase that reads the same forward and backward. The result is often kind of funny. See if you can make up palindromes of your own.

WORDS

mom
dad
noon
tot
bob
pop
race car
toot
sees
level
radar

PHRASES

Madam, I'm Adam.

Step on no pets.

Bald elf fled lab.

No panic, I nap on!

Ed is loopy poolside.

Ma's story rots, Sam.

No lemons, no melon.

Rats live on no evil star.

No way a papaya won!

Elk rap song? No sparkle.

Lee has a race car as a heel.

Some men interpret nine memos.

Go hang a salami, I'm a lasagna hog.

A man, a plan, a cat, a bar, a cap, a mall, a ball, a map, a car, a bat, a canal: Panama.

If you love palindromes (or if your name is Otto or Eve), check out *Too Hot to Hoot: Funny Palindrome Riddles* by Marvin Terban. It's all about these fun words and phrases.

Misspeled Wurds

Or should we say "Misspelled Words"? Spelling, no matter what anyone tells you, is important. If you don't spell words correctly, you risk having people misunderstand what you're writing. Spelling in English often can be done by sounding out words. However, here are just a few of the words that aren't spelled the way they sound and often trip up even good spellers.

answer	half
broccoli	league
business	license
chief	minute
committee	misspell
cough	necessary
debt	neighbor
desperate	often
disappear	once
doctor	scissors
dumb	separate
eighth	their
enough	through
exaggerate	truly
exercise	vacuum
February	Wednesday
gauge	where
guess	whole

PSSST

Each year, America's best speller is crowned at the National Spelling Bee. Pratyush Buddiga from Colorado won the 2002 title by correctly spelling the final word — *prospicience*. It means the act of looking forward.

Tongue Twisters

A tongue twister is a phrase that is difficult to pronounce. The words are difficult to speak rapidly because of a succession of similar sounds (which is actually sort of a tongue twister itself). See how fast you can say these. For extra credit, say them fast over and over.

Sam shaved seven shy sheep.

Nat's knapsack strap snapped.

A proper copper coffeepot.

Fred's friend Fran flips fine flapjacks fast.

She sells seashells by the seashore.

If Peter Piper picked a peck of
    pickled peppers,
How many pickled peppers would
    Peter Piper pick?

A skunk sat on a stump.
The stump thunk the skunk stunk.
The skunk thunk the stump stunk.

A tutor who tooted a flute
Tried to tutor two tooters to toot.
Said the two to their tutor,
"Is it harder to toot or
To tutor two tooters to toot?"

Actors sometimes use tongue twisters to loosen up their mouths and vocal cords before a performance. One of their exercises is to say "toy boat" several times very quickly. See how many times you can say it.

Worn-out Words

Words that are superpopular today might seem like another language to kids 100 years from now (heck, they might be gone next summer). Words go out of fashion, they stop being used, or they're replaced by other words. Here are some words and phrases that your parents or grandparents probably thought would be around forever. They were wrong!

WORD	MEANING
bloomers	ladies' underwear
bee's knees	phrase for "cool"
besot	give
countenance	face
dapper	describes a fancy dresser
ewer	a water pitcher
forbearance	patience
gentleman caller	a boyfriend
knickers	kids' short pants
settee	small sofa
shan't	"will not"
spectacles	eyeglasses
steamer	cruise ship
thither	over there
thou	you
ye	the
Zounds!	expression of surprise

So now you know what this means:
"Thou shan't besot an ewer in your bloomers to a gentleman caller who is the bee's knees."

Prefixes and Suffixes

A prefix is a letter or group of letters at the beginning of a word that contributes to the word's meaning. Suffixes come at the end of words and affect the meaning of the whole word by combining with the "root" word.

PREFIX	MEANING
anti-	against
astro-	star
atmo-	vapor, gas
bi-	two
co-, com-, con-	with, together with
contra-	contrary to
de-	down, away from
dis-	not, off, away
ex-	out, from, former
extra-	outside
for-	away, off, from
fore-	before, previous
non-	not
omni-	all
ped-	foot
pedi-	child
post-	after
pre-	before
sub-	under, beneath
un-	not

SUFFIX	MEANING
-able, -ible	capable of
-ant, -ent	like, similar
-ation	action, state, result
-dom	condition of
-en	made of, like
-ess	feminine
-ful	full of
-fuge	away from
-gamy	marriage
-gon	angle
-hood	state of
-ish	like, pertaining to
-ism	practice of
-less	without
-ly	in the nature of
-ment	act of
-meter	instrument
-ness	state of
-ory, -ary	relating
-ous, -ose	full of
-ward	in the direction of

Latin is the source of many of the dozens of prefixes and suffixes in English. Words from that language can be called "Latinate," which has a suffix itself — "-ate," which means having or showing.

My Word Games

Enough learning . . . let's have some fun! Below are three word games you can do in the spaces provided. Check out page 319 to see the answers we came up with. Have fun!

WORDS WITHIN WORDS

See how many words of four letters or more you can find by using only the letters from "BOOK OF LISTS."

_____   _____   _____

_____   _____   _____

_____   _____   _____

_____   _____   _____

COUNTING TO DIEZ

Use the list on page 162 to "translate" this equation and find out the answer.

tres + neun − ithnin + saba − tisa + wu − huit + fünf = _____

:), LOL, OR JK!

The little symbols known as "emoticons" or "smileys," plus the many abbreviations used in e-mail, have created a whole new language. Can you match up the items on the left with their "translations" on the right?

:)	laugh out loud
TMI	rolling on the floor laughing
LOL	ta-ta for now
;)	smile, happy
JK	surprised
: 0	just kidding
: (	kisses
ROTFL	wink
TTFN	sad
:x	too much information!

CHAPTER SEVEN

The Arts

There is more to "art" than just drawing on your walls and making papier-mâché statues. Painting, sculpture, music, dance, and even architecture are all part of "the arts."

Art Periods

Like any work of art, the history of art itself is subject to people's opinions. Dating exactly when periods ended or began is open to debate. But here's a rough time line showing the different periods of art history from the prehistoric to the present.

Prehistoric
from dramatic cave art 25,000 to 35,000 years ago to the days around 2000 B.C.

Ancient
including Egyptian, Greek, and Roman art dating to a few hundred years A.D.

Medieval
early Christian, Roman, Gothic, and Byzantine art to the mid-15th century

Renaissance
the cultural revolution in Italy from 1480 to 1527

Northern Renaissance
in European countries north of Italy in the late 15th and 16th centuries

Mannerism
in post-Renaissance Italy in the 16th century

Baroque
the late 16th and 17th centuries in Europe

Rococo
the dominant style of the 18th century in Europe

Neoclassicism and Romanticism
these styles flourished in the late 18th and early 19th centuries in Europe

Impressionism
early to late 19th century; started in Europe

Postimpressionism
late 19th century to the early 20th century; started in Europe

Modern Art
since the early 20th century worldwide

For more information on some of these styles, please see page 184.

The Italian Renaissance spawned much of the classic art — such as works by Leonardo da Vinci, Raphael, and Michelangelo — that is familiar even to people who know little about the rest of the art world.

Artists to Know

Throughout the centuries and around the world, there have been thousands of people who made important contributions to art. We've come up with a list of some of the most important and influential. Impress your friends with knowledge of these Impressionists . . . and others.

Salvador Dalí (Spain, 1904-1989)
Creative modern artist who popularized the surrealist movement

Leonardo da Vinci (Italy, 1452-1519)
Multitalented painter, inventor, sculptor

Henri Matisse (France, 1869-1954)
With paint and papier-mâché, became one of the greatest modern artists

Michelangelo (Italy, 1475-1564)
Sculptor of marble statues; painted frescoes and ceilings in Rome

Claude Monet (France, 1840-1926)
Painter who helped create the Impressionist movement

Pablo Picasso (Spain, 1881-1973)
Painter of Cubist works who created some of the world's most valuable art

Jackson Pollock (United States, 1912-1956)
Created splattery, multicolored Abstract Expressionist style

Rembrandt van Rijn (Netherlands, 1606-1669)
Influential Renaissance painter, specialized in portraits

Vincent van Gogh (Netherlands, 1853-1890)
Unknown during his lifetime, his Expressionist work was later world famous

Andy Warhol (United States, 1928-1987)
Combined painting and photography to create pop art

One hundred years after Vincent van Gogh's death, his *Portrait of Dr. Gachet* was auctioned for a record $82.5 million.

Name That Art!

What kinds of art are there? You've got sculpture, painting, drawing, and more. Art experts, however, use many other terms to describe types of art. These terms are used when talking about styles and movements of art from the past two millennia.

Abstract
little or no reference to realistic appearance or natural objects

Baroque
ornate and elaborate art of the late 16th century and all of the 17th century

Byzantine
religious art that emerged from the early Christian world

Cubism
rearranges natural forms through different shapes and colors

Dadaism
unconventional art movement that avoided traditional art forms

Fauvism
conflicting and intense colors and images

Impressionism
captures the impression of a subject and shows how it is affected by sunlight

Neoclassicism
modeled on traditional Greek and Roman art

Pop
utilizes images from popular culture

Postimpressionism
an extension of Impressionism that bridged the gap to modern art

Realism
portrays ordinary people in everyday situations

Romanticism
emotional and graphic art created to be the opposite of Neoclassicism

Surrealism
portrays alternate realities, including dreams and fantasy

Dadaism comes from the French word "dada," which means hobbyhorse. It was chosen randomly out of a dictionary in 1916 at a meeting of artists in Switzerland.

Most Expensive Art

Going once . . . going twice . . . sold! Paintings are some of the most valuable pieces of art in the world. Collectors and museums pay big bucks for the right to own these paintings and hang them in their homes or galleries. These paintings are the most expensive works of art ever sold on the auction block.

PAINTING (ARTIST, YEAR SOLD)	PRICE
Garcon a la Pipe Pablo Picasso, 2004	$104,000,000
Portrait of Dr. Gachet Vincent van Gogh, 1990	$82,500,000
Au Moulin de la Galette Pierre-Auguste Renoir, 2002	$76,700,000
Au Moulin de la Galette Pierre-Auguste Renoir, 1990	$71,000,000
Portrait de l'artiste sans barbe Vincent van Gogh, 1998	$65,000,000
Rideau, Cruchon et Compotier Paul Cezanne, 1999	$55,000,000
Les Noces de Pierrette Pablo Picasso, 1989	$51,671,920
Irises Vincent van Gogh, 1987	$49,000,000
Le Reve Pablo Picasso, 1997	$44,000,000
Self-portrait: Yo Picasso Pablo Picasso, 1989	$43,500,000

More than 200 of legendary Spanish artist Pablo Picasso's paintings have sold for $1 million or more.

Odd Art

In art, beauty is in the eye of the beholder. After all, where else is one man's shovel another man's work of art? Here are several well-known works of art that can be described as "off the wall."

Campbell's Soup I (Tomato)
By Andy Warhol
Warhol became famous in the 1960s for his paintings of products such as Coca-Cola™ bottles and Brillo™ pads, and of celebrities such as Marilyn Monroe and Jackie Onassis. Perhaps his most recognizable work is this painting of a solitary can of Campbell's tomato soup.

In Advance of the Broken Arm
By Marcel Duchamp
Duchamp is the best example of Dadaism (see page 184). This piece was simply a snow shovel presented as art. Critics coined it "ready-made" art.

Surrounded Islands
By Christo and Jeanne-Claude
Christo and Jeanne-Claude wrapped 11 islands in Biscayne Bay, Florida, with bright pink fabric. In their artwork, the couple wrap huge objects in various types of sheeting. Among their other works: wrapping the German Reichstag (government building) and the Pont Neuf (a bridge) in Paris, and installing "The Gates" in New York City's Central Park.

Whaam!
By Roy Lichtenstein
Like Andy Warhol, Lichtenstein was a leader in the pop-art movement of the 1960s. His paintings drew heavily from commercial products and advertising. He is best known for his paintings, such as Whaam! that were done in comic-book style.

Marcel Duchamp earned additional notoriety in 1920 with *La Joconde aux Mustaches* — a reproduction of the *Mona Lisa* with a beard and mustache painted on her face!

Color Your World

Color is one of the artist's main tools for creating different looks or effects. The possibilities multiply as the artist mixes primary colors, then secondary and tertiary colors.

Primary colors are the basic colors and can't be made by mixing any other colors.

- Blue ● Red ● Yellow

Secondary colors are made by mixing primary colors.

- Green (mix blue/yellow)
- Orange (mix red/yellow)
- Violet (mix blue/red)

Tertiary colors, also known as intermediate colors, are made by mixing a primary color with a secondary color.

- Blue-green
- Yellow-green
- Yellow-orange

Colors of the rainbow

- Red ● Orange ● Yellow
- Green ● Blue
- Indigo ● Violet

PsSST

To remember a rainbow's colors in order, think of the name Roy G. Biv. Those letters match up with the first letters of the colors.

Musical Terms

Like painting, archaeology, and teenagers, music has a language all its own. Specialized terms are used to describe different parts of how music sounds, how music is made (or "composed"), or how people sound when they're singing. Many of these terms come from Latin or Italian. If you don't know an alto from a soprano or a baritone from a tenor, here's your chance to learn a few basic musical terms.

A cappella music performed without instrumental accompaniment

Alto low, female singing voice

Aria solo song accompanied by an orchestra, as in an opera

Baritone male singing voice higher than a bass but lower than a tenor

Bass low, male singing voice

Beat basic unit of time in music

Bridge the musical transition between two parts of a composition

Chord three or more notes sounded simultaneously

Crescendo music that gradually grows louder and/or more intense

Encore an additional performance requested by extended applause from the audience

Falsetto male singing voice unnaturally produced above the normal range

Harmony the simultaneous combination of notes in a chord

Libretto the text of an opera

Measure rhythm grouping that contains a fixed number of beats

Melody closely related sequence of single tones that are heard as a unit

Meter organization of music into measures or bars

Overture introductory music for an opera or other long musical work

Refrain verse that is repeated throughout a song

Rhythm the regulated movement of music in time

Scale an ascending or descending series of tones

Soprano the highest natural human singing voice, usually found in women or young boys

Tenor high, male singing voice

Want to know more about these terms? Check out www.essentialsofmusic.com. In many cases, you can hear examples of each of the terms. Hearing might be believing!

Instrumentally Speaking

Instruments can be used to play different styles of music. Violins, for example, are used for classical, country, rock, and jazz. Here are some of the traditional instruments in popular music categories.

COUNTRY
Banjo
Mandolin
Guitar
Fiddle
Organ
Harmonica
Piano

JAZZ
Trumpet
Trombone
Saxophone

Clarinet
Guitar
Bass
Tuba
Drums
Oboe

ROCK 'N' ROLL
Electric guitar
Bass guitar
Drums
Piano or keyboard

Hip-hop and rap musicians depend more on their voices and a turntable than on instruments. What was the first rap/hip-hop song to achieve national hit status?

Answer: *Rapper's Delight*, by the Sugarhill Gang, was released in 1979. Though many people are responsible for creating hip-hop and rap, this was the first hit song.

World Music

In the past few years, music from many parts of the world has become popular in the United States and Canada. There are just about as many types of music as there are countries, but here are the names and home countries of some music you might have heard on the radio or on TV.

MUSIC	HOMELAND	MUSIC	HOMELAND
Bhajan	India	Mariachi	Mexico
Bomba	Puerto Rico	Merengue	Dominican Republic
Cajun	Louisiana		
Calypso	Trinidad	Reggae	Jamaica
Celtic	Ireland, Scotland	Rumba	Cuba
		Samba	Brazil
Flamenco	Spain	Slack key guitar	Hawaii
Gamelan	Indonesia	Salsa	New York City*
Isicathamiya	S. Africa	Tango	Argentina
Juju	Nigeria	Zouk	Martinique
Kodo	Japan	Zydeco	Louisiana

* Developed in the 1950s by people from Puerto Rico who were living in New York.

The Cajun people of Louisiana were originally French Canadians from the region called Acadia. They were kicked out in the 1800s and ended up way down south in "Loos-ee-ana." A mispronunciation of their original home changed Acadia to "Cajun."

Inside the Orchestra

An orchestra is composed of instruments in four families: string, woodwind, brass, and percussion. Here are the members of each family, most of which are found in large orchestras.

STRINGS

Violin
Viola
Cello
Double bass
Harp

WOODWINDS

Flute
Oboe
Clarinet
Bassoon
Piccolo
English horn
E-flat clarinet
Bass clarinet
Contrabassoon

BRASS

French horn
Trumpet
Trombone
Tuba

PERCUSSION

Snare drum
Timpani
Cymbals
Bass drum
Tam-tam
Glockenspiel
Celesta
Maracas
Chimes
Triangle
Castanets
Piano
Xylophone

PsSST Maracas are made from a hollowed gourd, a relative of the squash. The gourd's hard rind is filled with dried seeds or beads that make a rattling sound when the maraca is shaken.

Famous Orchestras

Orchestras are large groups of musicians assembled to play music, usually classical music. For most of the musicians, this is a full-time job. Orchestras are led by conductors and music directors; often these people are among the most well-known in the classical music world. Here are a dozen of the world's most famous orchestras.

Academy of St. Martin in the Fields (London)
Berlin Philharmonic
Boston Symphony Orchestra
City of Birmingham (England) Symphony Orchestra
London Philharmonic Orchestra
Los Angeles Philharmonic
Moscow Chamber Orchestra
National Symphony Orchestra (Washington, D.C.)
New York Philharmonic
New Zealand Symphony Orchestra
Royal Philharmonic Orchestra (London)
Vienna Philharmonic

Vienna, Austria, was home to legendary composers Wolfgang Mozart and Ludwig van Beethoven in the late 1700s and early 1800s, but each failed to create a successful orchestra for the city. It wasn't until 1842 — 51 years after the death of Mozart and 15 years after the death of Beethoven — that the Vienna Philharmonic was founded.

Delightful Dancers

Dance is perhaps the most beautiful of the performing arts. Classical ballet and modern dance, which these dance companies specialize in, demand incredible balance, grace, strength, and timing. It can be as athletic as a basketball game, but all set to music. There are thousands of companies dancing on stages and in theaters around the world. Here are some of the most well-known and accomplished.

Alvin Ailey American Dance Theater
American Ballet Theater
Bolshoi Ballet
Joffrey Ballet of Chicago
José Limón Dance Company
Martha Graham Dance Company
Moscow Ballet
New York City Ballet
Paris Opera Ballet
Paul Taylor Dance Company
Royal Ballet (London)

A dancer in the Moscow Ballet goes through about two pairs of shoes per performance. At about 200 performances a year, that adds up to . . . a lot of shoes!

Dance Styles

Gotta dance? Choose your style and hit the floor. Here are some of the most popular and well-known styles of dancing.

African	**Hip-hop**
Asian	**Jazz**
Ballet	**Latin**
Ballroom	**Modern**
Belly	**Square**
Break	**Swing**
Country	**Tap**
Disco	**Waltz**
Folk	

PsSST

Hip-hop and jazz dancing are obviously very athletic. But ballet can be a real workout, too. A male ballet dancer might have to lift as much as one and a half tons (1,359 kg) of ballerinas in a single performance (though not all at once, of course).

Awesome Kids' Museums

No, the museums on this list are not filled with mummies of kids or art by kids or airplanes flown by kids (though that would be cool, wouldn't it?). Instead, these are museums *for* kids, in cities all across America. There are more than 200 such museums, some focused on science, others on history or art, but all of them are chock-full of fun for you and your whole family. This is a list of what some experts consider the biggest, best, and coolest. Next time you take a trip, take along this list and stop by for some fun.

Brooklyn Children's Museum

Brooklyn, New York: Play drums, examine ancient objects, and dig in a greenhouse in America's oldest kids' museum, first opened in 1899.

Center for Puppetry Arts

Atlanta, Georgia: Try out more than 350 hand-, string-, and other types of puppets from throughout history.

Chicago Children's Museum

Chicago, Illinois: Dinosaurs, boats, planes, construction gear, and more.

Children's Discovery Center

San Jose, California: Science is a big focus here, but you and your friends can also put on a play.

Children's Museum

Boston, Massachusetts: Go rock climbing, dig for treasure, or dress up like a sailor.

Children's Museum of Houston

Houston, Texas: Make a TV show and check out rotating multicultural exhibits.

Children's Museum of Indianapolis
Indianapolis, Indiana: Build a skeleton and see a life-size *T. rex* skeleton.

City Museum
St. Louis, Missouri: A five-story playground features a full-size airplane.

Discovery Center
Rockford, Illinois: Explore a giant maze or pretend to be an astronaut.

Exploratorium
San Francisco, California: Tons of hands-on science experiments for you to try.

Liberty Science Center
Jersey City, New Jersey: Always-changing exhibits have included heart surgery and moviemaking.

Please Touch Museum
Philadelphia, Pennsylvania: You've just got to love that name — it says it all!

Port Discovery
Baltimore, Maryland: "Fly" in a hot-air balloon or climb a three-story tree house.

In 2003, *Child Magazine* named the Children's Museum of Indianapolis the best kids' museum in the country. It's the biggest, for sure, and also includes a working steam engine, a huge carousel, and more than 10,000 artifacts on display.

Famous Opera Singers

You don't have to be an opera fan (opera fans are called "aficionados") to recognize the names Luciano Pavarotti, Plácido Domingo, and José Carreras — the Three Tenors. Here are some other famous opera singers, past and present.

SINGER	HOME COUNTRY
Cecilia Bartoli	Italy
Maria Callas	United States
José Carreras	Spain
Enrico Caruso	Italy
Plácido Domingo	Spain
Kirsten Flagstad	Canada
Ben Heppner	United States
Marilyn Horne	Germany
John McCormack	Ireland
Nellie Melba	Australia
Lauritz Melchior	Denmark
Birgit Nilsson	Sweden
Jessye Norman	United States
Luciano Pavarotti	Italy
Leontyne Price	United States
Beverly Sills	United States
Ebe Stignani	Italy
Renata Tebaldi	Italy
Jon Vickers	Canada
Frederica von Stade	United States

PsSST Have you ever eaten melba toast or peach melba? These tasty foods were named for opera singer Nellie Melba, who was very popular in the late 1800s and early 1900s.

Many Voices as One

Some of the most beautiful musical sounds come from choirs or choruses, small or large groups of people singing together as one voice. Here are some of the world's most famous choirs.

CHOIR	HOME CITY
Boys Choir of Harlem	New York City
King's College Choir	Cambridge, England
London Chapel Royal Choir	London, England
Mormon Tabernacle Choir	Salt Lake City, Utah
National Cathedral Choir	Washington, D.C.
St. Thomas Church Choir	Leipzig, Germany
Sistine Chapel Choir	Vatican City
Vienna Boys Choir	Vienna, Austria

Members of the Vienna Boys Choir wear sailor suits. The tradition started in the 1920s when the choir needed uniforms for singing away from churches. Most boys of the era already owned a sailor suit, which was a popular fashion choice at the time, so that became their standard performance costume, too.

Architectural Styles

Just as music, art, and literature have special words to describe things, architecture also has its own vocabulary. Throughout history, buildings have changed as new materials were created, new ideas were thought up, and new ways of building were invented. Here are just a few of the many architectural styles from which a builder can choose.

Art nouveau

Art deco

California ranch

Cape Cod

Colonial

Federal

Georgian

Gothic

Greek revival

Mission

Modern

Romanesque

Tudor

Victorian

Check out www.archkidtecture.org for more information on types of buildings, architectural and building terms, and pictures of some of these styles of architectural design.

Brag About Bricks

The world of architecture is also full of colorful words that describe parts of buildings. For instance, a widow's walk is a rooftop observation deck originally designed to watch for boats returning to port after long voyages. Here are some other terms that you can use to show off your knowledge of the building world.

Baluster
pillar or post that supports a handrail

Campanile
a bell tower often near, but not attached to, a church

Facade
the face of a building

Gable
triangular wall section at the end of a pitched roof

Gargoyle
a rooftop figure carved as a grotesque human or animal

Jamb
vertical posts of a door or window frame

Joist
wall-to-wall beam used to support a floor or ceiling

Lintel
horizontal beam that bridges an opening such as a door frame

Mullion
the vertical post or strip that divides window panes

Niche
recess in a wall, often used for a statue or other ornament

Pergola
trellised walkway in a garden covered by climbing plants

Soffit
the underside of an architectural element

Stanchion
a vertical supporting pole or post

Stud
upright post in a wall for supporting drywall

Transom
small, hinged window above a door

In Pisa, Italy, there is a building that is perhaps the world's most famous example of a campanile. The building, however, has something odd about it. What is it called?

Answer: The Leaning Tower of Pisa is a tall marble campanile, which, because of soft ground beneath, is leaning over at an angle.

My Own Art

This should be a fun one . . . you'll need something to draw or color with. Markers, crayons, pencils — whatever medium works for you (*medium* is a fancy art word for the stuff you use to make the art). Then create a brand-new (and sure to be valuable someday) work of art! It can be in any style you choose (see page 184) or you can invent your own! Make sure to sign your work, like all the famous artists do.

CHAPTER EIGHT

Pop Culture

"Pop" means popular and "culture" means all that stuff you spend your hard-earned allowance on, like movies, books, comics, video games, roller coasters, and other fun stuff.

Makin' Comic Books

Comic books are created overnight by elves. No, that's not right. Comic books are drawn by magic wizards using wands? Nope. Actually, a whole team of creative people uses a variety of skills to put together comic books. This list shows what those team members do.

Step 1 The Script

A writer creates the story of the comic book, including setting, plot, and some dialogue (what the characters say).

Step 2 The Pencils

From the script, an artist known as a penciller draws all the panels of the comic book using only a pencil, telling the story visually.

Step 3 The Dialogue

When the pencils are finished, the writer then creates all the final dialogue, reflecting any changes in the story created by the artist.

Step 4 The Inks

Using special black ink, an artist called an inker draws over the penciller's work, adding depth, shadows, and dimension.

Step 5 The Colors

After the inked pages have been scanned into a computer, an artist called a colorist creates all the colors of the page, other than black.

Step 6 The Letters

Often using a computer but sometimes working by hand, the letterer puts in all the dialogue created by the writer. This is also the step in which many of those cool "Pow!"s "Zap!"s and "Kerblam!"s are put in.

Step 7 The Printing

The combined computer files are sent to enormous printers that print and bind the comic books. They are then ready for delivery.

All these steps can take as much as two months to complete for a regular-sized comic book. The longest time is spent by the penciller, who can take about 25 days, or about a page a day, to complete his or her work.

Becoming Super

One of the best things about comic-book superheroes is discovering how they started. Were they strange visitors from another planet? Did they get bathed in cosmic rays? Were they bitten by radioactive spiders? Or were they just born super? Here's a list of some comic-book favorites along with how they got their super-powers.

Batman
Actually has no powers, but has trained his mind and body to fight crime

Daredevil
After he became blind, his other four senses hyperdeveloped.

Fantastic Four
All four space travelers were changed after being hit by cosmic rays.

Flash
Soaked by accident in electrified chemicals

Green Lantern
Chosen by aliens to wear mighty power ring

Hulk
Hit by rays from top-secret gamma bomb

Iron Man
Scientist developed amazing metal suit

Spider-Man
Bitten by a radioactive spider

Superman
Born on Krypton under a red sun, he has super-powers under Earth's yellow sun.

Thor
Thunder God of Norse mythology born with control of elements

Wolverine
One of the X-Men, born as a mutant; later had metal skeleton grafted to bones

Wonder Woman
An Amazon princess, daughter of a goddess

According to the *Guinness Book of World Records*, the most expensive comic-book ever sold was a mint-condition copy of *Marvel Comics #1* from 1939, which sold for $350,000 in 2001.

Famous Fictional
Places

You can visit the following places, but only in your mind. These locales sprung from the pages of classic books. (Can you name the books or series in which each place originated? Answers are upside down in the right-hand column.)

Camelot
King Arthur legends

Hundred-Acre Wood
Winnie-the-Pooh

Middle Earth
The Lord of the Rings

Narnia
Chronicles of Narnia

Neverland
Peter Pan

Oz
Wizard of Oz

Gotham City
Batman Comics

Utopia
Utopia

Hogwarts
Harry Potter

Wonderland
Alice's Adventures in Wonderland

The word "utopia," from Sir Thomas More's book about an imaginary island, now means any perfect condition or situation.

Famous Fictional
Characters

Some characters seem real, even if they never existed. Here are some characters who were born from the pens of innovative authors and live on in our imaginations. We're sure you can add your own favorites to the list.

Big Bird

Captain Ahab

Charlotte the Spider

Dracula

Dr. Frankenstein

Dr. Jekyll & Mr. Hyde

Ebenezer Scrooge

Encyclopedia Brown

E.T.

The Grinch

Hamlet

Hardy Boys

Harriet the Spy

Harry Potter

Huckleberry Finn

James Bond

Nancy Drew

Odysseus

Robinson Crusoe

Scarlett O'Hara

Sherlock Holmes

Tarzan

Tom Sawyer

Willy Wonka

Winnie-the-Pooh

PsSST "Frankenstein" is the name of the doctor who created the monster in Mary Shelley's classic novel, not the name of the monster itself.

Caldecott Books

Each year since 1938, the Caldecott Medal has been awarded by the Association for Library Service to Children to the most distinguished American picture books for children. Here are recent winners.

2006 *The Hello, Goodbye Window*
Illustrated by Chris Raschka, text by Norton Juster

2005 *Kitten's First Full Moon* by Kevin Henkes

2004 *The Man Who Walked Between the Towers* by Mordicai Gerstein

2003 *My Friend Rabbit* by Eric Rohmann

2002 *The Three Pigs* by David Wiesner

2001 *So You Want to Be President?*
Illustrated by David Small, text by Judith St. George

2000 *Joseph Had a Little Overcoat* by Simms Taback

1999 *Snowflake Bentley*
Illustrated by Mary Azarian, text by Jacqueline Briggs Martin

1998 *Rapunzel* by Paul O. Zelinsky

1997 *Golem* by David Wisniewski

1996 *Officer Buckle and Gloria* by Peggy Rathmann

1995 *Smoky Night* Illustrated by David Diaz, text by Eve Bunting

1994 *Grandfather's Journey* by Allen Say, text edited by Walter Lorraine

1993 *Mirette on the High Wire* by Emily Arnold McCully

1992 *Tuesday* by David Wiesner

1991 *Black and White* by David Macaulay

1990 *Lon Po Po: A Red-Riding Hood Story from China* by Ed Young

1989 *Song and Dance Man*
Illustrated by Stephen Gammell, text by Karen Ackerman

1988 *Owl Moon* Illustrated by John Schoenherr, text by Jane Yolen

Randolph Caldecott, for whom the medal was named, was a nineteenth-century English illustrator.

Newbery Books

The Newbery Medal annually honors the most distinguished contributions to American literature for children. Here are recent winners.

2006 *Criss Cross* by Lynne Rae Perkins

2005 *Kira-Kira* by Cynthia Kadohata

2004 *The Tale of Despereaux . . .* by Kate DiCamillo

2003 *Crispin: The Cross of Lead* by Avi

2002 *A Single Shard* by Linda Sue Park

2001 *A Year Down Yonder* by Richard Peck

2000 *Bud, Not Buddy* by Christopher Paul Curtis

1999 *Holes* by Louis Sachar

1998 *Out of the Dust* by Karen Hesse

1997 *The View from Saturday* by E. L. Konigsburg

1996 *The Midwife's Apprentice* by Karen Cushman

1995 *Walk Two Moons* by Sharon Creech

1994 *The Giver* by Lois Lowry

1993 *Missing May* by Cynthia Rylant

1992 *Shiloh* by Phyllis Reynolds Naylor

1991 *Maniac Magee* by Jerry Spinelli

1990 *Number the Stars* by Lois Lowry

1989 *Joyful Noise: Poems for Two Voices* by Paul Fleischman

1988 *Lincoln: A Photobiography* by Russell Freedman

1987 *The Whipping Boy* by Sid Fleischman

John Newbery was an eighteenth-century British bookseller. The Newbery Medal was first awarded in 1922.

American Idol

When it debuted in 2002, *American Idol* quickly captured enormous attention. Millions tuned in to watch — the singers *and* the judges! — as singer after singer was voted off, until there was one champion. Did your favorites win? The final four are listed here for each season — the champion and the final three runners-up, as chosen by viewers.

SEASON 1
CHAMPION: Kelly Clarkson
RUNNER-UP: Justin Guarini
3RD: Nikki McKibbin; 4TH: Tamyra Gray

SEASON 2
CHAMPION: Ruben Studdard
RUNNER-UP: Clay Aiken
3RD: Kimberley Locke; 4TH: Joshua Gracin

SEASON 3
CHAMPION: Fantasia Barrino
RUNNER-UP: Diana DeGarmo
3RD: Jasmine Trias; 4TH: LaToya London

SEASON 4
CHAMPION: Carrie Underwood
RUNNER-UP: Bo Bice
3RD: Vonzell Solomon; 4TH: Anthony Fedorov

According to the company that did the counting, how many votes did Underwood and Bice receive combined in 2005's competition?

Answer: Would you believe 500 million? It's true!

Kids' Web Sites

Whether you go online at school, at home, at the library, or all of those places, you're not alone! Millions and millions of kids in the United States and around the world visit the World Wide Web every day to look for information, send e-mail, check out their favorite stars, do some shopping, or even look for homework help. All of these Web addresses begin with http://www.

disney.com
home of the Walt Disney entertainment empire

discoverykids.com
features content from the Discovery Channel

foxkids.com
includes the characters from FOX TV shows

dccomics.com
the online home of Superman, Batman, and more

kids.warnerbros.com
read about Warner Brothers movies

lego.com
tips and fun for fans of Lego® building blocks

sega.com
admit it — you're really online for the video games

nick.com
the characters from Nickelodeon TV shows

nintendo.com
more for the video-game nuts of the world

yahooligans.com
a directory to thousands of other kids' Web sites

What's the address? A Web site's address is known as the URL, which stands for Uniform Resource Locator. Each Web page has its own unique URL. But while you see mostly letters, your computer really reads the URL as a long series of numbers.

Bestselling Musicians

According to the Recording Industry Association of America, these are the bestselling recording artists of all time. Are your favorites on the list?

1. Elvis Presley
2. Garth Brooks
3. Billy Joel
4. Barbra Streisand
5. Elton John
6. Bruce Springsteen
7. Madonna
8. Michael Jackson
9. Mariah Carey
10. George Strait
11. Whitney Houston
12. Kenny Rogers
13. Neil Diamond
14. Kenny G
15. Celine Dion
16. Shania Twain
17. Willie Nelson
18. Eric Clapton
19. 2Pac Shakur
20. Alan Jackson

Michael Jackson's *Thriller* **(1982) has sold more copies than any other album by an individual. The overall record is held by a group, however: the Eagles, whose** *Greatest Hits: 1971-75* **has sold more than 27 million copies, just ahead of** *Thriller*'s **26 million.**

Bestselling Groups

The Beatles are history's bestselling group, according to the Recording Industry Association of America — and it's not even a close race. The Fab Four's sales are more than 50 percent better than runner-up Led Zeppelin. Here are the top 20 groups.

1. The Beatles
2. Led Zeppelin
3. Eagles
4. Pink Floyd
5. AC/DC
6. Aerosmith
7. The Rolling Stones
8. Metallica
9. Van Halen
10. U2
11. Fleetwood Mac
12. Alabama
13. Santana
14. Journey
15. Simon and Garfunkel
16. Silver Bullet Band
17. Chicago
18. Guns 'n' Roses
19. Foreigner
20. Backstreet Boys

The Beatles remain popular more than three decades after their last concert. *1*, a collection of their number-one singles, was released in 2000 and immediately soared to the top of the album charts.

Grammy® Winners

Sir Georg Solti was an internationally renowned conductor who led the Chicago Symphony Orchestra and the London Philharmonic, among others. Never heard of him? Well, he's the all-time Grammy® champ! Here's the list of the top 15 winners of the coveted Grammy® award, which is named after the gramophone, the first version of the record player. (Ask your mom what a "record" was. . . . She will probably sigh.)

ARTIST	AWARDS	ARTIST	AWARDS
Sir Georg Solti	31	Eric Clapton	16
Quincy Jones	27	Paul Simon	16
Pierre Boulez	25	Aretha Franklin	16
Vladimir Horowitz	25	Pat Metheny	16
Stevie Wonder	22	Vince Gill	16
Henry Mancini	20	Robert Shaw	16
Alison Krauss	17	Sting	16
Leonard Bernstein	16		

What do Elvis Presley, the Beatles, Bing Crosby, the Rolling Stones, and Boyz II Men have in common? None of those successful performers ever earned a Grammy® for Record of the Year. Paul Simon, on the other hand, has won the award an all-time best three times.

Animated Oscars®

In 2002, the Motion Picture Academy of America, the folks who give out the Oscars®, debuted a new award for Outstanding Animated Feature. Animated short films have been honored for a long time, but this was the first big award for the growing number of animated features. This list shows the nominees for the first four years of the award. The winners for each year are listed first.

2005
WINNER
The Incredibles
OTHER NOMINEES
Shrek 2
Shark Tale

2004
WINNER
Finding Nemo
OTHER NOMINEES
Brother Bear
The Triplets of Belleville

2003
WINNER
Spirited Away
OTHER NOMINEES
Ice Age
Lilo & Stitch
Spirit: Stallion of the Cimarron
Treasure Planet

2002
WINNER
Shrek
OTHER NOMINEES
Monsters, Inc.
Jimmy Neutron, Boy Genius

PsSST

The first full-length animated movie released in America was *Snow White*, by Walt Disney, in 1937. The first movie to be made entirely with computer animation was *Toy Story*, which was released in 1995.

Rated L for Lists

Wonder why Mom and Dad don't want you to see that scary/bloody/ violent/cool movie playing at the mall? They've considered the Motion Picture Association of America ratings. Here's what the letters mean.

G   General Audiences—All Ages Admitted.
The film does not contain material that would be offensive to parents of younger children who may view it.

PG   Parental Guidance Suggested. Some Material May Not Be Suitable for Children.
Parents should decide if they want their children to see the film, which may contain adult themes, some profanity, violence, or brief nudity.

PG-13   Parents Strongly Cautioned. Some Material May Be Inappropriate for Children.
A stronger warning to parents regarding the film's level of adult themes, violence, nudity, sensuality, language, or other contents.

R   Restricted. Under 17 Requires Accompanying Parent or Adult Guardian.
The film contains adult material, and parents are strongly encouraged to find out more about the film before allowing their children to accompany them.

NC-17   No One 17 and Under Admitted.
The film contains elements that most parents would consider off-limits for viewing by their children.

The system has been tinkered with occasionally since its creation in 1968. The original ratings were G (general audiences), M (mature audiences), R (restricted), and X (no one under 17 admitted).

Biggest Movies

These flicks have big B.O.! No, they don't stink. . . . In fact, just the opposite. The movies listed here have taken in more money at the box office ("B.O." — get it?) than any others. Of course, this list is always changing as Hollywood creates more amazing movies. How many on this list have you seen? Note: This list includes movies released in the United States through July 2005, and it doesn't include video or DVD sales.

MOVIE (YEAR)	MILLIONS
Titanic (1997)	**$600.7**
Star Wars (1977)	**$460.9**
Shrek 2 (2004)	**$437.0**
E.T.: The Extra-Terrestrial (1982)	**$434.9**
Star Wars: The Phantom Menace (1999)	**$431.1**
Spider-Man: The Movie (2002)	**$403.7**
The Lord of the Rings: The Return of the King (2003)	**$377.6**
Spider-Man 2 (2004)	**$373.3**
The Passion of the Christ (2004)	**$370.2**
Jurassic Park (1993)	**$357.1**

Movie studios compete to have the biggest "opening" of their movies. That means how much money a movie makes in its first day, its first weekend, or its first week. A movie that opens big can often turn into a mega-blockbuster, while a movie that doesn't open well can turn into a flop.

Very Rich Cartoons

Shrek 2 blew away the competition (we won't say how . . .) to become not only the most successful animated film ever, but also one of the all-time top-ten box-office hits in motion-picture history. Guess the other films are the ones that are, um, green. Here are the top-ten moneymaking full-length animated movies. How many have you seen?

1. Shrek 2

2. Finding Nemo

3. The Lion King

4. Shrek

5. The Incredibles

6. Monsters, Inc.

7. Toy Story 2

8. Aladdin

9. Toy Story

10. Snow White and the Seven Dwarfs

When you watch *Shrek 2*, pay close attention to the details. More than two dozen other movies or other fairy tales are referenced in either the dialogue or visuals.

Cartoon Families

You might think that you live in a cartoon family, but you don't. Sorry. So your family's not on this list, but this list does include the members of some of the most well-known families in cartoons and comics. We left a line at the end to include your favorites, in case they didn't make our list.

CARTOON CHARACTERS/
KEY FAMILY MEMBERS

Arthur the Aardvark
Dad, Mom, Arthur, D.W., Kate

Babar
King Babar, Queen Celeste, Flora, Pom, Isabelle, Alexander, Cousin Arthur

The Ducks
Donald and his nephews Huey, Dewey, and Louie

The Flintstones and the Rubbles
Fred, Wilma, and Pebbles; Barney, Betty, and Bam-Bam

The Jetsons
George, Jane, Judy, and Elroy

The Powerpuffs
Bubbles, Blossom, and Buttercup

CARTOON CHARACTERS/
KEY FAMILY MEMBERS

The Pickles (from *Rugrats*)
Stu, Didi, Grandpa Lou, Tommy, and Dylan, plus Grandma Minka and Grandpa Boris, Uncle Drew, and Cousin Angelica

Rolie Polie Olie
Mom, Dad, Olie, and Zowie

The Simpsons
Homer, Marge, Bart, Lisa, and Maggie

The Thornberrys
Nigel, Marianne, Debbie, Eliza, Darwin, and Donnie

_____

_____

_____

The Simpsons characters originally appeared in short films on *The Tracey Ullman Show*. Creator Matt Groening supposedly made them up while waiting to go into a meeting with that show's producers. The shorts were so popular that *The Simpsons* got its own half-hour show in 1990.

Who Owns TVs?

There are more than four television sets for every five people in the United States, the highest ratio in the world. How many do you have? How many do you wish you had? These countries have the most TV sets.

COUNTRY	SETS PER 1,000 PEOPLE
United States	**806**
Canada	**710**
Japan	**686**
Finland	**622**
France	**595**
Denmark	**594**
Germany	**567**
Australia	**554**
Czech Republic	**531**
Italy	**528**

More than 98 percent of all U.S. homes in 2000 had at least one television set. Ninety-four percent of the homes had a VCR, and 68 percent had basic cable. DVD players lagged behind at 15 percent.

Top Kids' TV Shows

What did you watch on TV last night? What are you watching tonight? You and millions of other kids answer those questions all the time, and the A.C. Nielsen Company is listening to your answers. They track and study what shows people watch. Here are the programs that kids ages 2 to 11 watched the most in 2002. Prime time is defined as 8 to 11 P.M.

SATURDAY MORNING

SHOW	WHO SHOWED IT	RATING*
SpongeBob SquarePants	Nickelodeon	5.8
Pokémon	WB	5.2
Adventures of Jackie Chan	WB	5.2
Rugrats	Nickelodeon	5.1
Hey Arnold!	Nickelodeon	5.0
Fairly Odd Parents	Nickelodeon	4.8
Chalkzone	Nickelodeon	4.5
Scooby-Doo	WB	4.4

PRIME TIME

SHOW	WHO SHOWED IT	RATING*
Boo to You, Winnie-the-Pooh	ABC	9.4
Super Bowl Postgame Show	FOX	8.9
Dinotopia, Part I	ABC	8.9
Winter Olympics Opening Ceremonies	NBC	8.8
Frosty Returns	CBS	8.5
Kids' Choice Awards	Nickelodeon	8.4
It's the Great Pumpkin, Charlie Brown	ABC	7.8
Rudolph the Red-Nosed Reindeer	CBS	7.7

The numbers are a percentage of the 25 million kids the Nielsen Co. includes in its ratings.

There were **333 shows aired during prime time during the 2001-2002 television season.** Sixty-three more aired on Saturday mornings. Among kids 12 to 17, the top programs were the Super Bowl Postgame Show, the Winter Olympics, and Game 7 of the World Series.

Your Parents'
Favorite Shows

The list on page 221 shows what you like to watch. But what did your parents watch when they were younger? Here are some shows that were popular 20 or 30 years ago. Ask an older family member about these and watch them get all misty-eyed and nostalgic.

Bozo the Clown

The Brady Bunch

Captain Kangaroo

The Electric Company

Fat Albert and the Cosby Kids

Flipper

H.R. Pufnstuf

Land of the Lost

Lancelot Link, Secret Chimp

Lassie

Lost in Space

Mister Rogers' Neighborhood*

Sesame Street*

Wonderama

ZOOM

* These are shows that both you and your parents probably watched!

Fred Rogers hosted a popular kids' show from his "neighborhood" for more than 30 years before retiring from TV in 2001.

Kids on TV

You love to watch yourself on TV. That is, you love to watch kids on TV. There have been kid stars on TV from Jerry Mathers on *Leave It to Beaver* to Mary-Kate and Ashley Olsen on *Full House*. Here are a few top kid stars from yesterday and today, and the shows they appeared or appear on.

YESTERDAY

STAR	TV SHOW
Melissa Sue Anderson	*Little House on the Prairie*
Tempestt Bledsoe	*The Cosby Show*
Soleil Moon Frye	*Punky Brewster*
Melissa Gilbert	*Little House on the Prairie*
Ron Howard	*The Andy Griffith Show*
Jay North	*Dennis the Menace*
Butch Patrick	*The Munsters*
Jonathan Taylor Thomas	*Home Improvement*

TODAY

STAR	TV SHOW
Amanda Bynes	*The Amanda Show*
Hilary Duff	*Lizzie McGuire*
Tia & Tamera Mowry	*Sister Sister*
Frankie Muniz	*Malcolm in the Middle*
Li'l Romeo	*Romeo!*
Ben Savage	*Boy Meets World*
Raven Symone	*That's So Raven!*
Camille Winbush	*The Bernie Mac Show*

Frankie Muniz was nominated for an Emmy® as Best Actor in a Comedy in 2001, but at 11 years old, he wasn't the youngest nominee ever. In 1990, Fred Savage of *The Wonder Years* was a few months younger than Frankie when he was nominated. He didn't win, either!

Computer and Video Games

Face it — if you're a kid, somewhere along the line you're going to play and/or own a computer game or a video game of some sort. You're not alone. Here are the top-selling video games (through July 2005) for a variety of platforms.

Nintendo
Super Smash Brothers
Super Mario 64
Mario Kart 64
The Legend of Zelda
Donkey Kong 64

Sega Dreamcast
Sonic Adventure
Sonic Adventure 2
Sega GT
Sega Bass Fishing

Game Boy Advance
Pokémon Emerald
Star Wars Lego
Super Mario 4
Madagascar

XBox
Star Wars Lego
MVP Baseball
FIFA Soccer 2005

Sony PlayStation 2
Star Wars Lego
MVP Baseball
Madagascar
NBA Live 2005
Madden NFL 2005

Games for PC
I Spy Fantasy
Sid Meier's Pirates!
FIA GT Racing
The Sims
The Sims Vacation
    Expansion Pack

Computer Games for Macintosh
I Spy Fantasy
Oregon Trail: 5th Edition
The Incredible Machine

You probably know this already, but most game makers insert secret points or parts of the game called "Easter eggs." Players need to know secret codes or combinations of keys to make the "eggs" appear.

Hall of Fame Games

Games magazine is the top publication for people who love games of all sorts: word games, math games, board games, picture games, etc. The editors of the magazine have created the "Games Hall of Fame" to honor board games that are popular favorites. Here is their list of the greatest games. We can't believe they didn't include Candyland!

Acquire

Axis and Allies

Blockhead!

Bridgette

Clue

Civilization

Diplomacy

Dungeons and Dragons

Mille Bornes

Monopoly

Othello

Pente

Risk

Scrabble

Sorry!

Stratego

Taboo

TriBond

Trivial Pursuit

Twister

Twixt

Yahtzee

Note: All game names are trademarked by their manufacturers.

Monopoly is the bestselling board game of all time, with more than 200 million copies sold since it was first produced in 1935. There are now versions for cities, countries, colleges, and sports teams, as well as editions in 26 languages. The streets' names in the original game are all named after streets found in Atlantic City, New Jersey.

Yu-Gi-Oh!

The latest card game imported from Japan hit North American shores in 2002, and it has quickly surpassed Pokémon, Digimon, and other similar series. Now also a popular TV show, Yu-Gi-Oh remains basically a player vs. player battle card game. Cards are sold in decks of various sizes and types that players then rearrange to create their own decks to use in games. This list shows the decks sold in the United States through summer 2005.

Starter Decks

Joey
Kaiba
Kaiba Evolution
Pegasus
Yugi
Yugi Evolution

Structure Decks

Blaze of Destruction
Dragon's Roar
Fury from the Deep
Zombie Madness

Booster Packs

Ancient Sanctuary
Dark Beginnings
Dark Crisis
Dark Revolution
Flaming Eternity
Invasion of Chaos
Labyrinth of Nightmare
Legacy of Darkness
Legends of the Blue Eyes
The Lost Millennium

Magic Ruler
Magician's Force
Metal Raiders
Movie Exclusive Pack
Pharaoh's Servant
Pharaonic Guardian
Rise of Destiny
Soul of the Duelist
White Dragon

What does Yu-Gi-Oh mean?

Answer: The name of the game means "King of Games." It was invented in Japan by artist Kazuki Takahashi.

Famous Cowpeople

The cowboy image we have from Hollywood comes from seeing the likes of John Wayne and Kirk Douglas on the big screen. The cowgirl image started out as pretty frilly, but it's gotten rougher and tougher (and more real). Here are some famous people who made their living on the ranches or frontiers of the Old West and not necessarily on the screen.

COWBOYS

Jesse Chisholm

John Chisum

Charles Goodnight

John Wesley Iliff

Richard King

Oliver Loving

John Lytle

Samuel Maverick

Joseph McCoy

Nelson Story

Alexander Swan

Andrew Voigt

COWGIRLS

Calamity Jane
(Martha Jane Canary)

Mary Ann Goodnight

Charmayne James

Henrietta King

Florence LaDue

Goldia Bays Malone

Lucille Mulhall

Annie Oakley

Narcissa Prentiss Whitman

Lizzie Williams

Ya say ya ain't heard 'bout lotta these cowfolks? Well, check out www.cowboyhalloffame.org and www.cowgirl.net on that newfangled Internet!

"Cowgirl" was first used to describe Lucille Mulhall in the early 1900s, and the name stuck. Various reports credit Theodore Roosevelt or Will Rogers with coining the term.

Biggest Amusement Parks

More people annually visit Tokyo Disneyland than any other amusement park in the world. Here were the most frequented parks around the globe in 2000.

AMUSEMENT PARK	LOCATION
Tokyo Disneyland	Japan
The Magic Kingdom at Walt Disney World	Florida
Disneyland	California
Disneyland Paris	France
Epcot at Walt Disney World	Florida
Everland	South Korea
Disney-MGM Studios at Walt Disney World	Florida
Disney's Animal Kingdom at Walt Disney World	Florida
Universal Studios Florida	Florida
Lotte World	South Korea
Blackpool Pleasure Beach	England
Universal's Islands of Adventure	Florida
Yokohama Hakkeijima Sea Paradise	Japan
Universal Studios Hollywood	California
SeaWorld Florida	Florida
Busch Gardens Tampa Bay	Florida
Nagashima Spa Land	Japan
Tivoli Gardens	Denmark
Huis Ten Bosch	Japan

The oldest amusement park in the world is Bakken, which is near Copenhagen, Denmark. It first opened in 1583. We hope they've cleaned out the popcorn machine a few times since then.

Fastest Roller Coasters

Roller coaster enthusiasts yearn for either wooden or steel roller coasters. Both sides claim that their type of roller coaster offers the most thrills. In the end, however, the biggest thrill may be the speed.

MILES/KM PER HOUR	ROLLER COASTER/LOCATION
128/206	**Kingda Ka**/Six Flags Great Adventure, New Jersey
120/193	**Top Thrill Dragster**/Cedar Point, Ohio
106/177	**Dodonpa**/Fujikyu Highland, Japan
100/167	**Superman–The Escape** Six Flags Magic Mountain, California
100/167	**Tower of Terror**/Dreamworld, Australia
95/163	**Steel Dragon 2000**/Nagashima Spa Land, Japan
93/155	**Millennium Force**/Cedar Point, Ohio
85/142	**Goliath**/Six Flags Magic Mountain, California
85/142	**Titan**/Six Flags Over Texas, Texas
82/137	**Phantom's Revenge**/Pennsylvania*
82/137	**Xcelerator**/Knott's Berry Farm, California
80.8/135	**Fujiyama**/Fujikyu Highland, Japan
80/133	**Desperado**/Buffalo Bill's Resort/Casino, Nevada
80/133	**HyperSonic XLC**/Kings Dominion, Virginia
80/133	**Nitro**/Six Flags Great Adventure, New Jersey

In Kennywood Park, Pennsylvania.

Steel roller coasters top the list for those thrill seekers wanting speed. The new speed champ, Kingda Ka, is also the world's tallest roller coaster, soaring 418 feet (127.4m) at its highest point!

Fabulous Fads

A "fad" is something that millions of people suddenly seem to be doing, wearing, or eating all at once — and then it's gone almost as quickly as it appeared. Fads can be clothes, dances, styles of music, toys, activities, or just about anything. Here are some of America's wildest, weirdest, and most popular fads. The years listed are the height of the fad's popularity.

1920s Raccoon coats
College kids wore enormous overcoats made of raccoon skins.

1924 Flagpole sitting
People tried to see how long they could stay atop a flagpole.

1939 Goldfish swallowing
. . . and we don't mean crackers! Don't try this at home.

1950s Bomb shelters
People afraid of atomic bombs built underground rooms in their backyards where they would be safe during an attack.

1950s Poodle skirts
Long, wide, colorful skirts with big appliqués of poodles on them.

1955 Coonskin caps
Kids everywhere wore these caps, modeled after the ones worn on the TV show *Davy Crockett.*

1959 Phone booth stuffing
How many bored college kids can you squeeze into a phone booth? They also tried this with Volkswagen Beetles.

1960s Tie-dyed T-shirts
A totally groovy fashion made by tying shirts into knots and then dying them, usually purple.

1962 Alvin and the Chipmunks
These squeaky-voiced cartoon "singers" were a huge hit for years. They were actually people's singing voices speeded up.

1970s Platform shoes
How high can you go? Platform shoes made girls stand out in the 1970s. This is one fad that has made a recent comeback.

1973   Puka shells
Little white seashells worn on chokers by both boys and girls.

1974   Streaking
Running through public places with no clothes on. Really.

1975   CB radios
CB stands for "citizens band," a type of radio first used by truckers. A song made them popular with many other people — but only for a while, good buddy. 10-4!

1975   Pet Rocks
Believe it or not, millions of people paid good money for a box with a rock in it. That was it, a rock that people kept for a pet.

1980   Rubik's Cube®
This extremely difficult multicolored puzzle was a rage for years; you can still find them in some people's toy closets.

1982   Smurfs
They were blue, they had a funny language, and they were everywhere! Smurfs were cartoon characters from Belgium.

1983   Cabbage Patch Kids
If you didn't have one of these dolls (which were so popular for a while, they were hard to get), you just weren't "in."

1989   Teenage Mutant Ninja Turtles
Four turtles who knew karate, talked like surfers, and lived in the sewer. America couldn't get enough of them.

1993   Macarena
You might have heard the song or done the dance, which was everywhere for about a year, but then vanished just as quickly.

1994   POGs
These were collectible cardboard disks, first created in Hawaii, that were pretty much the next Pet Rocks — hugely popular, then nowhere. POG stood for passion-orange-guava juice. The disks were originally inside bottle caps of that drink.

What fads are coming next? Kids in America should look to the West. Many of today's fashion, video-game, and music fads are coming from Japan. They usually hit America's west coast and then travel east.

Black Cats and Rabbits' Feet

See a penny, pick it up, all the day you'll have good luck. Most of us learned that one a long time ago. Here are some other common signs that things are going to go your way. The other list is one of bad luck signs.

GOOD LUCK

A four-leaf clover

A cricket inside the house

A horseshoe hung above the doorway

A rabbit's foot

A rainbow

Eating black-eyed peas on New Year's Day

Crossed fingers

Carrying the bride over the threshold

Keeping a chain letter going

When the first butterfly you see in a new year is white

Finding a penny that is facing heads-up

BAD LUCK

A black cat crossing your path

Walking under a ladder

The number 13 (especially Friday the thirteenth)

Breaking a mirror

Opening an umbrella inside the house

Stepping on cracks

Spilling salt (unless you throw a pinch over your left shoulder)

Killing a ladybug

Placing a hat on a bed

A groom seeing his bride before the ceremony on the wedding day

Seeing three butterflies together

Breaking a chain letter

When you hang that horseshoe above the doorway, be sure to keep the open end up. Otherwise, all the good luck will fall out!

Are You Listaphobic?

The word "phobia" is used to describe a condition in which a person is very, very scared of something. There are lots of things to be scared of, and there's a phobia for just about all of them. For instance, are you afraid of spiders? If so, you're not alone. In fact, fear of spiders (arachnophobia) is the most common phobia. Here are some of the fears with the most fearers, er, people.

Spiders	Arachnophobia
People and social situations	Anthrophobia
Flying	Aerophobia
Open spaces	Agoraphobia
Confined spaces	Claustrophobia
Vomiting	Emetophobia
Heights	Acrophobia
Cancer	Carcinomaphobia
Thunderstorms	Brontophobia
Death	Necrophobia
Heart Disease	Cardiophobia

So many folks associate the number 13 with bad luck (see the signs of good luck and bad luck on the opposite page) that there's a word for their fear: triskaidekaphobia.

More My Favorites

This chapter is full of top computer games, TV shows, books, and more. Here is some space for you to record your favorites in some categories.

WEB SITES FOR SCHOOL

1. _____
2. _____
3. _____
4. _____
5. _____
6. _____

WEB SITES FOR FUN

1. _____
2. _____
3. _____
4. _____
5. _____
6. _____

VIDEO/COMPUTER GAMES

1. _____
2. _____
3. _____
4. _____
5. _____
6. _____

BOOKS

1. _____
2. _____
3. _____
4. _____
5. _____
6. _____

MAGAZINES

1. _____
2. _____
3. _____
4. _____
5. _____
6. _____

CDS OR SONGS

1. _____
2. _____
3. _____
4. _____
5. _____
6. _____

CHAPTER NINE

Critters

Lions and tigers and bears . . . and dogs and cats and egg-laying mammals and flying monkeys and an exaltation of larks. Plus a horse named Ed and a cow that says "mu."

Endangered Animals

An animal species is endangered if its ability to survive is threatened. The reasons for this include disease, destruction of its habitat (where they live), too much hunting, or overfishing. Here are some animals from around the world that are officially recognized as endangered.

Asian elephant
Bison
Blue whale
California condor
Cheetah
Chimpanzee
Florida manatee
Flying squirrel
Giant armadillo
Giant panda
Gorilla
Jaguar
Komodo dragon
Lemur
Leopard
Marine otter
Ocelot
Orangutan
Tiger
Whooping crane

The bald eagle is the official National Emblem of the United States. It once was on the brink of extinction, but has made a comeback and now has been reclassified as "threatened."

Extinct Animals

Extinct means you won't be seeing any of these animals at the zoo anytime soon — or anywhere else for that matter. Some of these animals died out naturally; others were simply hunted by humans into extinction. Dinosaurs have been extinct for millions of years, though it's open to debate exactly what caused their demise. Here are some examples of other animals that ceased to exist a bit more recently.

ANIMAL	LAST ALIVE
Balinese tiger	1937
Blue pike	1970
Caribbean monk seal	1922
Dodo bird	1681
Great auk	1844
Heath hen	1932
Passenger pigeon	1914
Saber-toothed tiger	c. 9000 B.C.
Stellar's sea cow	1768
Tasmanian tiger-wolf	1936
Woolly mammoth	c. 2000 B.C.
Woolly rhinoceros	c. 8000 B.C.

The Tasmanian tiger-wolf was neither a tiger nor a wolf. Instead, it was a marsupial that had a front pouch for its young, much like a kangaroo.

Deeeeep Sleepers

How would you like to go to bed in November and wake up in March? Well, you'd miss out on New Year's, so maybe it wouldn't be that cool. However, some animals do sleep that long. Everyone knows about bears that "hibernate" in the winter, but here are some other animals that get some Big Sleep.

Bat
Box Turtle
Eastern Chipmunk
Ground Squirrel
Jumping Mouse
Raccoon
Skunk
Snake
Toad
Woodchuck

PsSST

Hibernation means much more than sleeping soundly. An animal's bodily functions almost come to a halt. Breathing rate and pulse slow down a lot, and body temperature may drop.

Get Me Out of Here!

That's what the babies of the animals in this list are saying. The word "gestation" means how long an animal is inside its mother before being born. Some animals really like to hold on to their babies and have very long gestation periods. These animals carry babies for the longest times.

ANIMAL	GESTATION PERIOD (IN DAYS)
Elephant	510–730
Whale	365–547
Donkey	about 365
Horse	329–345
Deer	197–300
Cow	about 280
Monkey	139–270
Hippopotamus	220–255
Bear	180–240
Goat	136–160
Sheep	144–152
Pig	101–130
Lion	105–113

For human beings, pregnancy generally is considered nine months. Technically, it's anywhere from 253 to 303 days.

Do German

Cows say "moo" all over the world, right? Well, yes and no. The sounds an animal makes are the same, but they are expressed differently in different

ANIMAL	ENGLISH	RUSSIAN
Bird	Tweet-tweet	Squick
Cat	Meow	Meau
Cow	Moo	Mu
Dog	Bow-wow	Guf-guf
Duck	Quack-quack	Quack
Goat	Meh-meh	Beee
Horse	Neigh-neigh	Eohoho
Owl	Whoo	Ooooo
Pig	Oink-oink	Qrr-qrr
Rooster	Cock-a-doodle-do	Kukuriki

When does a frog sound like a duck? When it's German, of course. In English, a frog says "ribbit." But in German, it comes out "quaak, quaak."

Cows Moo?

languages. Here are some common animal sounds and how they are expressed in five languages.

JAPANESE	FRENCH	GERMAN
Qui-qui	Choon-choon	Piep-piep
Nyeow	Meow	Meow-meow
Mo-Mo	Meu-meu	Muh-muh
Won-won	Whou-whou	Vow-vow
Qua-qua	Coin-coin	Quack
Mee-mee	Ma-ma	Eeh-eeh
He-heeh	Hee-hee-hee	Iiiih
Hoo-hoo	Oo-oo	Wooo-wooo
Boo	Groan-groan	Crr-cvl
KoKeKock-ko	Cocorico	Goockle

What is the loudest land mammal? Hint: Look up when you're in the jungle.

The howler monkey's shriek can be heard three miles (five kilometers) away!

Pigs (etc.) in Space

The first animal in space was a female Samoyed husky named Laika, who was aboard the Soviet Union's *Sputnik II* in 1957. Tossing your cat in the air does not qualify it for this list of animals that have traveled in space.

Beetles	**Monkeys**
Bullfrogs	**Rats**
Chimpanzees	**Snails**
Fruit flies	**Swordtail fish**
Medaka fish	**Wasps**
Mice	

BONUS BIT! Miss Baker was the name of a one-pound (2.2-kg) squirrel monkey sent to space aboard a U.S. missile in 1959. Despite traveling at more than 10,000 miles (16,690 km) per hour to an altitude of 300 miles (500 km), little Miss Baker had little trouble with liftoff, reentry, or weightlessness, which were important test results for manned flight. But the trek did make her a bit cranky. After the flight, she bit the person who removed her from the capsule!

PSSST Laika had a special doggy-shaped space suit made for her. It was made so her four legs stuck out of the suit, perhaps to make it easier for her to go for a "space walk."

Animals in History

One of the most important animals in history is the horse Paul Revere rode to warn American patriots of an impending attack by the British in 1775. No one knows for sure the name of the horse (which wasn't actually Revere's), though it is often called Brown Beauty. Here are some other famous animals in history.

Balto The Siberian husky that was the lead dog on a lengthy Alaskan trek to deliver lifesaving medicine in 1925.

Buddy The first Seeing Eye dog in 1928.

Chips German shepherd–collie–husky that was awarded a Purple Heart in World War II.

Koko Gorilla trained to use American Sign Language.

Laika Samoyed husky that was the first animal in space in 1957.

Mrs. O'Leary's Cow Sometimes called Daisy, Madeline, or Gwendolyn, she was the cow that allegedly kicked over a lantern that started the Great Chicago Fire of 1871.

Pickles The dog that found the stolen Jules Rimet (World Cup) Trophy in 1966.

Punxsutawney Phil The Pennsylvania groundhog whose emergence reportedly predicts the length of winter.

Seabiscuit The legendary racehorse who, according to his recent biography, was the biggest newsmaker of 1938 — bigger even than Franklin Roosevelt or Adolf Hitler.

PsSST Balto's heroic journey to deliver medicine to children in a remote Alaskan village inspired the Iditarod, the annual dog-sled race from Nome to Anchorage.

Not Just Us Chickens

Chickens lay most of the eggs that we eat. (What's your favorite? Scrambled, boiled, fried . . . salad?) All birds, in fact, lay eggs. But birds aren't the only animals that lay eggs. Here are a few more nest-sitters.

Butterfly

Crocodile

Duckbill Platypus

Echidna
(Spiny Anteater)

Fish

Frog

Ladybug

Snake

Toad

Turtle

Animals that lay eggs are called "oviparous." Animals that give birth to live offspring from the mother's body are called "viviparous."

Dogs and Cats Living Together

Talk about outnumbered! Believe it or not, there are more dogs and cats in the United States than people! Listed from most popular to least popular, here are the top breeds of cats and dogs in the United States, according to national dog and cat organizations.

DOGS

Labrador Retriever
Golden Retriever
German Shepherd
Dachshund
Beagle
Yorkshire Terrier
Poodle
Boxer
Chihuahua
Shih Tzu
Rottweiler
Old English Sheepdog
Pekingese
Saint Bernard
Saluki

CATS

Persian
Maine Coon
Siamese
Exotic
Abyssinian
Oriental
American shorthair
Scottish fold
Burmese
Cornish rex
Birman
Tonkinese

A dog is listed in the *Guinness Book of World Records* for something that's truly mouth-watering: *his* mouth, that is. His tongue is 15 inches (33 cm) long. It's almost always lolling out of his mouth like a red, wet snake!

Animal Group Names

Smack, prickle, and gulp. No, that's not the name of a new breakfast cereal. Those are words called "collective" nouns. Collective nouns are special words that describe a particular group of things — in this case, animals.

A **shrewdness** of apes

A **colony** of bats

A **wake** of buzzards

A **bed** of clams

A **gulp** of cormorants

A **bask** of crocodiles

A **murder** of crows

A **brace** of ducks

A **convocation** of eagles

A **business** of ferrets

A **stand** of flamingos

A **business** of flies

A **tower** of giraffes

A **band** of gorillas

An **army** of herring

A **bloat** of hippopotamuses

A **passel** of hogs

A **cackle** of hyenas

A **smack** of jellyfish

A **troop** of kangaroos

An **exaltation** of larks

A **pride** of lions

A **plague** of locusts

A **richness** of martens

A **labor** of moles

A **romp** of otters

A **parliament** of owls

A **muster** of peacocks

A **prickle** of porcupines

A **covey** of quail

A **warren** of rabbits

An **unkindness** of ravens

A **crash** of rhinoceroses

A **pod** of seals (or whales)

A **shiver** of sharks

A **nest** of snakes

A **murmuration** of starlings

A **streak** of tigers

A **knot** of toads

A **gang** of turkeys

See if you can make up some collective noun for your school or friends. Your class can become a "power" of kids and your neighbor can be a "pile" of people. Have fun with it!

Baby Animal Names

Some baby animal names are well known, like a bear cub or puppy dog. But did you know that a baby skunk is called a kitten or that a baby turtle is called a chicken? Here are some other baby names for animals, including the obvious and the not-so-obvious.

ANIMAL	BABY	ANIMAL	BABY
Ant	antling	Kangaroo	joey
Canary	chick	Lion	shelp, cub, or lionet
Cat	kit, kitling, kitten, or pussy	Opossum	joey
Chicken	chick, chicken, poult, cockerel, or pullet	Ostrich	chick
		Owl	owlet or howlet
Chimpanzee	infant	Penguin	fledgling or chick
Cow	calf	Rabbit	kitten or bunny
Duck	duckling or flapper	Raccoon	kit or cub
Eagle	eaglet	Rhinoceros	calf
Elephant	calf	Seal	whelp, pup, cub, or bachelor
Fish	fry, fingerling, minnow, or spawn	Shark	cub
Fly	grub or maggot	Sheep	lamb, lambkin, or shearling
Frog	poll	Squirrel	dray
Giraffe	calf	Swan	cygnet
Goat	kid	Tiger	whelp or cub
Goose	gosling	Toad	tadpole
Horse	colt, foal, stat, stag, filly, youngster, yearling, or hogget	Whale	calf
		Zebra	colt or foal

PsSST

A father Emperor penguin protects the penguin mother's eggs for 60 days, standing on his feet the whole time. He doesn't eat while waiting for the chicks to hatch, and he can lose up to 25 pounds (11.3 kg).

Dangerous Animals

Most animals will not harm you unless they are provoked or accidentally disturbed. Be careful when around any wild animal, but stay *far away* from the animals on this list — the most dangerous animals in the world.

ANIMALS	HOME	DANGER
African elephant	Africa	trampling
Bees, hornets, wasps	worldwide	stinging, venom
Black mamba snake	Africa	biting, venom
Black widow spider	worldwide	biting, venom
Blue-ringed octopus	Australia	biting, venom
Box jellyfish	Australia	venom through tentacles
Brazilian huntsman spider	Brazil	biting, venom
Crocodile	worldwide	biting
Gila monster	Mexico, U.S.	biting, venom
Great white shark	worldwide	biting
Hippopotamus	Africa	biting, trampling
King cobra snake	Southeast Asia	biting, venom
Moray eels	tropical waters	biting, toxic flesh
Piranha fish	South America	biting
Poison dart frog	South America	poisonous skin
Puffer fish	Indo-Pacific region	fatal when eaten
Short-tailed shrew	North America	biting, venom

PSSST

So, what is the most dangerous animal in the world? Because of the diseases they carry, many people consider the mosquito and the fly to be the most dangerous creatures in the world. The hippo, however, usually lands atop the annual list of animals who have killed or seriously hurt the most people.

Ewww! Spiders!

Two body parts, eight legs, spins webs — must be a spider. You can find more than 2,500 species of spiders (also called arachnids) in North America. This list includes many of the most common spiders found in North America.

Barn spider	Ground spider
Black widow spider	Jumping spider
Brown spider	Lynx spider
Cellar spider	Nursery web spider
Cobweb spider	Orb web spider
Comb-footed spider	Pirate spider
Crab spider	Sac spider
Dock spider	Spitting spider
Fishing spider	Tarantula
Funnel web spider	Trapdoor spider
Ghost spider	Wolf spider

Spiders are fascinating creatures. They actually have blue blood. And their skeletons are on the outside of their bodies in the form of an exoskeleton. Trivia time: Those daddy longlegs that you find around the house? Not really spiders. They belong to a different order of animals, called the Opiliones.

A Lot of Candles

The box turtle doesn't move very fast, but maybe that's because it's got lots of time on its hands: Its life expectancy is about 100 years. Here are some animals that usually live rather long lives.

ANIMAL	LIFE EXPECTANCY (IN YEARS)	ANIMAL	LIFE EXPECTANCY (IN YEARS)
Box turtle	100	Gorilla	20
Killer whale	90	Horse	20
Blue whale	80	Polar bear	20
Andean condor	70	White rhinoceros	20
Eletus parrot	50	Black bear	18
Asian elephant	40	Black rhinoceros	15
Bald eagle	30	Lion	15
Hippopotamus	30	Lobster	15
Grizzly bear	25	Rhesus monkey	15

The box turtle is a kid compared to the quahog (*KOH-hog*), a type of clam that can live to be more than 200 years old.

Celebrity Animals

Rin Tin Tin, Trigger, Lassie, Flipper, Mickey Mouse, Snoopy . . . Animals real and imaginary have entertained us since the earliest days of movies and television. Here are some celebrity animals you might know.

Air Bud Hoops-playing golden retriever from a movie

Babe The pig from the movie of the same name

Beethoven Saint Bernard dog from the movie of the same name

CatDog® Mixed-up cartoon animal

Clifford® Big red dog from books and TV

Dogbert® From the *Dilbert* comic strip

Garfield® The lasagna-loving cartoon cat

Keiko The whale in *Free Willy*

Marcel The monkey from *Friends*

Salem The cat from *Sabrina the Teenage Witch*

Scooby-Doo® The cartoon dog

Shamu The performing killer whale at SeaWorld

PsSST

A "talking" horse named Mr. Ed was one of the most famous celebrity animals. He starred in his own 1950s TV show. In the days before computer animation, stagehands used a small wire to make Mr. Ed "talk."

If I Were an Animal...

Judging by how well you keep your room clean, some might say you already are an animal! Ha! Of course, we're all human beings (well, most of us), so that makes us animals. But on this page, it's time for imagination. Fill in the blanks on this list to record what sorts of animals you would like to be. Be creative! Have fun!

If I wanted to run very fast, I'd be a

_____.

If I wanted to fly like a bird, I'd choose a

_____.

If I wanted to swim like a fish, I'd become a

_____.

If I wanted to be extremely strong, I'd wish to be a

_____.

If I wanted to be extremely small, I'd shrink to become a

_____.

If I wanted to live in the steamy, hot jungle, I'd become a

_____.

If I wanted to eat only plants to live, I'd change into a

_____.

If I wanted to eat only meat to live, I'd be a

_____.

The one animal I'd most like to become would be a

_____.

CHAPTER TEN

Grab Bag

We took all the stuff that wouldn't fit anywhere else and shoved it into this chapter. So stick in your hand and see what you get! Good luck!

What's Your Sign?

Astrologists believe that the position of stars, moons, planets, and other heavenly bodies at the time of a person's birth influences his or her destiny. Here are the 12 signs of the zodiac. What's your sign?

SIGN	SYMBOL	DATES
Aquarius	Water carrier	Jan. 20 to Feb. 18
Pisces	Fish	Feb. 19 to Mar. 20
Aries	Ram	Mar. 21 to Apr. 20
Taurus	Bull	Apr. 21 to May 20
Gemini	Twins	May 21 to June 21
Cancer	Crab	June 22 to July 22
Leo	Lion	July 23 to Aug. 22
Virgo	Virgin	Aug. 23 to Sept. 22
Libra	Scales	Sept. 23 to Oct. 22
Scorpio	Scorpion	Oct. 23 to Nov. 21
Sagittarius	Archer	Nov. 22 to Dec. 20
Capricorn	Goat	Dec. 21 to Jan. 19

The earliest versions of astrology existed as long as 5,000 years ago. Early civilizations put great faith in the ability of the stars to predict the future.

What Animal Are You?

Just like the Western world's zodiac, the Chinese zodiac is divided into 12 signs. But each sign, which is the name of an animal, corresponds to one year, not just one month or so. Here are the animals of the Chinese zodiac and the years that they represent. What year were you born in?

ANIMAL SIGN	YEARS
Sheep	1979, 1991, 2003, 2015
Monkey	1980, 1992, 2004, 2016
Rooster	1981, 1993, 2005, 2017
Dog	1982, 1994, 2006, 2018
Boar	1983, 1995, 2007, 2019
Rat	1972, 1984, 1996, 2008
Ox	1973, 1985, 1997, 2009
Tiger	1974, 1986, 1998, 2010
Hare	1975, 1987, 1999, 2011
Dragon	1976, 1988, 2000, 2012
Snake	1977, 1989, 2001, 2013
Horse	1978, 1990, 2002, 2014

Some years are considered luckier than others. Occasionally, Chinese families try to make sure their babies are born during years of the dragon, for instance.

Nobel Peace Prize

The Peace Prize is one of six Nobel Prizes awarded annually (the others are for literature, physics, chemistry, medicine, and economics). The Peace Prize was first awarded in 1901. Here are the Peace winners since 1963. Note that the prize can go to a group or organization, not just one person.

1963 International Committee of the Red Cross; League of Red Cross Societies (Switzerland)

1964 Rev. Dr. Martin Luther King, Jr. (United States)

1965 UNICEF (United Nations Children's Fund)

1968 René Cassin (France)

1969 International Labor Organization

1970 Norman E. Borlaug (United States)

1971 Willy Brandt (West Germany)

1973 Henry A. Kissinger (United States);
Le Duc Tho (North Vietnam; refused prize)

1974 Eisaku Sato (Japan); Sean MacBride (Ireland)

1975 Andrei D. Sakharov (U.S.S.R.)

1976 Mairead Corrigan and Betty Williams (Northern Ireland)

1977 Amnesty International

1978 Menachem Begin (Israel) and Anwar el-Sadat (Egypt)

1979 Mother Teresa of Calcutta (India)

1980 Adolfo Pérez Esquivel (Argentina)

1981 Office of the United Nations High Commissioner for Refugees

1982 Alva Myrdal (Sweden) and Alfonso García Robles (Mexico)

1983 Lech Walesa (Poland)

1984 Bishop Desmond Tutu (South Africa)

1985 International Physicians for the Prevention of Nuclear War

1986 Elie Wiesel (United States)

1987 Oscar Arias Sánchez (Costa Rica)

1988 U.N. Peacekeeping Forces

1989 Dalai Lama (Tibet)

1990 Mikhail S. Gorbachev (U.S.S.R.)

1991 Daw Aung San Suu Kyi (Burma)

1992 Rigoberta Menchú (Guatemala)

1993 F. W. de Klerk and Nelson Mandela (South Africa)

1994 Yasser Arafat (Palestine), and Shimon Peres and Yitzhak Rabin (Israel)

1995 Joseph Rotblat and Pugwash Conference on Science and World Affairs (U.K.)

1996 Carlos Filipe Ximenes Belo and José Ramos-Horta (both East Timor)

1997 Jody Williams and the International Campaign to Ban Landmines (United States)

1998 John Hume and David Trimble (both Northern Ireland)

1999 Doctors Without Borders (France)

2000 Kim Dae Jung (South Korea)

2001 United Nations and Secretary-General Kofi Annan

2002 Jimmy Carter, Jr. (United States)

2003 Shirin Ebadi (Iran)

2004 Wangari Maathai (Kenya)

2005 Mohammed ElBaradei; Intl. Atomic Energy Agency

Oddly, the Nobel Peace Prize is named for the man who invented dynamite. Swedish chemist Alfred Nobel originally funded the Nobel awards through money left in his will.

Odd "Official" Events

People in the United States will celebrate just about anything, it seems. To spread the word about events, causes, people, or local traditions, governments, as well as companies, give various parts of the year "National" status. Here are some of the more unusual "National Months" celebrated in America. There are also hundreds of official weeks and days.

MONTH	EVENT
January	Oatmeal Month
	Meat Month
February	Wild Bird Feeding Month
	Scottish Culture Month
March	Frozen Food Month
	Furniture Refinishing Month
April	Pets Are Wonderful Month
	Grass Month
May	Fungal Infection Awareness Month
	National Barbeque Month
June	Fight the Filthy Fly Month
	Zoo and Aquarium Month
July	Anti-Boredom Month
	Tahiti Awareness Month
August	Foot Health Month
	Catfish Month
September	Read-a-New-Book Month
	Be Kind to Writers and Editors Month
October	Hedgehog Month
	Doll Collectors Month
November	Peanut Butter Lovers Month
	Stamp Collecting Month
December	Hi Neighbor Month
	Bingo's Birthday Month

There are too many fun "National Weeks" to list here, but our favorites include: National Aardvark Week, TV-Free Week, Bubblegum Week, Pickled Pepper Week, and Tell Someone They're Doing a Good Job Week.

Dig These!

You're probably too young to remember most of the items on this list. But ask your mom, dad, grandma, or grandpa if they wore any of these out-of-date fad items — or if any of the clothes are hiding in their closets!

Acid-washed jeans

Bell-bottom pants

Go-go boots

Hot pants

Knickers

Leisure suits

Nehru jackets

Pedal pushers

Pillbox hats

Poodle skirts

Saddle shoes

Zoot suits

Nehru jackets, named for Indian prime minister Jawaharlal Nehru, had a banded collar and no lapels. They became a fashion hit after the Beatles took to wearing them in the 1960s.

Bestselling Wheels

The Ford F-Series pickup truck was the bestselling passenger vehicle in America in 2004, with more than 450,000 vehicles sold. But at that rate, it would take half a century to equal the sales of the Toyota Corolla, the bestselling passenger vehicle in history. Here are the most popular:

CAR	TOTAL SOLD	1ST YEAR AVAILABLE
Toyota Corolla	22 million	1963
Volkswagen Beetle	21 million	1937
Ford Model T	15.5 million	1908
Volkswagen Golf/Rabbit	15 million	1974
Lada Riva	13.5 million	1970

A Box of Lemons

According to the readers at CarTalk.com, here are the five worst cars of all time. Not the worst-selling — just the worst to own or drive, said the people who voted. Any of these in your garage?

1. Yugo
2. Chevy Vega
3. Ford Pinto
4. AMC Gremlin
5. Chevy Chevette

Volkswagen stopped production of the Beetle in the late 1970s, but the "Bug" made a comeback in 1998 and once again became a popular car.

Biggest Trucks

s it just us, or do trucks rule? Seriously, doesn't every kid want a big, giant
ruck to drive to school? Okay, maybe not every kid, but we're guessing it's
lot. Anyway, here are some of the biggest trucks in the world.

Largest Dump Truck

-282 (made by Liebherr Mining Equipment Co.)
t can carry more than 700,000 pounds (317,000 kg).

Largest Crane

)emag CC 12600 (made by Demag Mobile Cranes)
Height: 557 feet (169 m). It can lift 1,600 tons (1.45 million kg).

Largest Land Vehicle

RB293 Bucket-wheel Excavator (made by Man Takraf)
his earthmover is 722 feet (220 m) long, 310 feet
94 m) tall, and weighs 31 million pounds (68 million kg).

Largest Monster Truck

3igfoot 5 (built by Bob Chandler)
More than 15 feet (4.5 m) tall; weighs 38,000 pounds
17,214 kg); has tires 10 feet (3 m) high.

The RB293 Bucket-wheel Excavator can shift nearly 8.5 million cubic feet (170,000 cubic meters) of earth per day. Think what that could do at your school yard!

That Is a *Big* Donut!

Wonder what the world's largest culinary creations are? Here's a tasting.

Largest Bowl of Soup/61.99 gallons (234.6 l)
It was beef and vegetable soup.

Largest Hamburger/24 feet (7.29 m) wide
It weighed 6,040 pounds (2,736 kg) and took two hours to cook.

Largest Chocolate Bar/5,206 pounds (2,358 kg)
It was the equivalent of 22,800 four-ounce (10 g) bars.

Largest Cookie/81 feet, 9 inches (26.6 m) around
It was chocolate chip, of course.

Largest Donut/3,739 pounds (1,700 kg)
It was more than 15 feet (4.9 m) across!

Longest Hot Dog/13 feet, 4 inches (4.1 m)
It weighed more than 200 pounds (90 kg) and came complete with bun, mustard, ketchup, and pickles.

Largest Jar of Jelly Beans/6,050 pounds (2,704 kg)
It included 2,160,000 Jelly Bellys®.

Largest Pizza/122 feet, 8 inches across (37.3 m)
It contained nearly 4,000 pounds (1,812 kg) of cheese.

Largest Popsicle/20,020 pounds (9,069 kg)
It was 21 feet (6.3 m) long, 7 feet 5 inches (1.7 m) wide, and was an average of 3 feet 7 inches (.86 m) thick.

Largest S'more/789 pounds (357 kg)
It included more than 9,000 toasted marshmallows.

Largest Sushi/4,851 pounds (2,197 kg)
It stretched for three quarters of a mile (1.2 km).

The world's largest food fight is an annual event in Buñol, Spain, called La Tomatina. In 1999, 25,000 people hurled more than a quarter million tomatoes in an hour!

Foods of the World

You'd be right at home eating the following foods in their native countries. Of course, if you've been to any of those big, fancy food courts at the mall, you could probably find a lot of these things right there.

Australia
Meat pie

Canada
Maple syrup

China
Egg roll

England
Fish and chips

France
Brie

Germany
Bratwurst

Greece
Baklava

Hungary
Goulash

India
Curry

Ireland
Corned beef and cabbage

Israel
Matzo

Italy
Pizza

Jamaica
Jerk chicken

Japan
Sushi

Mexico
Burrito

Nigeria
Fufu

Philippines
Adobo

Poland
Kielbasa

Russia
Borscht

Spain
Paella

Sweden
Gravlax

Thailand
Pad thai noodles

Turkey
Shish kebab

While many of the United States' favorite dishes have their origins in other countries, there's nothing quite as American as apple pie with vanilla ice cream.

Gross Stuff People Eat

Warning: Don't try these at home . . . unless you're really brave! No, it isn't the menu for the next edition of *Survivor*. But people actually eat this stuff in various parts of the world. Listed with each food is just one of the countries where you can enjoy these delicacies.

FOOD/COUNTRY

Beef tongue and brains/Mexico

Chocolate-covered ants/United States

Cricket lollipops/United States

Deep-fried beetles/Thailand

Dog stew/South Korea

Dried sea slugs/China

Fried locusts/Thailand

Grasshopper paste/Zambia

Iguana soup/Mexico

Pigeon stew/Thailand

Sheep eyeballs/India

Tarantula kebabs/Cambodia

Toasted termites/South Africa

Edible snails are considered a delicacy even in the United States. Of course, they sound a lot more appetizing when they're smothered in garlic and butter — and called *escargot*!

Dentists Beware!

Think of all the chocolate, chewy, hard, soft, sticky, sour, nutty candy you've ever eaten. Check out these candy names and make a list of all the ones you have personally tried. Check out when your favorite brand-name candy appeared!

YEAR FIRST SOLD/CANDY NAME

1893/Good & Plenty
1896/Tootsie Rolls
1900/Hershey's Bars
1901/NECCO Wafers
1906/Hershey's Kisses
1912/LifeSavers
1913/GooGoo Clusters
1920/Baby Ruths
1923/Mounds
1926/Milk Duds
1928/Heath Bars
1928/Reese's Peanut Butter Cups
1930/Snickers
1931/Tootsie Roll Pops

YEAR FIRST SOLD/CANDY NAME

1931/Kit Kats
1932/3 Musketeers Bars
1936/5th Avenue Bars
1940/York Peppermint Patties
1941/M & M's
1949/Jolly Ranchers
1952/Pez
1960/Starbursts
1960/Lemonheads
1976/Jelly Belly Jelly Beans
1979/Twix
1981/Skittles
1982/Reese's Pieces
2000/Bertie Bott's Every
Flavor Beans

Here's an easy one: What holiday generates the most candy sales? Here's a hard one: When is National Candy Month?

Answer: Duh! It's Halloween! National Candy Month, however, is June.

What's on That Pizza?!

Ah, pizza! Easily the world's greatest food. Add pepperoni and you've got all the major food groups in each slice. But while you're probably used to seeing sausage or peppers or onions on pizza, here's a list of what people in other countries slap on top of their pizza pies.

COUNTRY	TOPPING
Australia	Eggs
Bahamas	Barbecued chicken
Brazil	Green peas
Chile	Mussels and clams
Colombia	Guava
Costa Rica	Coconut
England	Tuna and corn
France	Fresh cream
Guatemala	Black bean sauce
India	Pickled ginger
Japan	Squid, mayonnaise, potato
Pakistan	Curry
Russia	Red herring

Americans eat more than three billion pizzas each year! Our favorite toppings are Pepperoni ● Mushrooms ● Extra cheese ● Sausage ● Green Pepper ● Onions.

Hold the anchovies! The list of favorite pizza toppings varies from establishment to establishment, but almost every one ranks the small fish as the least popular topping.

World's Stinkiest Cheeses

Phew! Here's a list of the stinkiest cheeses in the world, according to people who love cheese, no matter how it smells! All these cheeses are from France, with the exception of Appenzeller, which is made in Switzerland, and Limburger, from Germany.

Appenzeller

Banon

Brie de Meaux

Camembert au Calvados

Epoisses

Limburger

Livarot

Muenster

Ossau Iraty

Pont l'Eveque

Raclette

Reblochon

Roquefort

Vieux Boulogne

PsSST

The scientists who helped choose this list used their own noses as well as a computer-controlled electronic sniffer that responded to chemicals in the cheeses.

Take a Day

You probably have all the holidays in America memorized. That's when you get a day off from school! But kids (heck, everyone!) in other countries enjoy different holidays. Here's a sampling of international holidays.

DATE	HOLIDAY/COUNTRY
January 15	**Adult's Day**/Japan For people turning 20, making them adults
Jan./Feb.*	**Vietnamese New Year**/Vietnam A seven-day festival called *Tet Nguyen Dan*
February*	**Full Moon Day**/India and elsewhere Commemorates Buddhist teachings
February 6	**Waitangi Day**/New Zealand Recalls 1840 treaty signed by native Maori people
April*	**Sechseläuten**/Switzerland Celebrates the beginning of spring
May 5	**Children's Day**/Japan An official day to celebrate kids? Cool!
May 5	**Cinco de Mayo**/Mexico Celebrates 1861 victory over the French military
May 24	**Victoria Day**/Canada Birthday of late Queen Victoria of Great Britain

Off, World!

DATE	HOLIDAY/COUNTRY
July 1	**King Kamehameha I Day**/Hawaii Honors first king to rule all of Hawaii's islands
July 1	**Canada Day**/Canada Honors creation of Canadian nation in 1867
July 14	**Bastille Day**/France Celebrates start of French Revolution in 1789
July/Aug.*	**Brother and Sister Day**/India Day that siblings have to be nice to one another
November 1-2	**Day of the Dead**/Mexico Honors ancestors and others who have died
November 5	**Guy Fawkes Day**/Great Britain Celebrates foiling of traitorous plot in 1605
December*	**Las Posadas**/Mexico Celebrates the coming of Christmas
December 26	**Boxing Day**/Gt. Britain, Canada, Australia A bonus day for giving gifts after Christmas

These holidays are celebrated on different days each year, usually in the months listed.

In Japan, there used to be one holiday for girls and one for boys, but in 1948, they put them together. On Children's Day, kids go to shows, get new toys, and make cool crafts.

Easy Magic Tricks

Like almost anything else, it takes a lot of practice to become a skilled magician. But here are a few simple tricks you can start out with to amaze your friends and family.

MAGIC FINGERS

Ask someone to interlock his fingers and squeeze tightly. After a minute or so, have him or her stick his index fingers straight out while leaving his hands clasped together. The fingers should not be touching. Wave your hand over them and watch the fingers magically move toward each other. Try this one with your own hands first.

COLOR YOUR MIND

You need six crayons of different colors. Put the crayons on a table. Gather your audience in front of you. Put your hands behind your back, then turn your back and ask someone to hand you one crayon and hide the rest. Tell your audience that you will now read their minds and reveal what crayon is in your hands. Here's the secret. With your thumb, scratch off a very tiny part of the crayon you're holding. While keeping the crayon in the *other* hand, turn around and put your hand on someone's head to "read" their mind." As you do it, carefully sneak a look at your thumb and see the color you've scratched on your thumbnail. Build up the suspense by acting like you're "sensing" the color, then reveal the answer.

SIMPLE CARD TRICK

Look at the deck and pick out your "favorite card." Set it aside face down on the table. Ask someone to pick a favorite card from the deck. Cut the deck and have the card placed on the top half. Put the bottom half over the top half. Cut the deck several times, then place your card anywhere in the middle. Cut it again. Tell him your favorite card. His will be right next to it in the deck. How does it work? Because the card you choose as your favorite isn't really the one you took out of the deck. It's actually the top card of the deck, which you need to note mentally and tell him that it was your "favorite."

The secret to most magic tricks is that the audience members don't see everything that happens — and they believe they see things that don't really happen.

Famous Magicians

Harry Houdini, an escape artist in the 1920s, is perhaps the best-known magician in history. Here are some famous magicians who have baffled audiences with feats of illusion, along with some of their specialties.

John Henry Anderson   first to pull a rabbit from a hat

Harry Blackstone, Sr.   expert in large illusions

Joseph Buatier   famous for disappearing birdcage trick

David Copperfield   makes big things disappear

Doug Henning   popular on TV in the 1970s

Adelaide Hermann   late-19th-century female magician

Alexander Hermann   famous for "dancing pants" illusion

Harry Houdini   world's greatest escape artist

Servais LeRoy   Belgian inventor of magic tricks

John Maskelyne   created levitation (floating body) trick

Penn and Teller   combine comedy and magic

Giuseppe Pinetti   used robotlike machines in tricks

Jean Robert-Houdin   created stage magic, invented tricks

Siegfried & Roy   used white tigers in their shows

Chung Ling Soo   died trying to catch a bullet in his teeth

Howard Thurston   made cars vanish, people float

PsSST Chung Ling Soo was a world-renowned magician in the early 1900s. Perhaps his greatest illusion was the fact that he really was an American named William Robinson!

Packing for Camping

We know you'll remember to bring a tent and a sleeping bag the next time you're ready for the great outdoors. But a good camping list also includes — but is not limited to — these items.

Batteries

Camera and film

First-aid kit

Fishing gear

Games

Hiking boots

Insect repellent

Lantern (or flashlight or other light source)

Matches (or a lighter)

Plastic garbage bags

Plastic tarp

Playing cards

Radio

Rain gear

Rope

Sewing kit

Soap, toilet paper, deodorant

Sunglasses

Sunscreen

Swiss Army knife

Toothpaste and toothbrush

Water

Don't forget the ingredients you'll need to make s'mores, everyone's favorite camping dessert: graham crackers, chocolate bars, and marshmallows. Roast the biggest marshmallow you can find and stick it on top of a chocolate bar between two graham crackers. It's gooey, but it's good — and you'll definitely want "some more"!

Space Junk

NASA provides just about everything an astronaut needs on his or her flight into space. But astronauts also can carry some personal items aboard. Here are a few of the more unusual items that have traveled in space, according to *Air & Space/Smithsonian Magazine* and other sources.

Astrolabe (a navigation tool) from the 17th century

Bible on microfilm

Corned-beef **sandwich**

Doorknob from the Wisconsin state capitol

Four-star **insignia** of U.S. General Omar Bradley

Hand fan used by officials in sumo wrestling matches

Silk socks worn by Cornell University President Ezra Cornell in 1831

Small **piece of Stonehenge**, the ancient stone monument in Great Britain

Spurs owned by President Ronald Reagan

A **sternpost** from Captain James Cook's ship *Endeavour*

Swatch of **fabric** from the Wright brothers' first airplane

Vial of **sand** from Kitty Hawk, North Carolina, site of the Wright brothers' first flight

PsSST

Astronaut Alan Shepard carried golf balls along on the *Apollo 14* mission. He needed something to hit them with, so he attached the head of a 6-iron to a tool handle and swung away on the moon!

My Grab Bag

This chapter is a big mix of all sorts of things . . . and so is this page. Fill in the answers to these questions, which are based on most of the lists in this chapter. You might just find out some interesting things about yourself!

My astrological sign is _____. (page 254)

The Chinese year I was born in is the year of the _____. (page 255)

The "official" event I'd most like to celebrate would be _____. (page 258)

The type of car I'd most like to drive (and it doesn't have to be on this list) would be a _____. (page 260)

The biggest food item I've ever eaten is _____. (page 262)

The "food of the world" I'd most like to try is _____. (page 263)

The "food of the world" I'd least like to try is _____. (page 263)

The "gross" food that I'd actually try (if any!) is _____. (page 264)

My favorite pizza topping is _____. (page 266)

If I went to space, I'd make sure to take _____ with me. (page 273)

CHAPTER ELEVEN

Sports

Kick it, throw it, pass it, catch it, ride it, drive it, surf it . . . whatever you like to do in the world of sports, you'll find it in here. We've got the winners of all the big events, the champions from all the big sports, and even the story of what Eskimos do with their ears. Really!

NBA Champions

The NBA was formed officially in 1948 with the merger of the National Basketball League and the American Basketball Association. The Boston Celtics have won the most titles: 16.

1946-47	Philadelphia Warriors	**1976-77**	Portland Trail Blazers
1947-48	Philadelphia Warriors	**1977-78**	Washington Bullets
1948-49	Minneapolis Lakers	**1978-79**	Seattle SuperSonics
1949-50	Minneapolis Lakers	**1979-80**	Los Angeles Lakers
1950-51	Rochester Royals	**1980-81**	Boston Celtics
1951-52	Minneapolis Lakers	**1981-82**	Los Angeles Lakers
1952-53	Minneapolis Lakers	**1982-83**	Philadelphia 76ers
1953-54	Minneapolis Lakers	**1983-84**	Boston Celtics
1954-55	Syracuse Nationals	**1984-85**	Los Angeles Lakers
1955-56	Philadelphia Warriors	**1985-86**	Boston Celtics
1956-57	Boston Celtics	**1986-87**	Los Angeles Lakers
1957-58	St. Louis Hawks	**1987-88**	Los Angeles Lakers
1958-59	Boston Celtics	**1988-89**	Detroit Pistons
1959-60	Boston Celtics	**1989-90**	Detroit Pistons
1960-61	Boston Celtics	**1990-91**	Chicago Bulls
1961-62	Boston Celtics	**1991-92**	Chicago Bulls
1962-63	Boston Celtics	**1992-93**	Chicago Bulls
1963-64	Boston Celtics	**1993-94**	Houston Rockets
1964-65	Boston Celtics	**1994-95**	Houston Rockets
1965-66	Boston Celtics	**1995-96**	Chicago Bulls
1966-67	Philadelphia 76ers	**1996-97**	Chicago Bulls
1967-68	Boston Celtics	**1997-98**	Chicago Bulls
1968-69	Boston Celtics	**1998-99**	San Antonio Spurs
1969-70	New York Knicks	**1999-2000**	Los Angeles Lakers
1970-71	Milwaukee Bucks	**2000-01**	Los Angeles Lakers
1971-72	Los Angeles Lakers	**2001-02**	Los Angeles Lakers
1972-73	New York Knicks	**2002-03**	San Antonio Spurs
1973-74	Boston Celtics	**2003-04**	Detroit Pistons
1974-75	Golden State Warriors	**2004-05**	San Antonio Spurs
1975-76	Boston Celtics	**2005-06**	

Now you will know why the Lakers are called the Lakers when there aren't really any lakes in Los Angeles: Minnesota, the team's original home, is called the "Land of 10,000 Lakes."

Scoring Machines

Rack 'em up. Fill the bucket. From downtown. With authority. However you say it, scoring is the name of the game in basketball. Here are the all-time highest scorers in the NBA.

PLAYER	POINTS
Kareem Abdul-Jabbar	38,387
Karl Malone	36,928
Michael Jordan	32,292
Wilt Chamberlain	31,149
Moses Malone	27,409
Elvin Hayes	27,313
Hakeem Olajuwon	26,946
Oscar Robertson	26,710
Dominique Wilkins	26,688
John Havlicek	26,395
Alex English	25,613
Reggie Miller	25,279
Jerry West	25,192
Patrick Ewing	24,708
Charles Barkley	23,757

It's no surprise that Wilt "the Stilt" Chamberlain is among the all-time scoring leaders. He once averaged 50.4 points per game for an entire season! He scored 40 or more points in a game 271 times. And he is the only NBA player to score 100 points in a single game, which he did in 1962.

WNBA Champs

Following the American women's awesome gold-medal performance in the 1996 Olympics, the first pro basketball league for women was born in 1997. Fans around the country can now enjoy top-flight pro women's hoops. Here are the champs and MVPs for the WNBA's first few seasons.

YEAR	CHAMPION	MVP, TEAM
1997	Houston Comets	Cynthia Cooper, Houston
1998	Houston Comets	Cynthia Cooper, Houston
1999	Houston Comets	Yolanda Griffith, Sacramento
2000	Houston Comets	Sheryl Swoopes, Houston
2001	Los Angeles Sparks	Lisa Leslie, Los Angeles
2002	Los Angeles Sparks	Sheryl Swoopes, Houston
2003	Detroit Shock	Lauren Jackson, Seattle
2004	Seattle Storm	Lisa Leslie, Los Angeles
2005	Sacramento Monarchs	Sheryl Swoopes, Houston
2006		

On the college side, the top women's hoops team ever is the University of Tennessee, which has won six national titles. Of course, the folks at the University of Connecticut, who went 38-0 in 2002 to win their third of five titles, might argue that point.

Tennis Grand Slams

The four "major" tennis tournaments are the Australian, French, and U.S. Opens, and Wimbledon, played in England. Both male and female tennis players are compared through the years on how many of these "Grand Slam" tournaments they win. Here are the top Grand Slam singles–title winners for both men and women.

WOMEN

PLAYER	AUSTRALIAN	FRENCH	U.S.	WIMBLEDON	TOTAL
Margaret Smith Court	11	5	5	3	24
Steffi Graf	4	6	5	7	22
Helen Wills Moody	0	4	7	8	19
Chris Evert	2	7	6	3	18
Martina Navratilova	3	2	9	4	18

MEN

PLAYER	AUSTRALIAN	FRENCH	U.S.	WIMBLEDON	TOTAL
Pete Sampras	2	0	5	7	14
Roy Emerson	6	2	2	2	12
Bjorn Borg	0	6	0	5	11
Rod Laver	3	2	2	4	11
Bill Tilden	0	0	7	3	10

Perhaps the greatest feat in tennis is winning all four Grand Slam events in one calendar year. Rod Laver accomplished it in 1962 and 1968. For the women, Margaret Smith Court did it in 1970, and Steffi Graf aced a clean sweep in 1988.

World Series Winners

The champions of Major League Baseball are the winners of the annual World Series, played between the winners of the National and American leagues. The New York Yankees have won the most World Series with 26, almost three times as many as the next-best total.

1903	Boston Pilgrims	1928	New York Yankees
1904	No series	1929	Philadelphia Athletics
1905	New York Giants	1930	Philadelphia Athletics
1906	Chicago White Sox	1931	St. Louis Cardinals
1907	Chicago Cubs	1932	New York Yankees
1908	Chicago Cubs	1933	New York Giants
1909	Pittsburgh Pirates	1934	St. Louis Cardinals
1910	Philadelphia Athletics	1935	Detroit Tigers
1911	Philadelphia Athletics	1936	New York Yankees
1912	Boston Red Sox	1937	New York Yankees
1913	Philadelphia Athletics	1938	New York Yankees
1914	Boston Braves	1939	New York Yankees
1915	Boston Red Sox	1940	Cincinnati Reds
1916	Boston Red Sox	1941	New York Yankees
1917	Chicago White Sox	1942	St. Louis Cardinals
1918	Boston Red Sox	1943	New York Yankees
1919	Cincinnati Reds	1944	St. Louis Cardinals
1920	Cleveland Indians	1945	Detroit Tigers
1921	New York Giants	1946	St. Louis Cardinals
1922	New York Giants	1947	New York Yankees
1923	New York Yankees	1948	Cleveland Indians
1924	Washington Senators	1949	New York Yankees
1925	Pittsburgh Pirates	1950	New York Yankees
1926	St. Louis Cardinals	1951	New York Yankees
1927	New York Yankees	1952	New York Yankees

1953	New York Yankees	1980	Philadelphia Phillies
1954	New York Giants	1981	Los Angeles Dodgers
1955	Brooklyn Dodgers	1982	St. Louis Cardinals
1956	New York Yankees	1983	Baltimore Orioles
1957	Milwaukee Braves	1984	Detroit Tigers
1958	New York Yankees	1985	Kansas City Royals
1959	Los Angeles Dodgers	1986	New York Mets
1960	Pittsburgh Pirates	1987	Minnesota Twins
1961	New York Yankees	1988	Los Angeles Dodgers
1962	New York Yankees	1989	Oakland Athletics
1963	Los Angeles Dodgers	1990	Cincinnati Reds
1964	St. Louis Cardinals	1991	Minnesota Twins
1965	Los Angeles Dodgers	1992	Toronto Blue Jays
1966	Baltimore Orioles	1993	Toronto Blue Jays
1967	St. Louis Cardinals	1994	No series
1968	Detroit Tigers	1995	Atlanta Braves
1969	New York Mets	1996	New York Yankees
1970	Baltimore Orioles	1997	Florida Marlins
1971	Pittsburgh Pirates	1998	New York Yankees
1972	Oakland Athletics	1999	New York Yankees
1973	Oakland Athletics	2000	New York Yankees
1974	Oakland Athletics	2001	Arizona Diamondbacks
1975	Cincinnati Reds	2002	Anaheim Angels
1976	Cincinnati Reds	2003	Florida Marlins
1977	New York Yankees	2004	Boston Red Sox
1978	New York Yankees	2005	Chicago White Sox
1979	Pittsburgh Pirates	2006	

FACT: The Series was not held in 1904 because of a dispute between the leagues. The Series was canceled in 1994 due to a labor strike by players.

NFL Champions

The National Football League began in 1920. Through 1932, the champion simply had the best regular-season record. From 1933 to 1965, the NFL Championship Game determined who was number one. Since then, the new Super Bowl has been played to decide what team is the NFL champion.

1920	Akron Pros	1942	Washington Redskins
1921	Chicago Staleys	1943	Chicago Bears
1922	Canton Bulldogs	1944	Green Bay Packers
1923	Canton Bulldogs	1945	Cleveland Rams
1924	Cleveland Bulldogs	1946	Chicago Bears
1925	Chicago Cardinals	1947	Chicago Cardinals
1926	Frankford Yellow Jackets	1948	Philadelphia Eagles
1927	New York Giants	1949	Philadelphia Eagles
1928	Provid. Steam Roller	1950	Cleveland Browns
1929	Green Bay Packers	1951	Los Angeles Rams
1930	Green Bay Packers	1952	Detroit Lions
1931	Green Bay Packers	1953	Detroit Lions
1932	Chicago Bears	1954	Cleveland Browns
1933	Chicago Bears	1955	Cleveland Browns
1934	New York Giants	1956	New York Giants
1935	Detroit Lions	1957	Detroit Lions
1936	Green Bay Packers	1958	Baltimore Colts
1937	Washington Redskins	1959	Baltimore Colts
1938	New York Giants	1960	Philadelphia Eagles
1939	Green Bay Packers	1961	Green Bay Packers
1940	Chicago Bears	1962	Green Bay Packers
1941	Chicago Bears	1963	Chicago Bears

What secret weapon did the New York Giants use to win the 1934 NFL Championship Game?

Answer: They switched from football cleats to sneakers in the second half, and had better traction on the frozen field than the Chicago Bears. Good call!

1964	Cleveland Browns	1986	New York Giants
1965	Green Bay Packers	1987	Washington Redskins
1966	Green Bay Packers	1988	San Francisco 49ers
1967	Green Bay Packers	1989	San Francisco 49ers
1968	New York Jets	1990	New York Giants
1969	Kansas City Chiefs	1991	Washington Redskins
1970	Baltimore Colts	1992	Dallas Cowboys
1971	Dallas Cowboys	1993	Dallas Cowboys
1972	Miami Dolphins	1994	San Francisco 49ers
1973	Miami Dolphins	1995	Dallas Cowboys
1974	Pittsburgh Steelers	1996	Green Bay Packers
1975	Pittsburgh Steelers	1997	Denver Broncos
1976	Oakland Raiders	1998	Denver Broncos
1977	Dallas Cowboys	1999	St. Louis Rams
1978	Pittsburgh Steelers	2000	Baltimore Ravens
1979	Pittsburgh Steelers	2001	New England Patriots
1980	Oakland Raiders	2002	Tampa Bay Buccaneers
1981	San Francisco 49ers	2003	New England Patriots
1982	Washington Redskins	2004	New England Patriots
1983	Los Angeles Raiders	2005	Pittsburgh Steelers
1984	San Francisco 49ers	2006	
1985	Chicago Bears		

The Touchdown Zone

The point of the game is to score more points than the other guys. These players made it to the end zone more often than anyone else.

Jerry Rice*	207	Jim Brown	126
Emmitt Smith	175	Walter Payton	125
Marcus Allen	145	John Riggins	116
Marshall Faulk*	135	Lenny Moore	113
Cris Carter	129	Barry Sanders	109

(*Still active. Stats through 2004 season.)

World Cup Winners

The biggest sporting event in the world is not the Olympics. It's the World Cup of soccer, held every four years in a different country. More than 180 nations compete in the two-year tournament that sends 32 teams to the final playoffs. The World Cup final is always the most-watched sporting event of the year worldwide.

YEAR	CHAMPION	HOST COUNTRIES
1930	Uruguay	Uruguay
1934	Italy	Italy
1938	Italy	France
1950	Uruguay	Brazil
1954	W. Germany	Switzerland
1958	Brazil	Sweden
1962	Brazil	Chile
1966	England	England
1970	Brazil	Mexico
1974	Germany	Germany
1978	Argentina	Argentina
1982	Italy	Spain
1986	Argentina	Mexico
1990	Germany	Italy
1994	Brazil	United States
1998	France	France
2002	Brazil	Korea and Japan

The United States has only recently played a part in the World Cup. The national team qualified in 1990 for the first time in 40 years. In 2002, they reached the final eight — the quarterfinals — for the first time

Women's World Cup

In 1999, one of the biggest sports events in U.S. history occurred when the American soccer team won the first women's World Cup. Fans of soccer, of women's sports, and of sports in general rejoiced when the United States beat China to become the world champs. The success of the team helped jump-start creation of the WUSA women's pro soccer league in 2001. Here is a list of all the members of that historic 1999 championship team, whose head coach was Tony DiCicco (yes, a man).

PLAYER	POSITION	PLAYER	POSITION
Michelle Akers	Midfielder	Tiffeny Milbrett	Forward
Brandi Chastain	Midfielder	Carla Overbeck	Defender
Tracy Ducar	Goalkeeper	Cindy Parlow	Midfielder
Lorrie Fair	Defender	Christie Pearce	Defender
Joy Fawcett	Defender	Tiffany Roberts	Midfielder
Danielle Fotopoulos	Forward	Briana Scurry	Goalkeeper
Julie Foudy	Midfielder	Kate Sobrero	Defender
Mia Hamm	Forward	Tisha Venturini	Midfielder
Kristine Lilly	Forward	Sara Whalen	Defender
Shannon McMillan	Forward	Saskia Webber	Goalkeeper

For the 2002 season, there were eight teams in the WUSA women's pro league: Atlanta Beat, Boston Breakers, Carolina Courage, New York Power, Philadelphia Charge, San Diego Spirit, San Jose CyberRays, and Washington Freedom.

Hockey's Best

The champions of the National Hockey League receive the Stanley Cup, the oldest trophy in North America. Lord Stanley gave money to create the cup in 1893. At first, amateur leagues in Canada used it. In 1917, when the NHL was officially formed, the trophy went to its champion for the first time.

1917	Seattle Metropolitans	1941	Boston Bruins
1918	Toronto Arenas	1942	Toronto Maple Leafs
1919	Montreal-Seattle*	1943	Detroit Red Wings
1920	Ottawa Senators	1944	Montreal Canadiens
1921	Ottawa Senators	1945	Toronto Maple Leafs
1922	Toronto St. Pats	1946	Montreal Canadiens
1923	Ottawa Senators	1947	Toronto Maple Leafs
1924	Montreal Maroons	1948	Toronto Maple Leafs
1925	Victoria Athletic Club	1949	Toronto Maple Leafs
1926	Montreal Maroons	1950	Detroit Red Wings
1927	Ottawa Senators	1951	Toronto Maple Leafs
1928	New York Rangers	1952	Detroit Red Wings
1929	Boston Bruins	1953	Montreal Canadiens
1930	Montreal Canadiens	1954	Detroit Red Wings
1931	Montreal Canadiens	1955	Detroit Red Wings
1932	Toronto Maple Leafs	1956	Montreal Canadiens
1933	New York Rangers	1957	Montreal Canadiens
1934	Chicago Blackhawks	1958	Montreal Canadiens
1935	Montreal Maroons	1959	Montreal Canadiens
1936	Detroit Red Wings	1960	Montreal Canadiens
1937	Detroit Red Wings	1961	Chicago Blackhawks
1938	Chicago Blackhawks	1962	Toronto Maple Leafs
1939	Boston Bruins	1963	Toronto Maple Leafs
1940	New York Rangers	1964	Toronto Maple Leafs

Each member of a Stanley Cup-winning team gets to take the cup itself home for one day after the NHL Finals. Some players drink out of the cup, give babies baths in it, or take it to cheer up sick kids in hospitals.

1965	Montreal Canadiens	1987	Edmonton Oilers
1966	Montreal Canadiens	1988	Edmonton Oilers
1967	Toronto Maple Leafs	1989	Calgary Flames
1968	Montreal Canadiens	1990	Edmonton Oilers
1969	Montreal Canadiens	1991	Pittsburgh Penguins
1970	Boston Bruins	1992	Pittsburgh Penguins
1971	Montreal Canadiens	1993	Montreal Canadiens
1972	Boston Bruins	1994	New York Rangers
1973	Montreal Canadiens	1995	New Jersey Devils
1974	Philadelphia Flyers	1996	Colorado Avalanche
1975	Philadelphia Flyers	1997	Detroit Red Wings
1976	Montreal Canadiens	1998	Detroit Red Wings
1977	Montreal Canadiens	1999	Dallas Stars
1978	Montreal Canadiens	2000	New Jersey Devils
1979	Montreal Canadiens	2001	Colorado Avalanche
1980	New York Islanders	2002	Detroit Red Wings
1981	New York Islanders	2003	New Jersey Devils
1982	New York Islanders	2004	Tampa Bay Lightning
1983	New York Islanders	2005	Season canceled
1984	Edmonton Oilers	2006	
1985	Edmonton Oilers		
1986	Montreal Canadiens		

* The Cup was shared after a flu epidemic led to cancellation of the final playoff series.

He Shoots....He Scores!

In the National Hockey League, players who score a lot of goals are called "lamplighters." That's because a red light goes on behind the goal after a score. Here are the top ten goal-scorers in NHL history.

Wayne Gretzky	894	Mike Gartner	708
Gordie Howe	801	Mark Messier	694
Brett Hull*	741	Mario Lemieux*	683
Marcel Dionne	731	Steve Yzerman*	678
Phil Esposito	717	Luc Robitaille *	653

(* Still active. Stats through 2003–2004 season.)

NASCAR Champions

Stock-car racing has become one of America's most popular and fastest-growing sports. But those high-speed heroes have been racing around for more than 50 years. Here are the champions of NASCAR from the beginning. Since 1970, the top level of racing has been called the Winston Cup Series.

YEAR	CAR NO.	DRIVER	YEAR	CAR NO.	DRIVER
1949	22	Red Byron	1978	11	Cale Yarborough
1950	60	Bill Rexford	1979	43	Richard Petty
1951	92	Herb Thomas	1980	2	Dale Earnhardt
1952	91	Tim Flock	1981	11	Darrell Waltrip
1953	92	Herb Thomas	1982	11	Darrell Waltrip
1954	42	Lee Petty	1983	22	Bobby Allison
1955	300	Tim Flock	1984	44	Terry Labonte
1956	300	Buck Baker	1985	11	Darrell Waltrip
1957	87	Buck Baker	1986	3	Dale Earnhardt
1958	42	Lee Petty	1987	3	Dale Earnhardt
1959	42	Lee Petty	1988	9	Bill Elliott
1960	4	Rex White	1989	27	Rusty Wallace
1961	11	Ned Jarrett	1990	3	Dale Earnhardt
1962	8	Joe Weatherly	1991	3	Dale Earnhardt
1963	8	Joe Weatherly	1992	7	Alan Kulwicki
1964	43	Richard Petty	1993	3	Dale Earnhardt
1965	11	Ned Jarrett	1994	3	Dale Earnhardt
1966	6	David Pearson	1995	24	Jeff Gordon
1967	43	Richard Petty	1996	5	Terry Labonte
1968	17	David Pearson	1997	24	Jeff Gordon
1969	17	David Pearson	1998	24	Jeff Gordon
1970	71	Bobby Isaac	1999	88	Dale Jarrett
1971	43	Richard Petty	2000	18	Bobby Labonte
1972	43	Richard Petty	2001	24	Jeff Gordon
1973	72	Benny Parsons	2002	20	Tony Stewart
1974	43	Richard Petty	2003	17	Matt Kenseth
1975	43	Richard Petty	2004	97	Kurt Busch
1976	11	Cale Yarborough	2005	20	Tony Stewart
1977	11	Cale Yarborough	2006		

Winston Cup drivers get points for everything from victories to laps led. In 2004, Kurt Busch won the title over Jimmie Johnson by just eight points, the tightest race ever.

Daytona 500

Forty-three of the top drivers in the world speed for 200 laps around the Daytona International Speedway every February. The "500" has become the biggest race on the motor sports calendar.

YEAR	DRIVER	YEAR	DRIVER
1959	Lee Petty	1983	Cale Yarborough
1960	Junior Johnson	1984	Cale Yarborough
1961	Marvin Panch	1985	Bill Elliott
1962	Fireball Roberts	1986	Geoff Bodine
1963	Tiny Lund	1987	Bill Elliott
1964	Richard Petty	1988	Bobby Allison
1965	Fred Lorenzen	1989	Darrell Waltrip
1966	Richard Petty	1990	Derrike Cope
1967	Mario Andretti	1991	Ernie Irvan
1968	Cale Yarborough	1992	Davey Allison
1969	Lee Roy Yarbrough	1993	Dale Jarrett
1970	Pete Hamilton	1994	Sterling Marlin
1971	Richard Petty	1995	Sterling Marlin
1972	A. J. Foyt, Jr.	1996	Dale Jarrett
1973	Richard Petty	1997	Jeff Gordon
1974	Richard Petty	1998	Dale Earnhardt
1975	Benny Parsons	1999	Jeff Gordon
1976	David Pearson	2000	Dale Jarrett
1977	Cale Yarborough	2001	Michael Waltrip
1978	Bobby Allison	2002	Ward Burton
1979	Richard Petty	2003	Michael Waltrip
1980	Buddy Baker	2004	Dale Earnhardt, Jr.
1981	Richard Petty	2005	Jeff Gordon
1982	Bobby Allison	2006	Jimmie Johnson

PsSST The Daytona International Speedway in Florida is so big, it has a lake on the "infield," the part of the Speedway inside the roadway.

Golf's Grand Slam

Four annual golf tournaments make up the famous "Grand Slam." No golfer has won the U.S. Open, British Open, Masters, and PGA Championship in one year, but Tiger Woods won all four in a row, though over two years. The golfers listed here are the only ones to win all four tournaments during their career. Also listed are the winners of the most of each Grand Slam event.

CAREER GRAND SLAM
(Number of wins per tournament)

GOLFER	MASTERS	U.S. OPEN	BRITISH OPEN	PGA
Jack Nicklaus	6	4	3	5
Ben Hogan	2	4	1	2
Gary Player	3	1	3	2
Tiger Woods	3	2	1	2
Gene Sarazen	1	2	1	3

MOST VICTORIES IN "MAJORS"

The Masters
Jack Nicklaus, 6
Arnold Palmer, 4

British Open
Harry Vardon, 6
Tom Watson, 5
J.H. Taylor, 5

U.S. Open
Jack Nicklaus, 4
Ben Hogan, 4
Bobby Jones, 4
Willie Anderson, 4

PGA Championship
Walter Hagen, 5
Jack Nicklaus, 5
Gene Sarazen, 3
Sam Snead, 3

Unlike today's all-professional Grand Slam, the original included the U.S. and British Amateurs, along with the U.S. and British Opens. The great Bobby Jones was the only golfer to win an original Grand Slam (1927).

Ladies of the Links

Gaining membership into most halls of fame means getting enough votes from sportswriters or fellow athletes. That's not true for the LPGA (Ladies' Professional Golf Association) Hall of Fame. For many years the rules were simple: You got in if you won 30 tournaments, including two of the ones considered "majors"; won 35 tournaments with one major; or won 40 tournaments. In 1998 the rules were amended so that any player who piled up 27 "points" for winning tournaments, majors, and certain awards was automatically in. Here are the 21 women in the LPGA Hall of Fame.

PLAYER	YEAR ENTERED	PLAYER	YEAR ENTERED
Patty Berg	1951	Pat Bradley	1991
Betty Jameson	1951	Patty Sheehan	1993
Louise Suggs	1951	Betsy King	1995
Babe Didrikson Zaharias	1951	Amy Alcott	1999
Betsy Rawls	1960	Beth Daniel	2000
Mickey Wright	1964	Juli Inskter	2000
Kathy Whitworth	1975	Judy Rankin	2000
Sandra Haynie	1977	Donna Caponi	2001
Carol Mann	1977	Marlene Hagge	2002
JoAnne Carner	1982	Annika Sorenstam	2003
Nancy Lopez	1987		

Note: Singer Dinah Shore was named an honorary member in 1994 for her contributions to women's golf.

Babe Didrikson Zaharias was perhaps the greatest all-around female athlete who has ever lived. Along with her golfing greatness (she won 12 major tournaments), she also won Olympic gold medals in the javelin and hurdles, played baseball with men, and was an awesome bowler.

Triple Crown Horses

Thoroughbred horses that win the Kentucky Derby, Preakness, and Belmont Stakes races in one year earn the fabled Triple Crown. Only 11 horses have captured that prize. Only one jockey, Eddie Arcaro, has ridden two different horses to Triple Crowns.

YEAR	HORSE	JOCKEY
1919	Sir Barton	Johnny Loftus
1930	Gallant Fox	Earl Sande
1935	Omaha	Willie Saunders
1937	War Admiral	Charley Kurtsinger
1941	Whirlaway	Eddie Arcaro
1943	Count Fleet	Johnny Longden
1946	Assault	Warren Mehrtens
1948	Citation	Eddie Arcaro
1973	Secretariat	Ron Turcotte
1977	Seattle Slew	Jean Cruguet
1978	Affirmed	Steve Cauthen

In 1973, the mighty Secretariat won the Belmont Stakes by an incredible 31 "lengths." The distance between horses in a race is measured in lengths; that is, the distance from a horse's nose to its rear.

World's Fastest

The people who hold the record for the 100-meter (110-yard) dash are considered the "fastest man" and "fastest woman" in the world. The identities of those people change, of course, as people run faster and faster times. Here are the five most recent world-record times for men and women in track and field's fastest race.

ATHLETE, COUNTRY	YEAR	TIME*
MEN		
Asafa Powell, Jamaica	2005	9.77
Maurice Greene, U.S.A.	1999	9.79
Donovan Bailey, Canada	1996**	9.84
Leroy Burrell, U.S.A.	1994	9.84
Carl Lewis, U.S.A.	1991	9.86
WOMEN		
Florence Griffith–Joyner, U.S.A.	1988	10.49
Evelyn Ashford, U.S.A.	1984	10.76
Evelyn Ashford, U.S.A.	1983	10.79
Marlies Göhr, East Germany	1983	10.81
Marlies Oelsner, East Germany	1977	10.88

* In seconds   ** Record set while winning an Olympic gold medal

Scientists have debated just how low these 100-meter times will go. Some feel that human beings are already reaching their full potential; that is, that we can't go much faster. However, scientists also said that about 50 years ago, when the women's record was 11.5 seconds!

Olympic History

The Olympics were first held more than 2,000 years ago in ancient Greece. A movement to restart the Games led to the first modern Olympics in 1896. Today, Olympics are held every two years, alternating Winter and Summer Games.

SUMMER GAMES

1896 Athens, Greece	**1932** Los Angeles, California
1900 Paris, France	**1936** Berlin, Germany
1904 St. Louis, Missouri	**1948** London, England
1906 Athens, Greece	**1952** Helsinki, Finland
1908 London, England	**1956** Melbourne, Australia
1912 Stockholm, Sweden	**1960** Rome, Italy
1920 Antwerp, Belgium	**1964** Tokyo, Japan
1924 Paris, France	**1968** Mexico City, Mexico
1928 Amsterdam, Netherlands	**1972** Munich, West Germany

Olympic Tug-of-War?

Over the years, some sports have been removed from the Olympics. Here are some sports that are no longer golden.

Cricket	Rope climb
Croquet	Standing long jump
Jeu de paume (like tennis)	Standing high jump
One-handed weightlifting	Tug-of-war
Polo	Underwater swimming

1976	Montreal, Canada	1996	Atlanta, Georgia
1980	Moscow, Soviet Union	2000	Sydney, Australia
1984	Los Angeles, California	2004	Athens, Greece
1988	Seoul, South Korea	2008	Beijing, China*
1992	Barcelona, Spain		

WINTER GAMES

1924	Chamonix, France	1972	Sapporo, Japan
1928	St. Moritz, Switzerland	1976	Innsbruck, Austria
1932	Lake Placid, New York	1980	Lake Placid, New York
1936	Garmisch-Partinkirchen, Germany	1984	Sarajevo, Yugoslavia
		1988	Calgary, Canada
1948	St. Moritz, Switzerland	1992	Albertville, France
1952	Oslo, Norway	1994	Lillehammer, Norway
1956	Cortina d'Ampezzo, Italy	1998	Nagano, Japan
1960	Squaw Valley, California	2002	Salt Lake City, Utah
1964	Innsbruck, Austria	2006	Turin, Italy
1968	Grenoble, France	2010	Vancouver, Canada*

Scheduled as of 2005

The Olympics were not held as scheduled in 1916, 1940, and 1944. Do you know why?

The events were canceled in 1916 due to World War I and in 1940 and 1944 because of World War II.

Greatest Gold

Winning an Olympic gold medal remains one of sport's greatest individual achievements. Whether it is in the heat of summer for being the fastest swimmer, best gymnast, or longest jumper, or in the chill of winter for being the speediest skater or the most skillful skier, earning a gold is the peak of an athlete's career and one of the highlights of his or her life. Here are the top male and female career gold-medal winners in Olympic Games history.

ATHLETE, COUNTRY	SPORT
10 GOLD MEDALS	
Ray Ewry, United States*	Track and field
9 GOLD MEDALS	
Larissa Latynina, USSR**	Gymnastics
Carl Lewis, United States	Track and field
Paavo Nurmi, Finland	Track and field
Mark Spitz, United States	Swimming
8 GOLD MEDALS	
Matt Biondi, United States	Swimming
Bjorn Dahlie, Norway	Cross-country skiing
Kato Sawao, Japan	Gymnastics
Jenny Thompson, United States	Swimming
7 GOLD MEDALS	
Nikolay Andrianov, USSR	Gymnastics
Vera Caslavska, Czechoslovakia	Gymnastics
Birgit Fischer, Germany	Kayaking
Boris Shacklin, USSR	Gymnastics
6 GOLD MEDALS	
Aladar Gerevich, Hungary	Fencing

Medal Winners

ATHLETE, COUNTRY	SPORT
Edoardo Mangiarotti, Italy	Fencing
Neo Nadi, Italy	Fencing
Kristin Otto, Germany	Swimming
Michael Phelps, United States	Swimming
Vitaly Scherbo, Belarus	Gymnastics
Lydia Skoblikova, U.S.S.R.	Speed skating

5 GOLD MEDALS

Bonnie Blair, United States	Speed skating
Krisztina Egerszegi, Hungary	Swimming
Eric Heiden, United States	Speed skating
Tom Jager, United States	Swimming
Michael Johnson, United States	Track and field
Pal Kovacs, Hungary	Fencing
Takashi Ono, Japan	Gymnastics
Steven Redgrave, Great Britain	Rowing
Ingemar Stenmark, Sweden	Alpine skiing
Johnny Weissmuller, United States	Swimming

Two of Ray's medals came at a semiofficial 1906 Olympic event.

* "USSR" stands for the Union of Soviet Socialist Republics, or Soviet Union, a nation that broke up in 1991 to become Russia and many other smaller nations.

Gymnast Larissa Latynina won more Olympic medals of all types than any other athlete. Along with her nine golds, she won five silver (second-place) medals and four bronze (third-place) medals from 1956 to 1964.

Eskimo Games

You've heard of the Olympic Games, of course. But the Aleut people (also called Eskimos) of Alaska and Canada have been taking part in other athletic activities for generations. Different organizations hold Eskimo Games every year made up of some of the wildest sports you've ever seen. Here is a list of a few of the more unusual events held at the Eskimo Games.

One-foot high kick
Jumping off one foot, touch that foot as high up a pole as possible. There is also a two-foot high kick event.

Blanket toss
Perform gymnastic maneuvers as your teammates repeatedly fling you in the air from a blanket made of walrus skins.

Ear pull
This is tug-of-war — only you pull on a cord attached to your and your opponent's ears!

Ear weight carry
Hang a 16-pound (7.2-kg) weight from your ear and walk as far as you can.

Eskimo stick pull
Seated facing your opponent, have a tug-of-war with a short stick instead of a rope.

Greased pole walk
How far can you walk on a wooden pole covered in slippery seal grease?

Four-man carry
Four people climb on top of you and you walk as far as you can.

Kneel jump
Jump as far as you can, starting from a kneeling position.

Knuckle hop
Resting on only your knuckles and toes and with your elbows bent, hop until you can't hop anymore. The record is 191 feet (57 m)!

Indian stick pull
Using one hand, battle with your opponent for posses- sion of a two-foot (.6 m) greased stick.

Most of the events in the Eskimo Games were created to mimic things that hunters might have to do to survive in the wild. For instance, a hunter might have to carry a couple of injured partners (or a huge seal), as in the four-man carry event. The knuckle hop helped toughen up hunters' hands for hard work.

Hiiiii-YA!
Martial Arts Ranks

Most martial arts use colors to rank participants in their sports. People earn higher ranks, or colors, by learning new skills, perfecting techniques, or just whomping people at a competition. There are many different kinds of martial arts, but here are two examples of what colors are used to signify the levels or ranks.

Tae Kwan Do
(ranked from lowest to highest)

COLOR	MEANING
White	purity, innocence
Yellow	rising sun, source of life
Green	growing things
Blue	sky, open and boundless
Red	blood, the essence of life
Black	all colors combined

Judo
(ranked from lowest to highest)

1. white
2. yellow
3. orange
4. green
5. blue
6. brown
7. black
8. red and white

Every school of martial arts has its own way of ranking. Also, martial arts from different countries use different terms. In Japanese karate, for example, each rank is called *kyu*. In Korean, those *kyus* are called *gups*. So new karate students are called "guppies."

Skateboard

These are the world's best, most successful, most "radical" skateboarders. They do things on skateboards that most of us can't do even bouncing on a trampoline. They are a mix of street and vert-ramp skaters you might see on TV or at an arena near you. (And they all wear helmets when competing!)

Jake Brown

An Australian skater known for his "all-or-nothing" approach to vert skating; he's earned top-fives at numerous international skate events.

Bob Burnquist

This Brazilian is the best vert skater in the world.

Cara-Beth Burnside

Olympic snowboarder turned star vert skater.

Sandro Dias

A World Cup and world champ in vert, this Brazilian native became the third person ever to land the 900.

Pierre-Luc Gagnon

This Canadian native is one of the world's best vert skaters; among other wins, he was the 2003 world champ.

Tony Hawk

Simply the world's greatest and most famous skateboarder. Among other things, the only person to pull a 900 (2 ½ complete spins in the air) off a vert ramp.

Bucky Lasek

Three-time X Games gold medalist.

Superstars!

Andy MacDonald

Versatile, popular skateboarder with 10 X Games medals.

Chad Muska

Creative and innovative street skater.

Paul Rodriguez

This California-born street skate expert has steadily moved up the ranks and should be challenging for number one soon.

Ryan Sheckler

Radical 14-year-old (!) 2004 X Games gold medalist.

Elissa Steamer

Top women's skater, awesome on vert ramp.

Danny Way

Set world record for most air (65 feet/19.7 m) in 2002; jumped over the Great Wall of China in 2005.

Shaun White

This multitalented redhead is a gold medal winner at the X Games and the 2006 Winter Olympics (as a skater and a snowboarder).

Skateboards were invented in the 1950s when California surfers were looking for a way to stay in surfing shape during the off-season. They attached roller-skate wheels to wooden boards and used their surfing skills on the streets. In the 1970s, molded plastic wheels and boards changed the sport dramatically.

Ollies and Others

There are about as many skateboard tricks as there are skateboarders. You've probably made up a few of your own and given them names that will make you famous around the world . . . as soon as you can do your tricks at the X Games. Here are some names and brief descriptions of well-known skateboard tricks. It takes pros years to learn most of these, some of which can be dangerous, so **don't** try these by yourself at home!

Board slide

Ride a rail with your board and the rail forming a T. There's also a tailslide, with just the back part of the board sliding on the rail or obstacle.

Frontside 180

As you roll along, ollie (see below) and spin your body and board so that the back foot becomes the front foot.

Grab

A grab trick is any time you get air and reach down to grab the board with your hands. An indy grab is from behind, and there are also tail and nose grabs, among many others.

Grind

Ride a rail on your back wheels alone. You can nosegrind, tailgrind, or 50-50 (along one side of the board).

Kickflip

Ollie, but then spin the board around parallel to your feet.

Ollie

Kick the board tail-first off the ground and then land on it again.

Pop shove it

Ollie but spin the board like a propeller before landing.

360

This is a vert-ramp trick; you fly off the lip and do a complete spin before landing again. A 540 is one-and-a-half spins.

 You can ride a skateboard with either foot in front. If you ride with your right foot in front, you're riding "right." It's called "goofy-foot" if you ride with your left in front. Riding both ways lets you do the most tricks.

Whoa. Dude.

This list includes the most outrageous shredders . . . the most radical drop-down artists . . . the gnarliest surfers in the world! They're the bravest, the most outrageous, heck, just the coolest guys and gals around at this awesome sport. Cowabunga, dude!

Megan Abudo
Hawaii
Ranked number one in the world, 2001.

Lisa Andersen
Florida
Four-time women's world champion.

Layne Beachley
Australia
World champ in 1998, set women's record for prize money.

Serena Brooke
Australia
One of the top young surfers on the world tour.

Tim Curran
California
Talented young surfer, a future superstar.

Association of Surfing Professionals

Shane Dorian
Australia
Veteran surfer and one of the best on the ASP* Tour.

Sunny Garcia
Hawaii
World champion in 2000, 36 ASP Tour victories.

C. J. Hobgood
Florida
World champion in 2001, 1999 ASP rookie of the year.

Dan Malloy
California
Scored a big win early in 2002; a great technician.

Lynette McKenzie
Australia
World number one in 2002.

Kelly Slater
The best surfer ever? He has won a record seven world titles.

Hawaiian legend Duke Kahanamokou was one of the people most responsible for making surfing popular. A champion swimmer, his fame let him spread the word about surfing, a sport beloved by his fellow Hawaiians.

Weird World of Sports

Baseball . . . basketball . . . boring! There is much more to the wide world of sports than just the games you are used to watching and playing. We've scoured the globe to come up with a list of unusual sports that you won't see every day. Listed with each sport is a country in which it is popular.

Bungee jumping/New Zealand
A big drop from a high place on a long rubber band.

Caber tossing/Scotland
Strong men try to flip telephone poles.

Camel racing/Saudi Arabia
In other countries, people race on ostriches and elephants.

Elephant polo/Thailand
They use a huge rubber ball instead of a small hard one.

Mountain unicycling/United States
Like mountain biking, only with one wheel.

Road bowling/Ireland
Bowlers throw small metal balls along very long roads.

Sepak takraw/Thailand
A form of soccer that is played like tennis.

Sumo wrestling/Japan
Men as large as 600 pounds (270 kg) go belly to belly.

Underwater hockey/United States
Go for the goal . . . six feet (1.8 m) underwater!

Waterfall kayaking/Indonesia
They just keep paddling — straight down!

The sport of lacrosse is popular in the eastern part of the United States. It was originally a game played by Native Americans. Instead of playing on a field, however, they would play over miles and miles of open land with the goals located in neighboring villages.

Let's Get It Started

Basketball games begin with a tip-off and football games with a kickoff. But *when* did sports such as those begin? This list shows the first year that major sports were organized in an official way. Some of them, such as horse racing, soccer, or golf, had been around for centuries in various forms. But the years listed here are generally recognized as the "kickoffs" of these sports.

Auto racing, 1895	first organized race in Chicago
Baseball, 1845	rules first written down
Basketball, 1891	invented by James Naismith
Football (COLLEGE), 1869	Rutgers 6, Princeton 4
Football (PRO), 1895	Latrobe YMCA 12, Jeannette AC 0
Golf, 1754	St. Andrews (Scotland) sets first rules
Horse racing, 1665	first modern course in England
Ice hockey, 1885	first league organized in Ontario, Canada
Olympics (ANCIENT), 776 BCE	athletic contest created to honor gods
Olympics (MODERN), 1896	new version of ancient games
Skateboarding, 1963	first competition, Hermosa Beach, CA
Soccer, 1857	first English club founded (Sheffield)
Tennis, 1873	outdoor game created
Volleyball, 1895	invented by William Morgan

The two cars in the first auto race in the United States on November 28, 1895, averaged an amazing 8 miles per hour (12.8 kph)! You can run faster than that! Today's best race cars can reach more than 240 mph (386 kph). The six cars in the race went 55 miles (88 km) in about eight hours!

Little League World Series

Since 1947, Little League Baseball has held its national championship in Williamsport, Pennsylvania. Little League holds eight national tournaments for boys and girls in different age divisions of baseball and softball. The Little League division for 11- to 12-year-olds is the most famous. Beginning in 2000, 16 teams from around the world made the finals to compete for the title.

YEAR	COUNTRY or CITY, STATE	YEAR	COUNTRY or CITY, STATE
1947	Williamsport, PA	1977	Koh Hsing, Taiwan
1948	Lock Haven, PA	1978	Pin Kuang, Taiwan
1949	Hammonton, NJ	1979	Pu-Tzu, Taiwan
1950	Houston, TX	1980	Long Kuong, Taiwan
1951	Stamford, CT	1981	Taiping, Taiwan
1952	Norwalk, CT	1982	Kirkland, WA
1953	Birmingham, AL	1983	Marietta, GA
1954	Schenectady, NY	1984	Seoul, South Korea
1955	Morrisville, PA	1985	Seoul, South Korea
1956	Roswell, NM	1986	Tainan Park, Taiwan
1957	Mexico	1987	Hua Lian, Taiwan
1958	Mexico	1988	Tai Ping, Taiwan
1959	Hamtramck, MI	1989	Trumbull, CT
1960	Levittown, PA	1990	San-Hua, Taiwan
1961	El Cajon/La Mesa, CA	1991	Hsi-Nan, Taiwan
1962	San Jose, CA	1992	Long Beach, CA
1963	Granada Hills, CA	1993	Long Beach, CA
1964	Staten Island, NY	1994	Maracaibo, Venezuela
1965	Windsor Locks, CT	1995	Tainan, Taiwan
1966	Houston, TX	1996	Kao Hsuing City, Taiwan
1967	Tokyo, Japan	1997	Guadalupe, Mexico
1968	Wakayama, Japan	1998	Toms River, NJ
1969	Taipei, Taiwan	1999	Hirakata, Japan
1970	Wayne, NJ	2000	Sierra Maestra, Venezuela
1971	Tainan City, Taiwan	2001	Kitasuna, Japan
1972	Taipei, Taiwan	2002	Louisville, KY
1973	Tainan City, Taiwan	2003	Tokyo, Japan
1974	Tainan City, Taiwan	2004	Willemstad, Curaçao
1975	Lakewood, NJ	2005	West Oahu, Hawaii
1976	Chofu, Japan	2006	

In 1989, Chris Drury became a national hero by pitching his Connecticut Little League team to the title. Later, Chris switched sports and became an NHL star. He played for the U.S. team in the 2002 Winter Olympics.

Snow Good!
Superstars of the Winter X Games

These folks can shred! If you don't know what snowboarding is, trust us — being able to shred is a good thing. Winter sports have come a long way from your basic sled. Today's snowboarders fly down ramps like skateboarders, schuss through slaloms like skiers, and fly over ramps like, well, birds! Here are some of the big names in the world of snow.

Antti Autti
This flying Finn is the master of the halfpipe and was the 2004 world champ.

Gretchen Bleiler
Inventor of the Crippler 540, Gretchen was the female halfpiper of the year in 2004 and the 2006 Winter Olympics silver medalist.

Kelly Clark
Women's gold medalist in the 2002 Olympics; 2002 best action sports athlete at the ESPYs.

Andy Finch
He's the U.S. halfpipe champ and won six events in 2004.

Ross Powers
2003 U.S. halfpipe champ, 2002 Olympic gold medalist, 2000 superpipe world champ.

Hannah Teter
A popular snowboarder, Hannah soared to glory in Italy, winning the 2006 Winter Olympics halfpipe gold medal.

Shaun White
Called the Flying Tomato for his bright red hair, Shaun is not only a three-time Winter X Games and Olympic Games gold medalist, he's also a hot pro skateboarder.

The halfpipe looks exactly like it sounds, a pipe cut in half lengthwise. But this is nothing like you find under your sink. Snowboard halfpipes can be from 400-650 feet (120-200 m) long with snow-packed walls 15-20 feet (4.5-6 m) high!

My Sports

Okay, now you've seen how the world of pro and Olympic sports lines up. What's on your personal sports lineup?

My favorite sport to play _____

My favorite sport to watch _____

My least favorite sport _____

A sport I wish I played better _____

My favorite player in my favorite sport _____

My favorite player in another sport _____

My favorite team _____

My favorite pro sports memory _____

My school's team nickname _____

A league I play in _____

My team's name _____

My uniform number _____

Two hundred years ago, American kids didn't have pro or college or even high school sports teams to watch. They played games instead, including rounders, a sort of early baseball; bowls, which was like outdoor bowling; and probably good old-fashioned tag.

Index

Quiz Answers

Here are the answers to the quizzes on "My Word Games" on page 180.

1. Here are some words that we came up with. Let us know if we forgo any good ones (plus, you can add an *s* to many of these to get yet another word): bits, bliss, book, bilk, boil, bolt, boot, boss, fist, flit, f folk, fool, foot, look, loot, lost, silk, slit, soil, stool, toil, took, toss.

2. 3 + 9 – 2 + 7 – 9 + 5 – 8 + 5 = diez, dix, zehn, ashra, kumi, shi . . . o

3. :) is smile, happy; TMI is too much information; LOL is laugh o loud; ;) is wink; JK is just kidding; : 0 is surprised; : (is sad; ROTFL is rolling on the floor laughing; TTFN is ta-ta (good-bye :x is kisses.

How to Say Good-bye

Well, we've come to the last page in the book, our last list. We hope you've had some fun, learned a few things, and perhaps thought of new lists of your own. To send you off in style, this final list shows you how to say "good-bye" in 20 languages from around the world.

LANGUAGE	GOOD-BYE (HOW TO SAY IT)
Apache	Ka dish day (KAH dish day)
Chinese	Zài jiàn (ZAI-JEN)
Czech	Nashle (NAHSH-lay)
Dutch	Vaarwell (vahr-VELL)
French	Au revoir (AU reh-VOIS)
German	Auf wederhesen (au-VEE-der-zayn)
Greek	Yasou (YAH-soo)
Hawaiian	Aloha (ah-LOH-ha)
Hebrew	Shalom (shah-LOHM)
Hindi	Namaste (nah-mahs-TAY)
Indonesian	Daa daa (DAH dah)
Irish	Slán leat (slan LEESH)
Italian	Ciao (CHOW)
ɔanese	Sayonara (sy-oh-NAH-rah)
ʋihali	Kwaheri (kwa-HARE-ee)
ˈori	E noho ra (ay no-ho RAH)
	Até a vista (ah-TAY ah VEES-tah)
	Do svidanja (dohs vee-DAN-yah)
	ˈdios (AH-dee-ose)
	ˈlom (pah-ah-LOHM)

ʃst one way Americans say
ˈrewell," "see you later," "catch
flip-flop," "bye-bye," and, of
y'all come back now, you hear?"